I AM MEIR'S BROTHER

Biography of a Family Separated by Destiny

Ellen Brazer

Other books by Ellen Brazer:

* *Hearts of Fire*
* *Clouds Across the Sun* (being made into a movie)
* *And So It was Written*
* *The Wondering Jew, My Journey into Judaism*

Ellen Brazer is available for speaking engagements.

Contact the author at

Email: ellenb9815@bellsouth.net

Visit the Website: EllenBrazer.com

Cover art Designed: Barbara Glicken
Interior design and composition: Rick Soldin

ISBN: 979-8-7043-2039-5 (paperback)
ISBN: 978-0-578-85537-0 (hardcover)

Printed in the United States of America

To Mel Brazer, my husband and best friend—

thank you for holding my hand

and for being there always.

I will love you forever and a day

Contents

—— ••• ——

Acknowledgments

———— ••• ————

Thank you, Eli and Lily Huberman, for allowing me to share the story of your lives. It has been the most glorious experience of my writing career. I respect and admire you both, and I am honored to have taken this journey with you. Lily Prellezo and Orlando Rodriquez have been my writing partners for the last twelve years. We have laughed, cried, argued and prevailed. I am forever in your debt. Barbara Glicken designed the wonderful cover with her original painting. She is my confidant and forever friend. Cousin/sister Judi and Charles Wolowitz who were our *go-to buddies* that kept my husband and me sane during the pandemic. The following are the friends I consider family: Michele and Larry Kabat, Dr. Susan and Gary Weiner, Alan and Marjorie Goldberg, Drs. Anita and Jay Meinbach, Sam and Maxine Cahn, Barbara and Bob Roseff and Janet Wolk, the person I wish to emulate and her husband Peter. The most precious and important people in my life are my family. Thank you to my wonderful children and grandchildren: Todd, my firstborn and his girls, Jordyn and Emma. Carrie, for the school she founded and her dedication to special needs children and her boys Max and Jacob. Judd for always being my technical *go to* and his family, Tiffany and Julia. To my beloved blended family for their love: Ellen and Barry Brazer, Heidi Brazer Tacktill, Dr. Jordan Tacktill and Dylan and Dean. Evan and Samantha Brazer Rosenbaum and Wesley and Cameron. Becky and Mitchel Brazer, Matt, Jessie and Cameron, Megan Brazer Cribbs, Todd and Miles. Bonnie Brazer

Grote, Joe, Rachel, Ali and Ryan. My sister-in-law-Barbara and brother, Howard Glicken and Jason, Aaron, Stephen, Sarah and their families. I would be remiss if I did not add just a few more special names, people that have passed away but will always hold a special place in my heart. My mother, Esther Glicken, she was my best friend and champion who always believed in me. My cherished father, Irving Glicken, the patriarch of our family who showed all of us how to live every moment of every day. I feel their presence with every breath I take. To our beloved Monte Glicken and to all the loved ones we have lost. Your presence is reflected in every word that I write.

How it All Began

———————— ••• ————————

The Lincoln Road Apple store on South Beach was one of the busiest in the county. I am not a patient person and entered with trepidation. I gave my name and headed for a vacant seat at one of the high tables—the idea of having to wait grating on me before I even sat down. I began asking myself if I really even wanted the new iPhone X.

Across from me at the table was an attractive older couple. Needing to pass the time, I began a conversation. I think it went something like: "I cannot believe there are so many people here. Have you been waiting long?" They smiled, and a conversation ensued. Not shy by nature and intently curious, within just a few minutes, I learned that they lived in Chicago, had a condo on South Beach, were born in Poland and grew up in Israel. Then their names were called.

I just could not let them walk out of my life. And so I did something I have never done before: I asked complete strangers to come to my home on Friday night for a Shabbat dinner. They smiled and replied in the affirmative. The wife and I exchanged business cards, and they walked away. Her name was Lily Huberman, and she was listed as the president of a translation company. I did not really care what she did; I was just happy knowing I would see them again.

That Thursday, I got an email from the husband, Eli, asking if they were still invited or had I changed my mind? I remember smiling as

I read it, picturing the look on my husband Mel's face when I told him about my encounter and the invitation I had extended. The email was signed: Eliezer (Eli) Huberman, PhD, CEO NovaDrug. So of course, I was curious and Googled his name. The Wikipedia description almost sent me into cardiac arrest. He was a world-renowned cancer research scientist. I think my exact words to my husband were: "I am freaked! We are going to sound like two idiots. What are we going to talk to them about?"

They came that Friday night bearing gifts: face cream and a gorgeous scarf, both from Israel. We ate and talked for hours. By the end of the night, I felt as though I had found precious new friends. We saw them twice more before they went back to Chicago because regardless of the horrific winter weather, Lily did not like being away from her city or family.

In April during Passover, my rabbi commented that it was a perfect time for new beginnings, a time of miracles, when G-d parted the Sea of Reeds. Those words opened a window into the future for me. I loved science and had always believed that one day I would write about it. I talked with Mel, telling him that I was thinking about asking Eli if I could write his biography. I had written four books—historical fiction and a memoir—but this was territory I had never even considered. With my husband's encouragement, I wrote to Eli. It took days for him to reply. He said that after careful consideration, he would be happy for me to write his biography. My husband and I were invited to Chicago in order to begin the interview process in person. Because I would be working, Mel decided not to come along.

The taxi driver dropped me in front of a large condominium in the heart of downtown Chicago, telling me it was the repurposed Montgomery Ward department store headquarters. Their penthouse was magnificent. After I was given a tour, a private elevator inside their apartment took me to the rooftop and to my accommodations overlooking the city. I could not stop smiling. The moment I was alone, I called Mel to tell him I felt like I had landed in an alternative universe.

I was with them for three days. As for the work, Eli and I would begin at 7 am. He would still be in his bathrobe and we would talk, me recording on my Sony recorder and on my new iPhone, fearful of a technical failure. I also did extensive interviews with Lily. By the time the three days had passed, I probably knew as much about them as any non-family member ever knew.

One afternoon while sitting in Eli's office, I asked him what he wanted the book to be about. He said, "That I am Meir's brother." His younger brother, Meir Dagan, had been the Director of the Israeli Mossad and a hero in Israel. He had died two years earlier, his obituary appearing in newspapers throughout the world. I felt a chill of excitement as I said, "*I Am Meir's Brother* will be the name of this book." Numerous articles, a *60 Minutes* appearance, and several books have highlighted Meir's life, but few know what I learned about the non-public man in the ensuing interviews. That I was staying in the same rooftop garden apartment where he had stayed felt like a connection, a distant bond with this great patriot and man.

The interviews took place in between meals and in between being treated like royalty: a visit to the Chicago Museum of Art, a dinner party, a great restaurant, and one of the most fabulous plays I have ever seen in my life.

Over the next two years, many more interviews followed, over the phone, through emails and in person when they came back to Miami Beach. During that time, I fell in love with both of them. I knew then, and I know now that this book was *beshert*, a Yiddish word that means *it was meant to be.*

Chapter 1

— ••• —

1936, Lukow, Poland

Sixteen-year-old Mina Slushni was quiet and a bit shy. But beneath that exterior facade laid an obstinate streak of resolve that was focused on Shmuel Huberman, the young man she intended to marry. Three years her senior, Shmuel was friendly, outgoing and magnetically charismatic. Only 5' 6", he had a presence that seemed to take up more space than he actually did. Dashing and handsome, his face was shaped like a gentle "U," accentuated by intense dark eyes, a prominent nose and a contagious smile that radiated warmth.

Mina was short and compact with thick wavy raven-colored hair that cascaded down her back, wide set dark eyes, a straight nose and a pretty mouth that all seemed to fit perfectly on her oval-shaped face.

Mina's parents, Sara and Berl Slushni, were the proprietors of a successful dry goods store. And Mina was the niece of Rabbi Aaron Freiberg, a rabbi in the *shetetl* town whose Jewish population neared ten thousand. Rabbi Freiberg's influence as a spiritual leader was so profound his entire extended family was considered *yichus* nobility. As a sign of respect, Berl was known by the honorific name Reb (Rabbi) Slushni. Proud to be observant Jews, they did not even comb their hair on the Sabbath, for fear it might be considered working.

On the other hand, the boy was openly and proudly non-religious. To make matters more intolerable, he was an outspoken leader in the socialist-Zionist group known as *Hashomer Hatzair*, The Young Guard.

His mother, Rachel, had lost her husband to typhoid. Widowed, she had supported her young son and daughter by selling lamp kerosene from a pushcart. A beautiful woman with luxurious blond hair and penetrating blue eyes, she remarried after ten years of widowhood to Levi Shulshtein, a successful owner of a bakery. She no longer worked but that changed nothing. Shmuel's family would always be thought of as socially beneath the Slushni family. The very idea that their daughter, Mina, would even be seen in public with Shmuel Huberman was outrageous.

Consequently, Mina was absolutely forbidden to see Shmuel. She begged her parents to reconsider, but her entreaties fell on deaf ears. Refusing to turn away from each other, the young couple did the unthinkable. They eloped. Mina's parents were brokenhearted and furious, believing that Mina had dishonored their traditions and their name in an unforgivable act of disrespect. The result was a decision too often observed in orthodox religious homes: they declared their daughter dead and sat *shiva*, seven days of mourning.

• • •

Three Years Later

It was a bitterly cold winter day, the wind howling and icicles hanging in claws from the roof eaves, the streets and sidewalks slick and treacherous. Yet, tucked inside a stove-heated cozy room in the *shetel* of Lukow, Mina Slushni Huberman gave birth to a son they named Eliezer. It was February 8, 1939. Exactly eight days after the birth, as commanded in the Torah, a circumcision ceremony was performed. In attendance were both sets of grandparents.

The birth of their first grandchild obliterated the idealistic declaration Berl Slushni had made that his daughter was dead. That proclamation was reversed by the obligation he had to make sure that his grandson Eliezer, nicknamed Eli, would study Torah and Talmud and that he would be raised as an observant Jew.

Seven months later, on September 1, 1939, one and a half million Nazis under orders from Adolph Hitler invaded Poland. The attack was brutal and all-encompassing as the *Luftwaffe* bombed Polish airfields, and the German warships and U-boats decimated the Polish naval forces. In a series of cataclysmic and catastrophic events, bombs were dropped over Lukow, and dozens of innocent civilians were killed. Fear, panic and shock set in with the invasion. The hopes and dreams of a generation imploded in grief. It was a nightmare that would forever scar the soul and the conscience of humanity.

When the German's invaded Lukow, the resistance fighters of the Polish Home Army fought back and managed to kill several German soldiers. In retaliation, the Germans rounded up every Jewish man in the *shtetl*. They chased them through the streets, beating, maiming, shooting and setting Jewish buildings and homes afire.

During the chaos, Mina was shoved into the synagogue along with hundreds of other women, weeping and screaming for their fathers and husbands, their sons, and their grandsons. She clutched her little boy Eli to her chest, terrified, trembling and in shock.

Hours and hours passed before the doors of the synagogue were finally unlocked, and the women were allowed to leave. Mina ran through the streets, sheltering her son from the searing heat of the raging fires. Arriving home, she and Eli were greeted with wailing cries of joy, hugs and tears by her miraculously unharmed parents and husband.

Chapter 2

— ••• —

From 1939–1941, a nonaggression agreement known as the Molotov-Ribbentrop Pact was signed and in place between Hitler's Nazi Germany and the Soviets. The agreement allowed both countries full access to Polish POW's, dissidents and Jews. Desperately in need of workers, the USSR and Germany fed their war machines with workers forcibly exiled from Poland.

The Germans left, and soon Russian soldiers overran the city. The Jews were terrified, certain the Russians would be as violent as the Germans. Thankfully they were not. Ordered to appear at designated synagogues, on a certain day and time, Mina and Shmuel and the entire family made their way to Rabbi Freiberg's temple.

A handsome Red Army senior officer in an immaculate uniform stood on the *bimah* (platform) at the front of the synagogue. His piercing black eyes moved from face to face as the Jews silently filed in and found seats. When all were settled, the officer took a long deep breath and said in Yiddish, the language of the Jews, "I am here to offer you the chance to leave this place and save yourselves." The reaction of those assembled was stunned disbelief. "If you agree," he continued, "we will provide all of you with transportation to Russia." Bedlam erupted. The officer held up his hand for silence. "You *must* listen to me! I am offering you a way out. If you stay here," he pleaded, his voice catching, "the Nazis will . . ." he stopped speaking, the sudden silence deafening. "I swear to you, this is your only hope!"

"Why should we believe you?" someone called out.

"Because I am trying to save you. It won't be an easy life. It won't! You will be sent to work camps. But you will have shelter and food and a chance to live."

The Huberman/ Shulshtein family and the extended Slushni/ Freiberg family huddled together for hours in the synagogue after everyone left. They discussed staying in Lukow. After all, it was their home, the only home any of them had ever known. If they stayed, they would be surrounded by friends and could continue to run their businesses. But for how much longer would they be allowed to even do that?

In agony, they discussed going to Russia and leaving everything they had and everything they knew behind, all based on the word of a man they didn't even know. And yet, if what the soldier said was true, then what other choice did they really have?

"I believe with every fiber of my being that if we stay here, we are doomed!" Shmuel said, every word exuding desperation. "I know it's a risk, but it's a risk I believe this family must take if we are to survive." He picked up his two-year-old son, Eli, nuzzling his pudgy cheeks as he fought for control of his emotions. He turned to Mina's father, "Please, I beg you, we must stay together!"

"What we must do is have faith," Rabbi Freiberg countered. "Surely, the Russians will soon be gone. The Germans are smart and sophisticated and will soon come to their senses. This will all be over soon." He looked hard at Shmuel. "I believe we are better off staying right here with the danger we already know," he pronounced, having come to a final decision. "Who will stay with me?"

Mina's father, Berl, slowly raised his hand. "Sarah and I are too old to go to a work camp. We wouldn't last a week. Besides, when our beloved son, your brother," he looked at Mina with tears in his eyes, "returns from the war, if we leave, how will he ever find us? We must stay," he said softly, so pale he looked as if he might faint.

"No!" Mina cried, throwing her arms around her father. "This can't be happening. We must all agree! Please, Papa, come with us. I can't leave you!"

"I promise you, my beloved Mina, when the war is over, we will be together again," her father said softly, taking her face in his hands and kissing her forehead. "You will see."

Chapter 3

———————— ••• ————————

The Jews heading for Russia were ordered to bring only what they could carry and what would fit in their suitcases. Having only one day to prepare before heading to the train station, Mina and Shmuel gathered shoes, clothing, medicines, personal sundries, food and diapers for the baby.

With every suitcase stuffed to capacity, they took a sad final walk around their modest flat. In the kitchen, the photo albums were in a stack on the counter to be picked up by Mina's parents for safekeeping. Shmuel walked to the bookcase in the living room, running his fingers along the precious titles that would have to be left behind. His hand lingered on the book *Altneuland, The Old New World,* by Theodor Herzl. Translated from German into Yiddish, the Zionist manuscript had been the inspiration that fueled his Zionism and belief in a Jewish homeland. Pulling it from the shelf, Mina nodded her head and smiled as Shmuel tucked it into a suitcase.

Mina wore the only silk dress she had ever owned. It was a precious and expensive gift from her parents that she refused to leave behind. She knew it was foolish, but Mina had made a solemn promise to herself that no matter what might happen, she would never allow anyone take away her upbringing, traditions or dignity.

•••

Waiting on the train platform that cold winter day in 1941, bundled in their warmest clothing and heaviest coats and scarves were Mina, Shmuel and baby Eli. Along with them were Shmuel's family: his mother Rachel, stepfather Levi Shulshtein, his sister Lola, Shmuel's teenage stepbrother Shlomo, and stepsister Channah.

Mina's parents were there as well. Clutching Eli to her breast, Grandmother Sara's tears spilled on to the little boy's innocent face. Mina put her arm around her mother and leaned in, capturing the moment, the love and the loss. Her father, Berl, stood apart, a lone figure, shoulders sagging as he stared at his hands.

"Papa," Mina said softly, approaching and then gently touching his arm.

Berl did a sharp intake of breath before looking into his daughter's eyes. "My *shane maydl*, my beautiful daughter, can you ever forgive me for the pain I caused this family?" he begged. "You married a good man, a kind man. I should have accepted your decision. I would give my life to have that time back, time I wasted when I could have been with you."

"Of course, I forgive you, Papa," Mina said, gasping through her tears. "I love you… and I always will."

Berl opened his arms and Mina stepped into his embrace. "Go with G-d's blessings my child. Take care of yourself and your family," he whispered.

The agony of those final moments that would take them into exile would remain indelibly etched in Mina's heart and memory for the rest of her very long life.

...

Their train covered 1,500 miles in two days: its final destination an isolated labor camp in northern Russia, in the Ural Mountains that separated Europe from the Asian part of the USSR. The area was part of the Komi Republic known as the White Sea region. While the camp was not technically located in Siberia, it might as well have been, as the winter weather was the same: frozen rivers, winds howled and temperatures that would plunge well below freezing.

The exiled civilians: Jews, Poles and Russians were herded off the train. Exhausted and disorientated, they were force-walked to the labor camp. Upon arrival, they were led into a cavernous desk-filled room that they would later learn was the administrative building of the compound.

The ferret-eyed superintendent of the camp, a member of the NKVD, the Soviet Union's Secret Service greeted them with the words: "Welcome comrades to your new home." A wicked smile turned the corners of his mouth. "You will notice that there are no guards in this camp. And do you know why?" Silence greeted his question. "There are no guards because there is nowhere for you to go!" he laughed, showing crooked, brown-tinged teeth. "This is a logging camp. Tomorrow you will each be assigned your jobs. If you work hard, you will eat! You don't work hard, you don't eat! Sabotage the war efforts, criticize the government or the Communist Party, say a bad word about the Red Army or any of the country's leaders, and you will be sent away. And once you leave here . . .chances are no one will ever see you again."

Voices began to rise in anger. An NKVD officer shouted, "No talking!" He had a clipboard in his hand. "When you hear your name called, say present. I will give you a number. Remember it."

Thirty minutes later, the assembled were organized into grouped numbers. Shmuel felt helpless as he watched his mother, sister and the rest of the family file out the door. Questions careened through his brain: would they be okay, when would he see them again?

Their group number was called. Two comrades from the camp were there to assist them with their meager but cumbersome luggage, all of which had been thrown into a massive pile on the ice-crusted

A Depiction Of A Typical Russian Work Camp

ground. Shmuel was disconsolate, filled with rage and guilt for talking his family into leaving Poland. At the time, he had been so certain it was the right thing to do. What a fool I am, he thought, digging through the mound of luggage.

It felt like the longest walk in his life as they trudged over the barren, rock-strewn path. Looking around him, everything was brown and dark and dead. They finally stopped in front of a dilapidated wooden-planked one room box-like shack that was to be their new home. It was in that moment that the stark reality of what lay ahead struck him as surely as a knife being plunged into his belly.

One of the comrades checked the number on the door, shook his head in the affirmative and entered. "Thank you for your help," Mina said in Polish.

"May you live a long life," the old man said, his sunken face softening. With that simple phrase, Mina understood the shared and undeniable commonality that linked them all—the will to survive.

Inside the shack, the air was so cold it hurt to breathe. Baby Eli whimpered, too tired and cold to even cry. Mina opened her coat and wrapped him inside, hoping her body warmth would mitigate the cold causing him to shiver. Within seconds the child fell asleep.

Shmuel fell to his knees. "What have I done? There's no electricity and no toilet! I never imagined, not even in my worst nightmares that it could be this bad! Mina, I am so sorry!"

Mina held back her tears, refusing to allow herself the luxury of self-pity. She eyed the twin cots with their filthy threadbare mattresses and the cast iron stove that stood in the middle of the room, quite obviously their only source of warmth.

"We will make this work. We just need some heat," she said, her voice hard and determined. "We passed a wood pile on the way here."

"I saw it," he replied softly, heading for the door.

Shmuel and Mina lay together on one cot, Eli on the other, warm under a pile of sweaters and coats. Slowly, even though the ceaseless wind drove cold air into the hut through the closed window and gaps in the wood, it had warmed up enough to consider trying to sleep. Holding each other, arms and legs intertwined, desperate to feel safe and protected, Mina could no longer pretend to be strong. She wept into her hands, stifling her sobs for fear of waking Eli.

Shmuel had no words left to say. All he could do was hold Mina until she fell into a fitful sleep. Only then did he shed his own silent tears.

Chapter 4

——— ••• ———

It was dark outside when loudspeakers screamed them awake in the morning. Finding a chamber pot under a pile of rubble in the corner, they relieved themselves before donning their heavy coats and boots, tucking Eli into his sweater and jacket and three pairs of big boy pants.

Mina had believed that things would look better with a night's sleep. But after inspecting the mattresses they had slept on, she felt sick. She could only pray that little Eli had not been infected with bedbugs. She vowed to herself, *if it is the last thing I ever do, my son will have a bath before this day is over*!

Mingling with the other shell-shocked prisoners, hunger became the reigning subject of any conversation. Eventually, they were taken to a mess hall with long wooden tables and benches. Standing in line with a bowl, they were given watery buckwheat gruel and a small piece of black bread. Mina and Shmuel knew then that the Russian Jew in Poland had lied when he said they would not starve.

Ten minutes into their disgusting dining experience, the same ferret-eyed superintendent appeared. Standing on a crate, to make himself appear taller, he demanded silence.

"Two days ago, a baker was discovered stealing a piece of bread!" he said, scowling. "Perhaps that seems like an innocent offense to you. But in the Union of Soviet Socialist Republic, the punishment for such an offense is a bullet in the brain!" he paused for effect. "Now that you know this, who among you knows how to bake bread?"

Shmuel's stepfather Levi called out: "My son and I know how to bake."

"Where did you learn?" the Russian officer demanded, eyes circling their faces as a vulture might before consuming its prey.

"I had a bakery," Levi replied, knowing that even though Shmuel had never spent more than five minutes in the bakery, he could quickly teach him what he needed to know.

"You," the soldier said, pointing to Shmuel, "will work in the bakery. You, old man, will be assigned to something else."

Levi paled; his enthusiasm and lie could cost Shmuel his life. "Listen to me," he whispered in his stepson's ear. "It's not so difficult. I will tell you what you must do to prepare the dough."

• • •

Standing in the filthy kitchen, hands and legs trembling, Shmuel stared at the sacks of flour, the yeast and the pots of heated water. Levi's directions swirled in his brain as he introduced himself to the head baker. After introductions were made to the helpers, everyone returned to their perspective responsibilities.

Shmuel mixed the first batch of dough concentrating so hard he bit his cheek and drew blood. Once the loaves had been put in the pans, he placed them in the oven. Crossing his fingers, he prayed for success, knowing that his family would not starve if all went well.

While the bread baked, Shmuel decided to wash the mountain of dirty mixing bowls stacked on the floor and on the counter near the sink. It was clearly not his job, but he was too nervous to do nothing. And there was no way he was going to mix another batch of dough before seeing how his first batch turned out. Washing out the first bowl, he made a self-deprecating joke about the gooey mess reminding him of changing dirty diapers. Wanting to ingratiate himself to his comrades, he went on to tell a funny story about the first diaper he ever changed, and the penis shower he received as a thank you. Chuckles followed and others added their own stories. By the time the bread was ready to come out of the oven, Shmuel had made new friends.

The loaves were removed. The dough had not risen; rather the loaves looked like someone had smashed them down and then vomited. Shmuel was horrified, knowing that if his incompetence was reported, he could be sent away for trying to sabotage the war effort. But he was not reported. Instead, the head baker gave him secret tutorials, and within a few days, Shmuel became a passable baker.

Months later, his stepfather Levi was unexpectedly assigned to the bakery and Shmuel was transferred to a woodshop where he would spend the remainder of his incarceration building large wooden boxes. He never knew if he was building coffins or simply crates for transporting goods. He never knew and he never asked.

•••

The freezing winter months took their toll on Mina. She lost so much weight her clothing hung from her tiny body. Shmuel was emaciated as well, his plans of stealing bread from the bakery derailed by constant surveillance. Only Eli maintained a normal weight, his parents eating less so that their son would thrive.

All winter, the slave laborers were forced to work eight-hour days in the forest cutting down trees: wood was a desperately needed commodity for the Soviet war effort. The conditions and food rations were inhuman, and the work was backbreaking and horrifically dangerous. Untold numbers of prisoners lost their lives, crushed by falling trees.

With spring the snow stopped, and the rivers thawed. Temperatures hovered in the 60's. The warmer weather brought hope to the camp, as migrating ducks and cranes and songbirds served to remind the exhausted prisoners that there was life beyond the pale. The logs having already been hauled to the waterside, the next phase of the logging operation would now commence. Longtime prisoners often spoke to Shmuel about what took place at the river with dread. When Mina was ordered to join the workforce there, Shmuel was frantic. He begged every administrator he had befriended to help get Mina reassigned. It was to no avail.

Leaving Eli with a fourteen-year-old babysitter, Mina joined the large entourage of workers. Once at the river, the men were given huge hooks that were used to pull the floating logs together, thereby creating giant rafts. The women were ordered onto the rafts. Their job was to jump on the moving logs and tie them together. Russian prisoners worked side by side with Jews and the Poles. There was no anti-Semitism and no nationalistic leanings. Life was about living for one more day. The work was treacherous. Workers died when losing their balance and falling into the river where they would either be crushed by the careening logs or swept away with the current. They also died from starvation, gorging on their weekly bread allocation rather than spreading it out for the entire week. The medical facilities were poor, and medication was almost non-existent, so a minor infection could lead to death.

Having seen prisoners sent away for minor infractions, Mina never told anyone that she could not swim. Instead, she forged ahead without complaint, spending everyday wet and cold and terrified. The result, she was considered a *stachanovka*, a model worker. Her reward, an occasional bowl of soup and a small piece of cake, which she brought home to her little boy.

Mina's example served as a guiding light for her husband and her son for the rest of their lives. She would always say: under duress people can do anything!

Chapter 5

———— ••• ————

October 1944

Warmed by the radiating fire from the potbelly stove, Shmuel and Mina sat on rickety chairs as five-year-old Eli played at their feet with miniature boxcars carved by his father. Mina's hands rested protectively on her belly as she reflected over the previous five months, still thinking it incomprehensible that she had not realized she was pregnant.

She did not remember having a regular period, but menstruation was rare for the overworked half-starved women. As for feeling sick in the morning, it meant nothing. She always felt sick. As for the swelling of her belly, Mina saw it as a sign of malnutrition, not a sign of new life. It took a female friend who worked with her at the river to ask *how many months along are you* before Mina accepted the obvious.

Mina knew it was a miracle that she sustained the pregnancy, considering how many times she had fallen into the river, having to grab on to the shifting and careening logs, to keep from drowning as she fought to regain her purchase. Looking back, she believed it was a good thing she had not known about her pregnancy—fighting for two lives would have been too great a burden for her to carry.

Mina closed her eyes and let her mind travel back to their first year in the camp. She had never imagined how hard life could be, that she would hoard a sliver of soap to bathe her son, that she would always be hungry, worried and sad. She missed her parents and her brother so much at times she thought she would go mad. She thought about the vow she made to herself before leaving Poland: to keep her dignity and always honor her upbringing and traditions. How naive and foolish she had been. What did dignity even mean? Did anyone care that she had once had good manners or had observed the Sabbath? Her life was now about only one thing—the survival of her husband, son and unborn child.

...

Realizing they could not stop the encroaching Red Army, the Germans fled Kherson, a port city located on the Dnieper River near the Black Sea in southern Ukraine in March 1944. As a result, the inhabitants of Mina and Shmuel's labor camp were now being relocated.

Mina had found it almost impossible to allow herself to have hope during the past four years. But Shmuel believed the war was going to end and his optimism was contagious. As they packed their meager belongings, Mina permitted herself the luxury of imagining the look on her mother and father's faces when she saw them again. In her mind's eye, their expressions of love would be like radiating golden streaks of sunlight, their embrace and their warmth able to soothe and melt her hardened heart. She thought of how they would adore their five-year-old grandson Eli, a curious bright-eyed little boy. She placed her open palm on her stomach, "I love you, little one," she whispered. The baby kicked and Mina smiled, thankful that above all else, this child would not be born in the camp where so many mothers and so many babies died.

But even in the labor camps there was romance. Shmuel's beautiful sister Lola, despite her unkempt hair and tattered clothing, met, fell in love and married Izak Beldigrin. He was a sophisticated and highly trained medical professional, assigned as the labor camp *Feldsher*. In

Poland and the Soviet Union, a feldsher was a senior nurse who in sparse and rural settings provided primary, obstetrical and uncomplicated surgical care. Izak pleaded with the camp superintendent for desperately needed Sulfa drugs, surgical supplies, and anesthesia. His request was met with smug rejections. Consequently, he had to make do with medical supplies consisting of bandage rolls, needles and thread, a pair of tweezers, a knife and cupping glasses to treat serious colds and pneumonia.

Izak trained Lola as his assistant to be his desperately needed second pair of hands. Working around the clock, every life lost took its toll on him, especially when he knew that his patient would have lived if surgery or hospitalization had been available. But nothing affected him as deeply as losing a mother, an infant, or both due to complications that could have been either avoided or treated. In those dark times, he would lament, slipping into a bleak mood that could last for days.

In the midst of their never-ending days into nights of work, a beacon of light appeared. Lola became pregnant. Refusing to leave her husband's side, knowing that her presence was desperately needed, she moved through morning sickness and a cumbersome belly as if it were nothing more than a slight inconvenience. Seven weeks before her delivery date, Lola went into labor. Sadly, Izak Beldegrin could do nothing to save his own newborn daughter.

●●●

Two hundred and twenty-five refugees boarded the train that would be following the Red army transports to the Soviet-occupied city of Kherson. The refugees were not free but leaving the labor camp felt like a beginning. After so many years of scarcity and near isolation, the thought of being in a real city struck them all speechless until they arrived. The streets were littered with shattered glass, broken furniture and building debris.

They learned that the Germans had forced the residents of Kherson to flee or be shot. Pillaging the city, the Nazis then systematically destroyed all industry, burning homes and buildings. The displaced residents had returned and were now rebuilding their lives under Communist rule.

...

The nine members of Shmuel's family—his sister Lola and her husband Izak, his mother, Rachel and her husband Levi and his two teenage children, plus Mina and Eli— were taken to an apartment building in the city's center that had recently been occupied by Nazis. After the labor camp, being crowded into a two-bedroom apartment with an actual icebox, plus a bathroom down the hall with showers and heat was most certainly luxurious.

Eli would remember fragments of the time he lived in Kherson, like constantly being fed grapes and told they would make him strong. He remembered that Uncle Izak smoked a pipe. When Izak was home, which was not often since he was on medical call for the Jewish community twenty-four hours a day, he let Eli play with his pipe, a pipe that became a telephone in the hands and imagination of a little boy.

On January 30, 1945, Mina Huberman went into labor. Romantic fables would develop about the circumstances of Meir's birth. Some claimed Meir was born on a Russian train on its way to Poland. Other writings had him born on a Russian train fleeing the Nazis. Neither story was true.

The years of deprivation and hard work, and her ability to withstand fear and pain, enabled Mina to deliver her son Meir without even crying out. She remained in the clinic on Kherson for two days with her newborn, relishing every moment of rest.

Cloistered and cut-off from news, Mina would eventually learn that of the three hundred members of her extended and immediate family, only two people had survived: her brother and an uncle who was visiting the United States when Poland fell. The uncle married while in America. His new wife would become a precious and beloved addition to the family: precious because in the sad searching years that followed the Holocaust, familial bonds became the ultimate lifeline connecting the Jewish past to the Jewish future.

Chapter 6

— ... —

The war in Europe officially ended on May 8, 1945. Three months later, Russia's Communist Party forged an accord with Poland, allowing all Polish citizens to return to their homeland, that very same place where neighbors and so-called friends had turned a blind eye to the Jews who were beaten and maimed and killed during the reign of the Nazi occupation.

To repopulate the deserted German towns and villages that were taken over by Poland as compensation for the land grabbed by the Soviet Union, the Polish Communist government put in place a resettlement plan. They designated specific destinations for each family unit. Consequently, over a period of several weeks, one hundred eighty thousand Jewish prisoners were returned to Poland.

Shmuel, Mina and the entire family were assigned to Dzierzoniow, previously Reichenbach, a city located at the foot of the Owl Mountains in southwestern Poland. In an area known as Lower Silesia, it was five hundred and fifty miles from their home in Lukow. Mina was frantic and disconsolate and desperate to go home but they had no money for transportation.

Meanwhile in Poland, hundreds of disenfranchised ex-soldiers formed violent nationalistic splinter groups determined to stop the returning Jews from reclaiming their confiscated properties. They printed pamphlets accusing the repatriating Jews of being Communist puppets of the USSR. Knives in hand, when trains from the Russian regions entered stations all over Poland, the terrorists boarded, stabbing as many Jews as they could before jumping off the trains and running away. But those miscreants had miscalculated the effect their attacks would have. The Jews may have left Poland as meek and peaceful citizens, but they returned filled with rage and purpose. No one would stop them or turn them away.

...

Standing in the crowded square waiting to be assigned a place to live, the family inhaled their first breaths of freedom. Looking around in awe, they were enthralled by the richly embellished ornamental motifs and colorful buildings that were a mixture of Bohemian and German mannerist architecture.

Their joy was short-lived, surrounded as they were, by hundreds of emaciated women, men and scrawny looking teenagers. The adolescents, all innocence obliterated, seemed to have a single commonality: an attitude of challenging defiance and rage etched into their faces.

Mina searched the crowd, feeling that something was so very off, but she could not identify what it was. Suddenly realization hit. Tears filled her eyes as she clutched Meir tightly to her breast.

"Shmuel," she cried, "where are all the babies . . . the little children?"

Shmuel shook his head. There were no words to express what he was thinking as he reached for Eli's hand.

In time, they would learn that there were *no* babies or young children left alive. They had all been murdered in places like Dachau, Sachsenhausen and the Buchenwald concentration camps. Many of the parents of those children were survivors from the near-by Gross-Rosen labor camp, known as the 90-day camp—the number of days one would survive. The Red Army liberated them on February 14, 1945. At the peak of the war, the Gross-Rosen slave labor camp had one hundred substations spread throughout Europe. It would later be estimated that 40,000 men and women were worked and starved to death or died as subjects used to test the effects of radiation, nerve gas and chemical warfare. The German companies knowingly participating and profiting from those slave labor camps were Blaupunkt, Siemens, Krupp, IG Farben, Daimler-Benz and Volkswagen.

•••

Because the Germans had to flee so quickly, the previous occupants had left almost everything behind. The Huberman/ Shulstein families were each given their own apartments within the same building. There were real mattresses covered with clean sheets, feather pillows and a luxurious wool blanket. The main living area had an upholstered sofa that could be sat on without getting poked by the springs. There was even a dining table. The kitchen lacked a refrigerator, but the cupboards were filled with dishes, glasses and pots and pans, and there was a hotplate for cooking. Mina wandered about their new home, her eyes drinking in the luxury of her surroundings, joyous to have their privacy.

With his mother preoccupied with baby Meir, Eli was left free to explore without supervision for the very first time. His imagination and curiosity ignited, he spent hours exploring every nook and cranny, standing on chairs as he climbed on counters. He pretended to be a baker like his grandfather as he played with the pots and pans. In a small closet off the kitchen used for cold storage, he found a glass jar filled with what looked to him like green eyeballs. He carried the jar to his mother in the bedroom and presented it to her as one might present the most magnificent gift.

"What is this?" he asked, sucking his bottom lip, a habit he had developed since being a baby.

"Let's take a look," Mina said.

"I think its eyeballs," Eli said, a mischievous expression crinkling his big black eyes.

"I am pretty sure these are some sort of preserves," Mina said, examining the jar. "Shall we open them and try one?"

"Sure." Eli said, thinking about the stale green bread for breakfast, the gruel for lunch and dinner, and all the terrible food he had been forced to eat in his young life, simply to survive. *How bad could it be?*

"Let's go get a fork," Mina said, moving sleeping baby Meir into the middle of the bed.

"How brave are you?' Mina teased after opening the jar and spearing an olive. "Do you dare to go first?"

Eli giggled, taking the fork. He licked the olive, the briny taste tickling his tongue. He put it in his mouth and bit down. "Yuck!! It's awful," he said, spitting into his hand.

Mina tried one as well. She too spits it out. "Beyond terrible! Are there more jars?"

"No," Eli said.

The idea of throwing food away was distressing but the decision to do so empowering. It was Mina's way of taking back her life. "We shall never eat another thing in our lives that we don't want to eat!" she announced, smiling at Eli. "To the garbage, young man! To the garbage!"

Chapter 7

_____ ••• _____

The only book Shmuel took with him when they fled their home in Lukow was Herzl's book *Altneuland*. During their years of exile in the labor camp, he had memorized many pages. Determined to bring hope that the creation of a homeland for the Jewish people was possible, he secretly organized discussion groups with fellow Jews in the camp. If caught, he would have been charged as a dissident, and the punishment was death. Despite that, Shmuel refused to remain silent.

Now back in Poland, he re-established himself as a leader in the Socialist-Zionist group *Hashomer Hatzair*, just as he had in his youth. Notorious for their heroic resistance against the Nazis during the War, the focus of *Hashomer Hatzair* now shifted back to the Zionist dream of establishing a Jewish homeland in Palestine.

The regional headquarters of *Hashomer Hatzair* was located on Kolejowa Street. Because of Shmuel's leadership role, it was decided that his family should be relocated to number 20, a second story apartment in the same building. Mina was ecstatic. The apartment had two full bedrooms, a bathtub and a full kitchen complete with an icebox and stove. Large windows overlooked the busy street, and on sunny days the sun shone through like streaks of shimmering diamonds. The furniture left by the fleeing Germans was utilitarian, clean lines, and fine quality. However, there was not a comfortable chair in the entire apartment.

•••

Looking handsome with his thick black hair slicked back and a newly laundered shirt, Shmuel stood in front of the hundreds of men and women who had gathered in one of the many abandoned industrial buildings, its walls newly whitewashed removing all reminders of the Nazi presence.

"I stand before you today, at a podium the Nazis used to call for the annihilation of our people," Shmuel said sadly, face darkening. "NEVER AGAIN!" he shouted. "NEVER EVER AGAIN!" The gatherers screamed back his words, fists in the air, their rage all encompassing. "Tonight, I will use this same podium to speak about the future of the Jewish people. Look around you. We are the survivors, and we will be the ones to claim, in the name of the millions slaughtered, a home for our people in the land of Israel!" His face broke into an endearing smile, and tears filled his eyes as the crowd cheered.

Mina leaned over the pram to readjust the blanket around Meir. She glanced at Eli, who had found some friends and was off to the side of the room flicking marbles against a wall. Adoring and proud, she turned her full attention back to her husband's speech.

"Now allow me to share with you the words of Theodore Herzl, from the year 1902, words said then and applicable now:

What glory awaits those of us who fight unselfishly for our cause! Therefore, I believe that a wondrous generation of Jews will spring into existence. We Jews who wish for a State will have it! We shall live at last as free men on our own soil and die peacefully in our own homes. The world will be freed by our liberty, enriched by our wealth, magnified by our greatness. And whatever we attempt there to accomplish for our own welfare, will react powerfully and beneficially for the good of all humanity."

Shmuel paused, letting the message swirl and resonate before speaking again. "We must commit, each and every one of us, that when we are allowed to leave Poland, Israel will be our destination."

Not long after, representatives from the Joint Distribution Committee in America, known as the JDC, contacted Shmuel through the *Hashomer Hatzair* center in Warsaw. They gave him instructions to rent a warehouse in Dzierzoniow large enough to hold a large shipment of canned food and clothing that would arrive within weeks from the United States.

Working tirelessly, the JDC had done the miraculous job of raising over three hundred million dollars from the American Jewish community money donated by fellow Jews, the rich and the poor, to their brethren in Europe thousands of miles away.

•••

Shmuel directed the volunteers, many of them his friends who had come back with him from the Soviet Union, to sort and help distribute food and clothing to the survivors and to the destitute refugees that continued to arrive daily in Dzierzoniow.

Mina was exhausted. During the day, she worked at the warehouse, and in the evenings, she prepared dinner, spent time with her two boys, and did her best to keep up with the laundry and cleaning. Anxious to relieve the babysitter and to hear about Eli's day at school, she left the warehouse as the setting sun was turning the late fall day frigid. Suddenly, she heard her name and stopped in her tracks, shocked by the familiar voice. Spinning on her heels, she had trouble recognizing the two people before her—friends from Lukow, Dina and her husband David. Cadaver thin, with eyes glazed and hair knotted in filth they both looked on the verge of death. Frozen in place and overcome, the three of them just stood staring at each other and weeping. "Come with me," Mina said, gently taking Dina's hand and then David's. Walking slowly, cooing encouragement, she led them into the warehouse. "This way," she offered, turning down the long-deserted hallway that led to Shmuel's office. "I'll be right back. While I am gone, please take all your clothes off and throw them in here," she said, pulling a metal garbage can from the shadows.

"You want to take my clothes?" Dina shook her head vehemently.

"It's okay. Please just trust me," Mina pleaded. "You are full of lice and that makes you contagious. You need to bathe and get clean before I can help you. Please do it now. I'll be right back."

Mina returned with clothing for both of them, clean water, soap, a shaving brush, razor and towels. She helped them wash, modesty a luxury no longer honored. To these three survivors, if a body still breathed, that mattered. Anything else had long ago become irrelevant. Somewhere down deep, David knew he should be embarrassed, but that emotion had been crushed by the Nazis.

Once they had washed and were wrapped in clean towels, Mina began to drag the garbage can out the door. A volunteer was waiting to take it outside and burn the contents.

"What are you doing?" Dina cried near hysterics. "Those are my things! You can't have them!"

Mina looked at her devastated friend, understanding how important and precious these filthy garments were to her. "You won't need these anymore. They are in the past and it is time to let them go," Mina said softly.

An hour later, their heads were shaved, and their bodies were free of lice. Dressed in clean clothing, Mina brought her friends home until a place of their own could be secured. The healing would take time, a long time, but with gentle love and patience, their ravaged bodies and broken hearts would one day begin to heal.

Chapter 8

———— ••• ————

May 1946

Shmuel awoke every day at sunrise, vowing to himself and to G-d that not one of the refugee survivors would ever feel lost, alone, and without hope—at least while he still had breath. He worked until his eyes blurred and his body was on the verge of collapse. Food, clothing, a place to lay their head that was safe, and a future that included living in the land of Israel were what ruled his world.

For Shmuel being at home when he could be working seemed superfluous since Mina was more than capable of handling the children without him. In fact, had Mina not insisted, he might not have even come home for the evening meal or even remembered to eat.

He stood at the threshold of his apartment, forcing the memories of the day from his mind. A smile pasted on his face; he strode into the kitchen.

"What have we here?" Shmuel asked, embracing Mina from behind and nuzzling her neck. Taking the spoon from her hand, he stuck it in the pot of savory beef stew and took a taste. "Such a good cook my little wife has become," he said tauntingly.

She slapped his hand away and laughed. "Go see your boys. They miss you."

Shmuel walked carefully between the wooden blocks strewn about the floor, rays from a full moon glowing through the windows. He felt a sense of wellbeing as he looked around the cluttered living room, including the pile of unfolded cloth diapers needing Mina's attention. For a fleeting moment Shmuel thought, *if one's life appeared normal, then perhaps normalcy could begin to be achieved.*

He picked up one-year-old Meir, an adorable little boy with a head full of curls, twinkling eyes and a joyous smile. He held his son close, overcome by the softness and warmth of his little body. That infusion of love momentarily filled all the empty spaces in Shmuel's weeping soul.

Then reality came crashing in as he thought: *normal! What is normal? Could my life ever be normal after listening to the stories told by a thousand childless parents? Parents whose children were torn from their arms and murdered.* For what seemed like the hundredth time that day, Shmuel asked himself: *What would I do if someone tried to take my sons away from me?*

Forcing himself back to the present, he mumbled a few endearing words, hugged Meir one more time before gently placing him back down amongst his toys.

Eli, a precocious seven-year-old with a chubby face, ears he would grow into, questioning eyes and a smile that lit up a room, waited patiently, sitting in a chair beside his father's paper-stacked desk.

"Ah! And how is my brilliant son today?" Shmuel asked in Yiddish, as he collapsed in his desk chair next to Eli.

"Good." Eli smiled, basking in the compliment and the attention, understanding that this was his father's way of showing love, unlike his mother, who was always hugging, kissing and pinching his cheeks.

"Shall we begin your studies?" Shmuel asked, speaking to Eli as if he were an adult.

"*A kluger farshtait fun ain vort tsvai,* a wise man hears one word and understands two," Eli replied. It was the mantra that began every homework session.

Shmuel nodded approvingly and Eli beamed, his father's admiration meaning everything. An independent and mature child, Eli attended a Jewish day school run by a close family friend, Aba Lichtenstein. Gifted beyond his years and relishing the demanding curriculum, he was learning to read and write in Yiddish, was studying Hebrew and could already speak Russian and Polish.

Shmuel envisioned the day he would take his son to Palestine, where they would only hear the true language of Jews: Hebrew. But in the meanwhile, out of an obligation to the past, each night he sat with his son to study Yiddish. Birthed in the 10th century to connect Jews throughout Eastern and Central Europe, it was a concoction of dialects based on Medieval German with borrowed words from Hebrew, Aramaic, Roman and Slavic languages. It was inventive and often funny, its nuances and expressions so unique they never quite translated into any other language.

In time, Eli would lose the ability to write or read Polish, with its "rz," "dz" and "sz" consonants making words hard to spell. His aptitude to understand Russian would remain but he would never be comfortable speaking it. But Yiddish would remain fluid and viable for the rest of his life, the words always taking him back to that all-encompassing and precious time he had spent with his father.

•••

Keren Kayemet, the Jewish United Fund that was established to purchase and develop land in Palestine, and popular among both the left and right leaning Zionists, distributed blue and white charity boxes.

Shmuel gave Eli the very grown-up job of being in charge of one of the donation boxes. Eli felt so important going up to people and asking, "Can you please give some money for the Jewish people in Palestine?" More times than not, he would get a smile as a coin was dropped into the box.

The box full, Eli felt an enormous sense of satisfaction as he sat at the kitchen table watching his father count the coins.

"You did a terrific job, and I am very proud of you," Shmuel said, giving him the customary pat on the head. "And I want you to know that your hard work is appreciated by everyone." Eli gleamed with pride. "But" his father continued, "it has been decided by the board that you are just too young to be handling so much money. And so, the job will be given to an older boy."

After Shmuel took away his box, Eli cried for hours. He was crushed. In the eyes of a seven-year-old, it was the worst insult he had ever experienced.

•••

The Pilawa River and bridge were next to Eli's building, and it was the meet-up place after school. Splashing in ankle-deep water at low tide, the rocks protruding like misshapen heads, the boys looked for everything from bullet casings to beer cans.

"*Psia-krew cholera!*" shouted David, a skinny eight-year-old Eli knew from Ukraine lifting something from the river.

A dozen boys came running and stood with their mouths open in disbelief as they stared at the muck-covered Browning automatic rifle. It was a magnificent find even if it was so old and rusted and must have been from World War I. The boys took turns holding the rifle, yelling *tat, tat, tat* as they pretended to shoot Germans.

When it was time to leave, a long discussion took place as to where they should hide their find. Eli, their mild-mannered ringleader said, "We have to turn it in."

"Are you crazy? Why?" one of the bigger boys shouted. "It's ours!"

Eli shook his head. "It isn't a toy, and it isn't ours to play with. This was used to kill people. Maybe even Jews," he said angrily.

Silence followed as the boys marched back into town, their Browning automatic rifle in tow.

•••

Eli was a happy boy. He loved their apartment, the food, and most of all winter. Even though the temperature in Dzierzoniow was freezing and darkness fell by 4 pm, he didn't care. He loved bundling up in two sweaters, a coat, mittens, earmuffs and boots to go sleigh riding with friends. He would trek up the gigantic hill just to the left of his apartment building, a hill as big as a mountain in his minds' eye. Because it was too dangerous to take Meir, Eli was allowed to leave him behind, and that alone made for a perfect afternoon.

Eli learned early in his life that *kvetching* only made his mother feel bad, and in the end, was a waste of time. And so, he never complained or admitted that he resented having a brother six years younger that was always the center of attention, a position Eli held until Meir came along. To make matters worse, wherever Eli went, his baby brother was always dragging after him. Eli felt embarrassed to be babysitting and insulted that his own desires and personality were disregarded because he was expected to not only watch his baby brother but to guard him.

Eli did guard his brother throughout their growing up years, taking on the role of brother and sometimes parent. Little did he know that one day Meir Huberman Dagan would become the world-renowned guardian of the State of Israel.

Chapter 9

————— ··· —————

The British established a blockade during and after WWII to stop the Jews who were fleeing the Nazis from coming into Palestine. That blockade officially ended on May 14, 1948, when the United Nations terminated the British Mandate over Palestine that had existed since 1923. That very day in Tel Aviv, the entire Jewish world held its collective breath as David Ben-Gurion, chairman of the Jewish People's Council proclaimed the establishment of the State of Israel. Hours later, Israel was recognized by the Soviet Union and the United States.

When statehood was announced, Poland and the Soviet Union along with Czechoslovakia offered assistance to the State of Israel. They came to her aid because they all had a common enemy: the British. But soon after the alliances shifted. Israel and America, sharing a love for Democracy, aligned. That relationship angered Russia—now archenemy of the United States. The Cold War had begun.

The land once ruled by Rome, then later by the Christian Crusaders, the Ottoman Empire and Britain, was now officially a home for the Jewish people. Shmuel was ecstatic. That joy sweetened by knowing that he could now join his sister, Lola, and her feldsher husband, along with the one hundred and twenty thousand Jewish refugees already living in Israel. Most survivors were smuggled in despite the British mandate. His dreams nearing reality, he expected to hear any day that his family's passage had been arranged.

Instead, the unthinkable happened. Pacing the living room of the apartment, he tore at a cuticle. "This can't be happening! Not now!"

"Please just sit down and start from the beginning," Mina begged, thankful that the boys were sleeping would not see their father in such a state. Shmuel came to the sofa. He sat facing her, their knees touching. "A man accosted me on the street this afternoon, ordering me to follow him. He had a gun!" Shmuel hissed, fury slicing his words. "He took me to an abandoned house. Inside there were two other men sitting on boxes smoking cigarettes and sharing a bottle of vodka. I couldn't believe what was happening. I hated them on sight. Who the hell are you? I asked. A pudgy, mustached man with a rat-like smile told me he represented the Russian NKVD secret service. He went on to say that Poland and the USSR were intertwined, cooperating on every international and political problem and that they were here to recruit me to spy for them when I got to Israel. He said that my senior position in *Hashomer Hatzair* in Poland would translate into me having a high position in the Israeli government and that I would have access to valuable information. They offered money, immediate passage to Israel for our entire family and more. I didn't know whether to laugh or cry."

Mina cringed, fear enveloping her.

Shmuel continued; his voice strained. "I somehow managed to convince them that due to my commitments and promises during public talks that I would be expected to become a worker, probably constructing houses or paving roads. Moreover, I told them that I do not speak or write Hebrew, just Yiddish, which makes me unsuitable for any governmental position and definitely not to one with any access to important information. They released me but not before warning that if I ever repeated one word of this conversation to anyone, my life would come to a very unpleasant end!"

Mina shook her head as she reached for Shmuel's hands. "Shmuel, what are we going to do?"

"Get the hell out of Poland! That is what we are going to do."

Shmuel had been communicating regularly, through coded letters sent to Kibbutz Negba, with men he knew from his work with *Hashomer Hatzair*. Alerting them to his predicament, he insisted that he and his family be smuggled out immediately. He was proud yet frightened for his family by the coded communiqué he received back. *You are our eyes and ears on the ground. You must remain in Poland. Just be a good spy and tell them what you think they want to hear. When the time comes, if complications arise with your departure, arrangements are in place to smuggle you and your family out through Sweden.*

• • •

Shmuel received an urgent communiqué from Kibbutz Negba warning that the Russians would be closing the borders and that it was time for him to leave. In January of 1950, Shmuel and his family boarded a train with the last group of Jews departing from Poland. They traveled from Dzierzoniov, Poland to Vienna, Austria and then to the port city of Brindisi, Italy on the coast of the Adriatic Sea. Their ship was the Caserta-Napoli. Built in 1929 she was a 2,924 gross ton passenger/cargo ship. It was currently positioned 1,243 nautical miles to the port of Haifa, and if the weather held, it would take a little over five days to reach Israel.

The refugees boarded the ship, the wind assaulting the sea as white caps rolled atop the water. With temperatures in the low forties but feeling much colder, the passengers were herded below deck to their makeshift living quarters in the cargo hold of the ship. On the second day, nearing the Greek Island of Crete, the majority of the refugees were seasick and vomiting. The crew distributed *Brekhn* (vomit) buckets and blankets but it did little to alleviate a situation growing more onerous by the hour. A group of men that included Shmuel came up with a strategic plan. An area was cordoned off for bathrooms, the men agreeing to take turns dumping the waste overboard. In another corner far from the bathrooms, an area was cordoned off and designated for meals. The crew served the passengers tasteless and stale food, but it was still better than anything these Jews had been fed while incarcerated at the Nazi work and concentration camps.

Regardless, it proved impossible to maintain sanitary conditions; therefore, the situation deteriorated, and people became ill. Only when they were allowed on deck, escaping the putrid odors from unwashed bodies and illness did anyone find relief. Like a woman in the travails of childbirth, few people who took these shipboard crossings would remember the number of days at sea or the food or the illnesses. The hardships were insignificant when compared to the reward of arriving in Israel.

Everyone crowded on deck once land was spotted. With the ship rolling and sloshing, eleven-year-old Eli only cared about one thing: getting off the ship so he could stop feeling sick. Approaching Israel, a Jewish country already in existence for a year and a half, Shmuel wept. Kissing Mina and Meir, he then grabbed Eli and hugged him, elated because his dream had come true: a Jewish country, a Jewish land.

When they disembarked, Shmuel searched the crowd, certain that there would be a reception committee waiting to greet him. After all he was a crucial man in *Hashomer Hatzair,* having risked his life remaining in Poland. No one came. Not then and not later. It was a window into his future and that disregard colored the rest of Shmuel's life, bitterness taking root and planting itself into his heart.

• • •

This tiny country of Israel, only two hundred and sixty miles long and seventy-one miles across at its widest point, was in crisis. Four thousand refugees were arriving weekly, all in need of lodging, education, jobs, food, clothing, medical attention and hope. With lodging critical, centers were established throughout the country. Ma'abarot (temporary) refugee absorption camps were set up in Galilee in northern Israel and the northern part of the Negev Desert in the south. These Ma'abarot metamorphosed in the years that followed going from temporary tin huts and tents into thriving towns on the peripheral borders of the country.

Camps once used to detain illegal Jewish immigrants by the British were refitted to house the refugees. Upon arrival, Shmuel and his family were sent to a camp at Atlit near the port city of Haifa. From there they were transferred to Sarafand, a British Army base southeast of Jaffa near Lod and next to the Arab village of Sarafand al-'Amar. Located in the central district of Israel, the refugees called their new home Machne (camp) Israel.

The family lived in a large, elongated army barrack with a tin roof. It was divided into eight individual units by ropes overlaid with blankets that afforded them a bit of privacy. Bathrooms and showers were communal and in a separate area outside for recreation was shared by hundreds of people. Yet despite the difficult conditions, something unexplainable and magical was taking place. These new *Olim* (immigrants) from Europe's Germany, Austria, Italy, Bulgaria, Yugoslavia, Poland, Rumania and from Muslim countries in Asia and Africa such as Libya, Morocco, Tunis, Turkey and Iran—all with different customs, languages and wartime experiences—had one commonality. They were all Jews. This was their new home. It was a place where they would be free to mourn their losses, find their voices, learn to fight and raise their progeny to be educated warriors, strong, proud and resilient.

Chapter 10

— ••• —

1950

Israel was still reeling from its War of Independence that had begun the day Israel was declared a state. Surrounded by millions of Arabs vowing to drive the Jews into the sea, Lebanon, Transjordan, Syria, Egypt and Iraq attacked. The war lasted for two horrific years. Israel was eventually victorious, but over six thousand Jews died, one percent of the population of the new country. Many of the dead were the men and women survivors of the Holocaust. When those bodies were buried in the earth of *Eretz Israel*, the soil wept.

Desperately poor, with little hard cash and the huge influx of immigrants, Israel's first elected government had no choice but to institute emergency legislation, an austerity program that would ration all food, clothing, and essential provisions. Thankfully, the United States sent millions of pounds of dried eggs, dried skim milk, butter and dried codfish.

Every refugee family at the camp where the Huberman's were living was given a burner for cooking along with food ration cards, blankets, sheets and other basic essentials. As for sleeping, the boys shared one army cot and Mina and Shmuel shared the other. Mina did her best to make their miniscule space habitable. She picked wildflowers and carefully arranged them in a makeshift vase, invented recipes, scrubbed every inch of their living space and washed clothing every day so that the boys were always clean.

But privacy remained a huge problem. There were people everywhere. It was like living in a huge apartment building with no walls. Babies cried, people argued, and if your neighbor passed gas, you could smell it. Yet, because everyone was in the same situation, it seemed to take some of the stings out of the living conditions, that, and the realization that this was a temporary situation. They would all soon have a new beginning in their lives.

•••

One day, sitting on a cot, watching her boys eating lunch there was a sudden thump and scream. Pulling the sheet aside, Mina saw Mr. Szabo, their neighbor from Hungary, lying on the floor, his wife kneeling beside him. "He has diabetes! Please help me," she cried in Yiddish.

Within moments others came and lifted him onto his cot. Mrs. Szabo put a glucose pill into his mouth, and he was soon conscious. Mina brought both a glass of water and then stayed with them for a long time. Eli, an inquisitive child who wanted to know the "whys" of everything, stood beside his mother.

"What is diabetes?" he asked more than once, relentless until Mr. Szabo explained to him what diabetes was and why it made him sick. "Unfortunately," Mr. Szabo said, his eyes sad, "keeping diabetes under control is an ongoing problem. I'm sorry that you're going to be inconvenienced by my fainting episodes."

"Not inconvenienced," Mina said. "We are all family now and we will be here for you."

Eli did not understand the medical terms or even how the body worked, but he promised himself that one day he would know how the body worked so that he could help people get well when they were sick.

Eli had a friend in the camp whose father Aba Lichtenstein had been his Hebrew and Yiddish teacher while they were living in

Dzierzoniow, Poland. The two boys were inseparable those first weeks in the camp. They were together all the time. And that time would have been idyllic if not for one small problem: a strong-willed and determined little five-year-old boy with a heart-shaped face, dreamy eyes, a pouty mouth and an endearing personality who refused to let Eli out of his sight. Meir would throw screaming fits until he got his way. And because Eli couldn't stand to see his little brother upset, Meir always got to tag along.

...

It was Sunday afternoon in the middle of February. The sun shone in a silken blue sky, the temperature in the sixties as the breeze sifted across the swaying palm trees. Taking a fifteen-minute walk from the camp, Shmuel, Mina and the boys meandered over the red sandy soil searching for the perfect place to have a picnic as sparrows and blackbirds soared overhead.

Laying out the blanket, Mina unpacked the satchel. There were roasted eggplants, wild greens from the fields, olives that were actually delicious, dates, dried codfish and hummus. Sitting cross-legged, feasting in the surroundings and the food, Shmuel cleared his throat. Picking his words carefully he said,

"Eli, as you know, your Aunt Lola and Uncle Izak and your grandparents are all living in a suburb of Tel Aviv. Unlike living here in the camp, there are wonderful schools where you can learn to speak Hebrew quickly."

"We think you should go and live with them for a little bit," Mina said, forcing aside tears that threatened.

Eli stared at his parents, excitement and niggling trepidation churning in his stomach. The thought of living with his Aunt Lola was a glorious idea. She was beautiful, kind and best of all she adored him and always let him do whatever he wanted. And truth be told, Eli missed his grandmother more than he had ever missed anyone in his entire life. He only knew basic Hebrew and the idea of going to a real school where he would learn to speak the language of Israel thrilled him.

"What do you think?" Shmuel asked.

"I'll miss you, but I want to go," Eli said.

"No!" Meir shrieked. "You can't leave me!"

Eli picked up his little brother and hugged him. "I'll be back before you know it. I promise."

•••

Hagshama was a Hebrew word that had become Shmuel's mantra. It meant personal fulfillment of one's ideology, the realization of a dream and he was determined to live that dream, to be a part of building something practical and needed for Israel. Roads were critical in order to create a useable infrastructure; and so, Shmuel built roads, clearing and paving them for more than a year.

Still considering himself as a leader in the Zionist movement, from a personal point of view, it was a gratifying time for Shmuel. He was proud to be setting a good example while remaining true to his convictions that Jews would be the ones to work the land. His so-called friends, from the Young Zionist Labor Movement (Hashomer Hatzair), who ignored him and his past commitments, had a different agenda. They were studying Hebrew and positioning themselves to become big *machers* (influential) in the government, men who would eventually become cabinet members, ministers and members of the Knesset (Assembly).

Chapter 11

E li moved in with his Aunt Lola and Uncle Izak, and their two-year-old son Arie. They lived in Bitzaron, a neighborhood of Tel Aviv bordered by Hashalom Road to the north and Yitzhak Sadeh Street to the south. His aunt and uncle had a one-bedroom six hundred square foot apartment on the second floor of an immigrant-housing complex a few buildings away from his grandparents who lived on the first floor. The buildings were 16-unit apartment blocks, with two units stacked one above the other, eight apartments on each floor, each with its own entrance. Eli slept on the sofa.

Accompanied by his Aunt Lola, Eli walked the half-mile to his new school at Nachlat Itzhak, an established community filled with Jews born in Israel and known as *sabras*. Head down, hands shoved into his pockets and filled with trepidation, he entered his fifth-grade classroom.

Expecting Eli, the teacher stood and moved from behind her desk. "Hello! My name is Rachel Perlmutter," *Ha morah Rachel,* the teacher said. She was tall and slim with bright, sparkling blue eyes and a warm smile. "Class, this is Eliezer Huberman and he is from Poland. I expect all of you to make him feel welcome here. Shall we call you Eliezer?"

Eli shook his head. In halting Hebrew, he responded, "Please call me Eli."

"Then Eli it is," she said. "Take the second seat in the third row, please. You will find your books inside the desk."

Eli sat, sneaking looks at the boys and girls in the classroom. Despite it being winter, the temperature was in the 60's and the boys were all dressed similarly, short sleeve shirts, shorts and sandals. The girls all wore white blouses, some wearing skirts and others in shorts. Eli wanted to disappear, feeling so ridiculous in his sweater, long pants and tie shoes.

That day while in the classroom, the students were polite to him but once they were in the yard, during the break, they were hateful and cruel: teasing him unmercifully about his accent, how short he was, his dumb clothing, and anything else they could think of to hurt his feelings.

It was just the beginning. As the only immigrant child in his class, he became a target for every bully. Eli was miserable. He had no friends and hated school. Yet, despite his struggles socially, having learned to speak a bit and to read and write Hebrew at his previous Hebrew Yiddish School, he flourished academically. Learning out of desperation, every paper he turned in was outstanding, making the students dislike him even more. What saved Eli was his teacher. She became his mentor and protector.

One day soon after his arrival, Eli went to the back corner of the classroom where the students stored their belongings. All the boys in the class were gathered there. He pushed his way through only to find all his books, papers and school supplies scattered on the floor. Sneering at him, they ground their feet on his things, ripping and dirtying them. When he went to pick everything up, somebody shoved him to the ground. Eli lay there crying as the boys heckled him. Hearing Morah Rachel return to the classroom, the boys fled.

"I am so sorry, Eli," his teacher said, feeling guilty for going to the teacher's lounge to have a cigarette before the students had cleared the classroom. Lifting him, she asked, "Are you hurt?"

"No. Just mad," he said, swiping at his tears.

"Morah Rachel accompanied Eli to the street. "I will see you tomorrow," she said, patting his shoulder, wise enough to have not asked him to rat on his fellow students, knowing these Israeli kids could be mean and vindictive, and this boy did not need more problems than he already had.

•••

Eli suffered silently, not telling his aunt what he was going through because he didn't want to upset her. Besides, he had a refuge, a place where he could go to feel safe and loved and listened to: his grandmother's.

"So, how is my little man today? Are you hungry?" his *bubbe*, grandmother asked.

Eli nodded, fighting back tears.

"Another bad day?"

"Terrible."

"Okay, okay. This too shall pass. Soon your parents will find an apartment and leave the camp. Then you will go to another school and have lots of friends. And besides," she said smiling, her stern yet lovely face softening and her sea-blue eyes crinkling, "education is the precious legacy of our people and you are my little genius. Don't you ever forget that."

"They are so mean!" Eli said, sucking in his lower lip.

"I have just the thing to make you feel better," Bubbe said, wearing her ever-present apron. "I made your favorite, an angel food sponge cake with lemon. And" she said with flourish reaching for the teakettle that was always boiling, "a *gloz tey*, cup of tea with sugar."

Eli sipped his tea and ate the delicious cake while his grandmother took her cube of sugar and drank three cups of tea.

"I have a surprise for you," Bubbe said. "Your uncle Izak has arranged a reunion. He is going to pick up your parents on Sunday and bring them for a visit!"

Machne Israel was eighteen miles away, and the roads in Israel were narrow and abysmal. There were few cars and traveling by bus took forever. But his Uncle Izak had a three-wheel motorcycle with a boat-shaped sidecar for a third passenger, adjacent to the third wheel. Thus he could transport Mina and Shmuel.

"I can't wait!" Eli said, hugging his Bubbe.

"I know, my *sheyn eyngl*, beautiful boy. And won't they be proud when they see your happy smiling face that will assure them that they made the right decision sending you here?"

"Don't worry, Bubbe. I won't tell them the bad stuff, only the good."

"You are such a good boy," she said with a wink. "Here, have another piece of cake."

Chapter 12

— ••• —

Eli was twelve years old and fluent in Hebrew when his family relocated to Bat Yam, a small town with a population of 4,000, twenty miles from the homes of his grandparents, aunt and uncle. Perched on the coast of the Mediterranean Sea, just south of Tel Aviv, there were white sandy beaches, breakwater aquamarine lagoons and constant fan-like breezes that sifted and whispered through the air.

The family moved into a miniscule one-bedroom apartment that was part of the governmental housing complexes being built throughout Israel by *Amidar*, the Hebrew word meaning: *my nation housing*. To purchase one of these units was in all practicality almost free. It required a small initial down payment that enabled the buyer to have the right to purchase the property at a later date, for a relatively low price. Because Shmuel was working and had an income, he was able to purchase their unit.

They lived in a complex of six apartments. Theirs was on the first floor with a small fenced in garden that made it possible for the family to have a small black dog that lived outdoors and brought hours of entertainment to the boys. Mina and Shmuel slept in the bedroom, and Meir and Eli in the living room, which they called the salon. During the day, the living room was used to welcome guests, who often arrived unannounced, and as was the accepted behavior, stayed as long as they liked.

The elementary school Eli attended belonged to the Histadrut Trade Union. In socialist Israel, the Histadrut was established as a

47

workers movement to influence settlement, education, housing construction, defense, health care, trade, banking and culture.

The school was two miles away and there were no buses. In the summer months, the temperature often hovered in the nineties, but Eli didn't mind. As a confident sixth grader, he had made the decision that he would never be bullied again. Besides, unlike his school at Nachlat Itzhak, here all the kids had similar backgrounds—immigrants and survivors, who all had to learn a new language and new customs and make a new life.

Eli and his three friends trudged to school with their heavy book bags. Menahem, a boy from Minsk, who had lost most of his family and lived with his mother wandered into the brush. He came back with a long stick from a broken tree branch.

"I have an idea," Menahem said, slipping his heavy book bag on to the stick. The three boys added their book bags as well, and then Eli took one end of the stick and Menahem took the other. Ten minutes later, tired and their hands getting sore, they traded places with their friends. Perhaps in truth their jury-rigged contraption was not even about the weight of their books and more about sharing, because regardless, working together made their burden seem lighter.

•••

Shmuel, still hurt by the lack of respect he had been shown by his fellow Zionists, turned his attention to forming a *Shtetl* Association. *Shtetls* were the small towns throughout Russia, Poland, Galicia and Romania that had large Jewish populations. The goal of the association was to honor the memory of the Jews murdered in those small towns.

Of course, Israel had established its own memorial tribute. The first *Yom Hazikaron laShoah ve-laG'vurah*, Holocaust Remembrance Day, was held on December 28, 1949. The day was commemorated by the burial of ashes and bones from the thousands of Jews massacred at the Flossenburg concentration camp into a Jerusalem cemetery.

In 1951, the Knesset, the legislative branch of the Israeli government, passed a resolution establishing Holocaust Remembrance Day as a national holiday to be held on April 12th. Every year, on that day in Bat Yam, huge gatherings were held. Shmuel was the keynote speaker as the representative of the *Shtetl* Association.

The Association met every couple of weeks in the early evening in the Community Center. The floor was concrete and there were metal tables and folding chairs set up around the room. The walls were adorned with posters. Shmuel's favorites were one depicting a young man with a hoe in his hand, digging into the earth of Eretz Israel, another of two soldiers, a male and a female, superimposed over the Israeli flag, the six-pointed star of David in the middle of the flag. A dozen other posters celebrated immigration and settlement, the Bible, and vacation posters urging people to come to the land of milk and honey.

On any given evening five or six other groups met at the center. It was always noisy, but it made little difference as Shmuel warmly greeted the thirty members of his association who were sitting in a corner on the far-left side. He called the meeting to order. The discussion that night would be about arranging the first of what hopefully would be many trips by the organization back to Poland.

"Can we really make this happen?" asked Pinkus Feiner, a landsman from Lukow. He was a stocky and intense thirty-nine-year-old with salt and pepper hair, a scraggly beard, and a hitch to his walk from an injury obtained in a work camp.

"Why not?" Shmuel said. "The Jewish Agency will help us locate others in Israel from Lukow. I am certain they will join us. But regardless, you and I *can* and *should* go back. We owe it to the memory of those who perished."

The conversation continued for over an hour. In the end, it was decided the entire group would hold fundraisers and when the funds were secured, Shmuel and Pinkus would return to Lukow.

• • •

Shmuel, Pinkus and four of their compatriots from Israel arrived at the Lukow train station, now a strategic east-west line to Warsaw and Berlin, on April 20, 1953. The weather was in the sixties and clouds were building to the south. As they walked along the newly paved streets interspersed with pine, oak and birch trees, they kept searching faces, looking for a familiar Jewish face among the throng of people: there was not even one! Moving past the familiar and unfamiliar sights, they spied a new shoe factory and a meat plant. Turning down Warszawska Street toward their hotel, the front yards they passed were filled with red poppies, the national flower of Poland, as well as riots of yellow, purple and pink irises. Shmuel kept asking himself: *how can a place that looks so clean, and serene and lovely have harbored such horror?*

Shmuel learned before leaving Israel that 2,200 Jews were murdered in the city and dumped into execution pits. More than nine thousand other innocent souls were sent to the death camps. By War's end, only one hundred and fifty-Jews from Lukow had survived. That Shmuel was back in this evil place suddenly seemed like a really bad decision. His hands began to shake and the desire for revenge settled deep inside his psyche.

The next day the sun was peaking above the horizon, the dew still covering the ground when Shmuel and his compatriots arrived at the fields where their families, friends and neighbors had been shot and dumped into mass graves. Pushing wheelbarrows filled with picks and shovels they stopped, each man trembling in grief, their eyes blurred by tears.

"We will say *kaddish* first," Solomon, the most religious among them said, singing out the prayer Jews recited for their dead.

The years, the rain and the erosion had washed layers from the ground and bones had washed to the surface. Shmuel bent down and picked up a bone and placed it in the wheelbarrow. Horrified, he clutched his stomach, tasting hell. He vomited.

Over the next five days, the men went to the pits in the killing fields and collected the bones of the departed. Every night of those five days, they would scrub themselves until their skin was raw, wash their dirt-encrusted clothing, barely saying five words to each other.

When they could not endure their task for even one more moment, they gathered the precious remains they had recovered. Pushing the wheelbarrows, they walked defiantly and proud through the streets of the town. Glaring at the gawking pedestrians, ignoring faces they recognized from the past, they made their way to what was once the Jewish cemetery. Again, they dug, this time into consecrated ground. With silent devotion, their bodies aching, and hands bloodied, they reburied the remains of the Jews of Lukow. It was heartbreaking, back-breaking work that had seeped every ounce of their energy.

The Jewish cemetery was in shambles, headstones turned on their sides, graves littered, stones removed and then used to build the walls of homes and businesses.

"We can't just leave these headstones thrown on the ground," Shmuel said.

"And we won't. We will use the headstones to build a monument," Jacob Dressler replied, the youngest among them, who had been studying architecture before the War.

Commissioning workers to lay a foundation of concrete and a blacksmith to make a five-foot tall Star of David, they began their work. Using the displaced tombstones, six across on each side at the base, and decreasing the number of stones as they built higher, on the tenth level they stopped. Having built a pyramid, they then placed the Star of David atop and then affixed an Israeli flag to the Star. They said their prayers and shed their tears. It was time to go to their new Jewish home in the land of Israel.

Monument to the Jews of Lukow, Poland

Chapter 13

···

Shmuel sold their Amidar apartment in Bat Yam to a newly arrived immigrant family. With the money from that sale, he purchased a larger eight hundred square foot one bedroom unit on the third floor of a building that overlooked a major two-way avenue separated in the middle with trees and benches. In the living room there was a simple L-shaped sofa with black cushions and a matching coffee table, a new style that was considered to be very fancy. Meir slept on one side of the "L" and Eli slept on the other. It was an arrangement that would last well into adulthood for both boys.

The summers were brutal in Bat Yam, a shock after living in the frozen tundra of Russia and Ukraine. To fight the heat, the shades were always down. The apartment had tile floors, and Mina always inventive, cleaned the floors and then left a layer of water—the evaporating water, cooling the apartment a bit.

"We need to talk," Shmuel said, a month before Eli was to enter high school. They were sitting at the Formica kitchen table, Eli nibbling on a piece of ooga, a Hebrew word for cake commonly made from twisted dough and filled with marmalade. Mina stood at the stove stirring a pot, keeping a watchful eye as Eli ate.

"Meir come get a piece of ooga," Mina called.

"I don't want anything," the nine-year-old shouted back, too busy arranging his few toy soldiers and a tank to be bothered with food. Meir was an unusual little boy, mischievous in order to get attention and curious to the point of danger. If a fence was present, he wanted to climb it; if a door was closed, he had to see what was behind that closed door. Fascinated by adult conversation even as a young boy, he would park himself in the corner and listen to his father and friends talk politics.

Mina frowned. After so many years of going hungry, feeding her family was her mission. She knew it was an obsession, but G-d forbid there was even one day that she did not organize a meal which often included potatoes and small pieces of chicken with its fat to give the meal a meat taste. On Fridays she was able to get fresh carp and she made gefilte fish. In nature, carp is a scavenger, and it is smelly during cooking to the point of making it almost un-edible. But in Israel, the carp were raised in special clean sweet water ponds, and as a result, when the gefilte fish was prepared it was a wonderful Jewish delicacy that Meir and Eli hated.

"Eli, I have great news. Do you remember Dr. Felshaw?" Shmuel asked.

Eli shook his head no.

"He was a famous teacher, author, lecturer and a friend of mine. Dr. Felshaw has been appointed the new headmaster of a private high school in Jaffa, and he has invited you to be a student there," Shmuel said, not revealing that Dr. Felshaw had also arranged a scholarship for Eli because his school needed brilliant students in order to build their reputation.

"But I'm already going to go to a good school, the best school and besides I want to be with my friends," Eli replied, forcing his voice to remain neutral, knowing anger was an emotion that never evoked a positive response from his father.

"Listen to your father," Mina said, moving to wipe the cake crumbs from the plastic tablecloth. "You have a brain that needs filling, and your father knows what's best for you."

"But Jaffa is so far away," he whined, knowing that it was a poor rebuttal before the words even left his mouth.

"There's a bus," his father replied, his tone closing the discussion.

•••

The headmaster, Dr. Felshaw, was a very impressive man with his short beard and professorial bearing. Greatly respected as an educator, he believed that motivation and recognition influenced learning and to that end, he created a system to reward excellence. In the main hall of the school, where everyone passed by each day, he placed a large plaque on the wall that listed the top ten students in the school. Competitive in nature when it came to his intelligence, Eli made sure that his name was always at the top or near the top of that list.

Acceptance into Eli's school was based on a family's ability to pay the tuition, not on the student's academic prowess. Consequently, the intellectual caliber of the student body left much to be desired. The caliber of the faculty was an entirely different story. With the huge influx of immigrants to Israel, jobs were scarce. As a result, some of the finest educators in Europe found their way to the school.

In fact, Eli's art teacher was an art appreciation professor from the Corvinus University of Budapest. Showing photos depicting the paintings of the great masters, listening to stories of their lives and travails, the teacher's passion, insight and descriptive intellect ignited an appreciation for art that would become a lifelong passion for Eli.

His diminutive Polish history teacher was from the Jagiellonian University in Krakow and it was Eli's favorite class. Every lesson was enthralling and exciting as the teacher brought history alive.

"Don't worry about dates," the teacher said. "You will learn dates, but history is more conceptual. It's about examining the past from a distance. That way we can disassociate and examine, and G-d willing not make the same mistakes again. You see, human nature seems to be like a festering scab, always ready to be picked and ready to bleed. If only we could let that wound heal, then perhaps there will be hope for all of us."

In Israel, every student studied the Bible. Eli soon realized that while immersing himself in the Bible, he was also immersing himself in Hebrew. The result was grasping and understanding of the language in a more meaningful way. His lessons included the *Bava Metzia,* a section in the *Talmud,* the central text of Jewish religious law and theology that dealt with discussions on civil matters such as property, law and usury. His biblical studies also delved into the *Mishna,* commentaries from renowned scholars on the *Torah,* the first five books of the Hebrew Bible. As inconceivable as it seemed, his class spent an entire year covering only twenty pages of *the Talmud,* every word of the commentaries scrutinized, interpreted and reinterpreted.

Regardless of being non-religious by nature and upbringing, having not even been Bar Mitzvah, Eli was fascinated and challenged by the coursework. As he progressed in his biblical studies, he began to realize that spending an hour conversing about ownership of a donkey was in reality an intellectually stimulating and complicated exercise in logic.

• • •

Shmuel opened a Laundromat where customers could have their dirty laundry washed and ironed. In his wildest imagination, this was not how he had imagined his life would turn out. But it was an honest living, and so he did not complain. Closed only on Shabbat, Eli worked for his father every day after school, riding his bike to deliver the clean laundry and pick up the dirty.

Balanced and stacked precariously in his bicycle basket, Eli's job included wrapping the dirty clothing in bags, labeling them, schlepping them to be washed, then returning the bundles to the customers. He leaned his bike against the wall and lugged his first delivery of the day to the second floor. He knocked on the door.

"About time!" Mrs. Dvorkin said, her wig sitting askew, her hands dusted with flour. "Put it on the table and take everything out."

Eli scowled as he opened the package. He detested being ordered around by rude old ladies, especially when he knew what was coming next.

Wiping her hands on her apron she picked up a blouse. "This you call clean?" she said, pointing to a stain near the collar. "For this I should pay you?"

Eli knew that she knew the stain was permanent and could not be removed. Insulted and frustrated by her accusation and attitude, he could do nothing in response but shrug.

"Why do I bother sending anything?" she complained, handing Eli Israeli liras and another bag of dirty laundry.

Eli made three more stops before heading back to the Laundromat for more deliveries. His basket overflowing with smelly dirty laundry, he was mortified to see Shoshana Bronsk walking with three of her friends. She was the prettiest and smartest girl in his class, and he was smitten. Had he been paying better attention; he would have been able to turn around and avoid being seen. But it was too late for that now. *Did they see him? Should he wave? Should he say hello?* Insecure and inept around girls, he did neither. He just rode past knowing that his crush had just been crushed under a load of dirty laundry.

Chapter 14

―――――― ••• ――――――

1955

Eli made an appointment to see Dr. Felshaw after learning that his classmate, eighteen-year-old Zehava Roizman from Hungary was being tutored. The purpose of the tutoring was so that she could sit for a test that if passed, would allow her to skip from the sophomore year to the senior year. Eli did feel sorry for her: she was too old to be in his class. But she wasn't even very smart and that aggravated him.

Perspiration gathering on his brow, Eli sat nervously in the outer office watching as the secretary typed. At fifteen he was 5' 8" and would grow no taller. He had a thick head of black wavy hair, an elongated pudgy-cheeked face with midnight eyes, questioning, highly arched brows, and a wide, welcoming smile that made him instantly likable.

After waiting for twenty minutes, he was finally shown into the headmaster's inner sanctum. The room was filled with overflowing bookshelves, the walls adorned with past awards, diplomas and family pictures. The headmaster reached across his cluttered desk to shake Eli's sweaty hand.

"To what do I owe the honor of my star pupil requesting an interview?" Dr. Felshaw asked with a mischievous grin.

Eli took a deep calming breath before speaking, having rehearsed what he would say a dozen times. "I have learned that Zehava Roizman will be taking a test to skip to her final year of high school. I respectfully ask for that same opportunity but without the tutoring."

Dr. Felshaw sighed. He had no doubt that this brilliant young boy could easily pass the test, even without tutoring. The question remained. Was it the right decision? "Have you discussed this with your father?" he asked.

"Yes, sir. He said it was my decision," Eli replied, remembering the pride-filled expression on his father's face when they had the discussion.

"There are social aspects to be considered," Dr. Felshaw said. "The teenage years are difficult enough when you are surrounded by peers of your own age. It is important that you contemplate carefully what it will be like for you, being the youngest boy in the class."

"I have considered it carefully and I am fully prepared."

"Then you have my permission to sit for the exam."

...

Eli passed the exam and entered his senior year of high school at sixteen and a half. His classmates were eighteen and nineteen years old older than average due to the war and immigration. The boys in his class were obsessed with sex, always staring at breasts and bottoms and whispering their fantasies to one another. Eli always laughed when they told their jokes, but he was so naive he rarely understood the punch line. Wanting to be accepted and to feel a part of the group, he even started staring at the various lady-curves, enjoying it thoroughly, although it always embarrassed him.

Finding Eli adorable, the girls gently teased him until he blushed, naming him their *talmid chockom*, 'treasured sage' in Yiddish. Bewildered by and uncomfortable with the boy-crazy girls, who were constantly flirting and giggling, Eli soon realized that socially he had made a huge mistake. But he was willing to muddle through the social aspects of his life because, academically, it was the perfect decision. His classes included math, physics, chemistry, history, art and Latin. Feeling as though he was finally being challenged, he immersed himself in learning as a glorious new world opened to him.

•••

1956

Eleven-year-old Meir lay awake on his section of the "L"-shaped sofa. It had been a monumental day, watching his big brother graduate first in his class from high school. And as exciting as the day was, he knew it was about to get even more exciting. Tonight was the night the secret Eli told him weeks ago would be shared with his parents. He couldn't wait for the big moment.

Meir had his brother's coloring: dark eyes and dark hair, but that was where the similarity ended in both looks and personality. Where Eli was thoughtful and gentle, Meir was impetuous, his persona one of rugged and deliberate determination. Where Eli had a full sweet face, Meir's was etched tight. Even at his young age, with his straight masculine nose, full lips, and piercing inquisitive eyes, there seemed to be a man hiding just beneath the surface waiting for his moment to emerge. Eli would tease him and say that he would be a real *ladies' man* one day. He was not sure what that meant, but whatever his big brother said was good enough for Meir.

He heard the kitchen chairs scrape across the floor and knew they were all sitting. Thinking he was asleep; they were talking quietly. Meir slipped out from the covers and tiptoed to the closed kitchen doorway so he could hear every word.

"That is out of the question," Mina said, her voice strained and determined. "You are too young, and I will *not* give my permission."

"I can't apply to the university unless I have registered to enlist, and I can't enlist without your signatures," Eli insisted.

"I already lost my entire family. I will not lose you too!" Mina said, her voice breaking.

Chairs scrapped again. Meir peeked through a crack in the door. His father was embracing his weeping mother. Meir felt himself tear up. His mother never cried.

"Explain everything to your mother, and tell her exactly what your intentions are," Shmuel said softly. "When she has an entire picture, I think it will be easier for her to acquiesce."

"Mother, you know there is mandatory enlistment in the Army when I turn eighteen. All I am asking is for you to allow me to enlist a year earlier," Eli said, as Mina sat back down. "Otherwise, what was the point of me skipping a year in school? And if I don't enlist, I will have nothing to do because I won't be accepted to the university.

"I have already met all my requirements, including selecting two majors. My first choice is medicine and my second chemistry. Once I am accepted, as a university student I will have certain military privileges. They need doctors, mother. You don't have to worry. I won't be given a dangerous assignment. And two and a half years will be over before you know it"

As if struck by lightning, Meir realized that his big brother was actually going away. Without thinking, he shoved the door open, ran into the room and threw himself into Eli's arms.

"I'm coming with you!" he insisted. "I will be a great soldier."

Eli hugged his tough little brother. "I have no doubt that one day you will be a great soldier, little man: a really great soldier. But sadly, you will just have to wait until you grow up."

Chapter 15

————— ••• —————

Eli applied to Hadassah medical school immediately after his parents signed his induction papers for the Israeli army. He believed he would be a great doctor. It was his life's dream to heal, interact and help people. Unfortunately, there were only twenty medical school slots available in all of Israel. Discrimination was acceptable and applicable at that time and so the first students accepted were the children of doctors. Disappointed and angry but refusing to believe his dream was dead, Eli shunned an offer from Technion, the MIT of Israel to study chemistry. Instead, he decided to finish his stint in the army and then see if he could find a way into medical school.

•••

July 1956

Eli was sent to a Bahad Military Camp surrounded by eucalyptus trees located in a relatively flat area in central Israel. It was rocky, dry and dusty—the terrain a perfect location for his four months of basic training.

He was placed in an academic battalion that consisted of high school graduates who intended to go to universities right after basic training. He quickly became close with two of his tent-mates. Samuel Hakeem was thin and had a dark complexion. He was from Iraq, the son of a wealthy family with a villa in Ramat Gan near Tel Aviv. His other friend Joshua Noyman had a light complexion with reddish-brown hair. He was an Orthodox Ashkenazi Jew who was never without his kippah, a little round skullcap. As dissimilar as they were, the three boys established trust in one another. The result was intense philosophical discussions and conversations where they shared their deepest thoughts and aspirations.

Their tent held eight cots. In addition to his uniform, each soldier was given a mess kit that included eating utensils, a metal dish, a cup, a shaving kit and toiletries. That was the extent of their personal belongings supplied by the IDF, the Israeli Defense Forces.

Eli's being away and unreachable was extremely difficult for Mina and Shmuel. They were worried and desperate to see where their son was living and how he was doing. There were no buses and no other means of transportation, so they had no choice but to ask their brother-in-law Izak if he would drive them on his motorcycle. They traveled on dusty dirt roads with Shmuel sitting behind Izak. Meir squeezed in on his mother's lap in the sidecar. They arrived at the camp on Saturday, a week after Eli's induction. Of course, Eli's grandparents and his aunt insisted on going along as well. That meant three roundtrips for Izak but he was one to never refuse assistance. And so, from dawn till noon, Izak took the one-hour drive each way, transporting the entire family.

As it turned out they were not the only worried parents. In fact, there were hundreds of other families gathered by the front gate of the military camp to see their soldier sons and daughters.

"There he is," his grandmother shouted. "Eli, we are here!" she said waving her arms. The soldiers were not allowed to let any civilians inside the camp, but the new recruits were allowed to gather within a small perimeter outside the gates.

Eli waved back as he made his way through the mass of fellow-soldiers. Seeing that his *mishpucha,* his entire family had come to visit made Eli realize how homesick he was and how much his life had changed in only a week. He had never considered himself coddled or spoiled, having lived in difficult situations most of his life, first in Russia, then the Ukraine and Poland. But this was different. He had arrived a boy and within days, he was being treated like and expected to be a man.

And a man he would be, Eli thought as he adjusted his posture, standing just a bit taller. He wore a dark green beret that was folded on one side and had no official army insignia. His hair was cut short and while looking the part of a soldier for this occasion, when in training he wore a hodge-podge of used old, wrinkled army shirts and pants from the stockpiled clean clothing in the stockroom. With sizes never quite right, the khaki army belts were oftentimes the only thing keeping his pants from falling down.

"Oy!" his grandmother said, hugging him with all her might. "What, they don't feed you? Already you look skinny. But you shouldn't worry, I made your favorite sponge cake."

His mother kissed him on the cheek, her eyes glistening. "Are you okay? Are they working you too hard? You look thin." She patted his back. "I brought you ooga and cold gefilte fish in a glass jar."

His aunt Lola winked and smiled. Eli winked back.

The men stood aside, allowing the women their rightful place in this show of emotion. Eleven-year-old Meir tried to restrain himself, but his impulsivity won out as he ran into Eli's arms. "Come home," he said through tears. "I miss you."

"I miss you too, little man." He said softly, reaching to shake hands with his father, grandfather and uncle.

They all began to talk at once, throwing questions at him as they handed him dish after dish and watched him eat. "Enough!" Eli finally said. "I will take the rest back with me."

And so it went. Every Saturday, his uncle drove Eli's parents and brother to the camp. If Eli was not occupied with some training exercise,

Eli Huberman The Soldier

he would go to the gate. If he did not show up, his disappointed family would simply turn around and go back home.

Basic training was hard. Hours were spent cleaning and shooting guns, crawling under barbed wire, climbing up and jumping over walls and scrambling up ropes. They often walked an entire day or an entire night schlepping heavy backpacks through the mountains. The top brass decided that in order to toughen up their soldiers for situations they felt were inevitable, they would withhold liquid intake. That meant no water! It was a mistake and what transpired was dehydration and fainting. That practice was eventually abolished, but it was long after Eli had finished his training.

Growing up, Eli had participated to a limited degree in sports with his friends, but he never understood the fascination of kicking, batting or throwing a ball. Yet, he understood with perfect clarity that these training exercises were not a game and not some useless competition. They were a necessity that would enable the soldiers to survive combat thereby ensuring the survival of the State of Israel. He worked hard, did his best, and managed to get through most of the challenges, but not all. When his body would not respond with the intensity or power needed to complete a challenge, he was furious with himself. But he managed to push his body farther and harder than he had ever imagined he could.

His Sergeant Major was a tough taskmaster, demanding and rough, his normal-speaking voice a shout. He was known for his unannounced inspections. Eli lost count of the times his bed was flipped over because a corner was not perfect. Living in close quarters, it was no surprise that soldiers were stealing from one another as things began to disappear: dishes, utensils, razors, socks, etc. If you lost your fork in the army, you used your fingers, as things were not replaced.

It was a blistering August day, and the men were drenched in sweat as they entered the camp from a long and arduous march in the desert. They watched with distracted interest as two young soldiers stood with the Sergeant Major in the dusty patch of sand outside headquarters.

"Sheike, tell these men what happened," the Sergeant Major ordered, loud enough for the returning soldiers to hear.

"I caught Avi with my knife! I know it was mine because I carved my initials into it!" he shouted in response, glaring at Avi.

The Sergeant Major moved to within inches of Avi's face. "Look at me soldier! You are a schmuck, and do you know why?"

"Yes, sir," Avi shouted. "Because I stole my fellow-soldier's knife."

"Wrong!" the sergeant Major screamed. "You are a schmuck because you got caught!"

Chapter 16

— ••• —

The tentacles of war with Egypt had begun to spread the moment Israel was given statehood. Egypt's first move was to close the Suez Canal to Israeli shipping. One hundred and twenty miles long, the canal cut across Egypt and ran from Port Said on the Mediterranean Sea to Port Suez on the Red sea. The east side of the canal lay on Egypt's Sinai Peninsula and on the west side, Africa. The Canal allowed seafaring ships to avoid the South Atlantic and southern Indian Oceans. By not having to sail all the way around Africa, the journey was reduced by almost four thousand miles.

Egypt's next move was to introduce bloody terrorist incursions by the *fedayeen,* trained by Egypt to infiltrate Israel and to commit sabotage and murder. Hundreds of Israelis were killed, and hundreds injured. Vowing the obliteration of Israel, in 1955, President Gamal Abdel Nasser began importing arms from the Soviet Bloc. Nasser then signed an agreement with Syria and Jordan that gave him military command of all three armies. In July of 1956, Egypt nationalized the Suez Canal. That declaration infuriated the British and the French who had owned and operated the Suez Canal since its construction.

Israel was convinced that Egypt was preparing an onslaught and decided to preempt their attack. In a secret agreement, Britain and France, both desperate to render control over the Canal, agreed to help Israel with their war against Egypt, as long as the focus of the war was on the opening of the Suez Canal. Israeli agreed.

It was October 29, 1956. Eli was hard at work digging defensive trenches on a rocky hill in the Judean desert, his arms aching, and his hands callused and sore. In the middle of this very labor-intensive and tiresome task that was part of his basic training his group was ordered to come to attention as an officer approached.

"I am here to inform you that our Israeli Prime Minister David Ben-Gurion has ordered a preemptive surprise attack. Israel is now officially at war with Egypt!" the officer shouted, his face beet red, his expression a mixture of determination and rage. "You have now officially completed your basic training and will now be assigned to your army duties."

The soldiers dropped their shovels and cheered, ecstatic that they could stop digging trenches and would now have the opportunity to fight. How foolish and naïve they were, these eighteen-year-old adolescents who idealized conflict, not yet understanding the consequences and repercussions of war.

Eli was sent south to a guarding unit stationed near the Sinai, and his two closest friends and tent-mates were sent elsewhere. Sadly, that deployment would forever break the familiar bond created by the three young soldiers. Eli could never reconcile why he never looked for his two friends or understand why neither one ever looked for him. It was a loss that would haunt him even as he moved into the winter of his years.

The tiny Israeli Air Force bombed the unprepared and unprotected Egyptian airfields and airplanes into oblivion. At the same time, the infantry under the leadership of Moshe Dayan advanced on the Sinai, Israeli paratroopers landing near the canal at the Mitla Pass.

This prearranged landing opened the door for the British and French to call for an immediate ceasefire, demanding that both sides withdraw from the canal. The offer of a ceasefire was ignored by Egypt, as the French and British knew it would be. In response, Anthony

Eden, Prime Minister of Britain, and Rene Coty, President of France agreed to join Israel by positioning their paratroopers along the Suez Canal. Within one hundred hours, the infantry took over the Gaza Strip, much of the peninsula of the Sinai and Sharm el Sheikh, situated at the southernmost tip of the Sinai.

Eli's job was to defend the fully equipped French convoys heading toward the Sinai carrying armament that the Israeli army could only dream about. Seventeen-year-old Eli thought of himself as a hero-soldier, a protector of Israel's French allies. But in truth, he found himself standing around all day holding his primitive Czechoslovakian rifle. During the entire conflict, he never saw an Egyptian and never had to defend anybody. That was a good thing because he could barely defend himself.

Innocent and enjoying the experience, Eli felt like he was on a movie set. To make matters even sweeter, the French invited the Israeli soldiers, whose rations were meager and tasteless, to share their food. It was a culinary delight. The French had food packages filled with goodies Israelis could only fantasize about—rapped or canned; it contained chocolates, cheeses, pate and soups.

Egypt was defeated but not before blocking the canal to all shipping, rendering it impassable and useless for months. As a result of the war, Israel did obtain the freedom of navigation through the Straits of Tiran.

From a military point of view, the war was successful, but from a political point of view, it was a disaster. The United States threatened to withdraw all aid to Israel if they did not pull back to the armistice lines. Khrushchev threatened that the Soviet Union would launch nuclear-tipped ICBM rocket attacks on Britain, France and Israel if Israel did not acquiesce.

Israel had paid a devastatingly high price for its victory: the death of almost two hundred Israeli soldiers and the wounding of 817. With no other option, the army was forced to relinquish their hard-won territories. As the Israeli army retreated, they obliterated the Egyptian railroads but not before commandeering six locomotives. They then turned their attention on the infrastructure of the Sinai Peninsula destroying the roads and telephone lines.

When the war ended, Eli and a group of his comrades were assigned to the artillery division of the army, where he took a communication course. Passing his exams, he was assigned the job of communications instructor. His responsibility was to teach his students how to set up the lines of communication for use during conflicts and teach soldiers how to maintain, use and interact in the language of a walkie-talkie.

Soon recognized for his intelligence, Eli was reassigned to a top-secret artillery unit. The objective of this secret unit was to identify the coordinates of the enemy's cannon fire raining down on Israel from bordering Arab countries.

Arriving in the Negev, he disembarked from his transport, unloaded his gear and was immediately given a tour.

"We have three of these babies," a soldier not much older than Eli said, caressing the field gun. "Meet Long Tom. He's a one hundred- and fifty-five-millimeter cannon built in America. The gun has a range of 14.7 miles and a firing rate of forty rounds per hour."

Eli was awe-struck and proud. He had seen sophisticated French armament but had not seen anything like this in the ragtag Israeli armory. He thought he now understood why this was a top-secret base, but he was wrong. The big secret on this base was a mechanism created by Israeli mathematicians that could measure roads in order to establish direct angles of fire. When the calculations were complete, those big canons could be placed on the mountain and fire accurately at the enemy as soldiers hid on opposite sides of the pass waiting for their foes to approach.

During Eli's training, 155 mm Howitzer cannons were fired from various locations to represent enemy fire. It was the job of Eli's unit to identify the location of those cannons on the military maps. Once trained, his unit took up positions in the dead of night on the mountains or hilltops near the borders. Using map locations and theodolites, surveying instruments used for measuring horizontal and vertical angles, they would pinpoint the enemy fire and use walkie-talkies to relay the locations.

Math was Eli's expertise, and he was placed within the unit to oversee those calculations. It was a job he held until his military service was completed in 1959.

Chapter 17

His army service completed, twenty-year-old Eli Huberman opened the front door shouting, *I'm home!* Mina ran into the foyer and threw her arms around her elder son, hugging him with all her might. Eli laughed, untangling himself from her embrace to shake his father's hand.

"Where's Meir?" Eli asked.

"Where's Meir?" Mina mimicked. "He's fourteen and thinks he's a big shot. He shows up when it's dark outside and he's hungry."

Eli grinned, thinking how lucky Meir was to have the freedom to roam. It was something he had never experienced, his mother always so protective. Eli had to beg and cajole for permission to do anything outside the classroom: trips, parties or picnics. Mina claimed it was foolish to waste time. In truth, although she never admitted it, she was afraid to let Eli out of her sight for fear someone would take him away from her.

By the time Eli graduated from high school, Mina had made peace with her fears and Meir became the beneficiary. It was a good thing because Meir was not compliant and gentle like his brother. He was a tough kid who knew how to manage himself, willing to argue and fight for the things that he wanted. If he didn't get his way, there was the distinct possibility that he would do what he wanted anyway.

Eli came into the kitchen after taking a gloriously long hot shower. He was dressed in his favorite canary yellow T-shirt and tan shorts, smelling like he had dumped an entire bottle of aftershave on himself. He had a date with a girl he met in the army, a redheaded beauty he called Red. She was from Tel Aviv and had gorgeous big blue eyes. He really liked her but knew their time as a couple was nearing its end. Dating meant marriage to Jewish girls and he had zero intentions of settling down with Red. She was sweet and fun and beautiful but there was no way Eli could marry someone who was *smart like a teaspoon*. That was his favorite expression to describe someone with limited intellect because how much knowledge could a teaspoon hold. Still, she was a great distraction while he waited to hear about his admittance to the University.

Eli was shocked to discover that despite his outstanding academic achievements, there was competition to get into the University of Tel Aviv. When his admittance letter finally came, he was baffled. He had applied for microbiology, but this letter said they wanted him to take a test and then interview with a professor of statistics and mathematics.

At the interview, the professor said, "You did very well on your examination, but your integrals need improvement."

Integrals! Who cares about integrals? Eli thought, insulted by the criticism. Aloud he said, "Sir, I mean no disrespect, but I want to study microbiology, not statistics and mathematics."

"To what end?" the professor asked, irritation coloring his question.

"I intend to go to medical school; if not in Israel then I will try to go abroad."

"Perhaps you should reconsider your goals. You are good in mathematics and it is the future," the professor said, rising from his chair, the signal he was dismissing Eli. Fifty years later, Eli would still be asking himself why he had not reconsidered mathematics. Had he done so he would have been involved with the computer revolution that forever changed the world.

Two days after that interview Eli got a letter admitting him to practical mathematics. *They can't do this to me! I am not giving up on my dream. Not now and not ever!* Realizing that his life's ambition was in jeopardy, Eli waited in line for three hours to see an administrator in the admissions department. He was shown in at five o'clock that afternoon.

"Come in," Dr. Gold said, introducing himself in an American-accented Hebrew. His hair cut short and his beard expertly trimmed, he was a handsome man in his late fifties who obviously took very good care of himself. To Eli, the office looked like Doctor Gold had either just moved in or was moving out, as there was no photo or a personal effect to be seen.

"Have a seat," he said pointing to a wooden folding chair across from his desk where an open file laid.

"There has been a mistake," Eli said without preamble, placing his acceptance letter on the administrator's desk.

"This looks in order," Dr. Gold said after a cursory glance. "What seems to be the problem?"

"I didn't apply to this program. I applied to Microbiology."

"Hmm. I have looked over your transcripts and there is no doubt that you would be an excellent candidate for the school of microbiology. Unfortunately, there are only twenty-five spots available and they are all taken."

Eli's stomach dropped and his head swam. Microbiology was the trajectory he needed to open the door into medicine.

Dr. Gold perused Eli's transcripts again. "There has obviously been a mistake made and I am sorry! The only thing I can do for you is this: if someone declines, I promise you will be the first student offered this spot."

•••

Providence, G-d's will, whatever—a student dropped out and Eli Huberman was accepted into the department of microbiology. Because he could not afford housing in Tel Aviv, he lived at home. Over the summers, he worked at a medical facility giving out numbers to patients waiting for appointments and did menial administrative projects.

Living at home was a challenge. The center of his mother's universe was Eli and Meir. The center of his father's universe was his landsman and his Zionist friends. Consequently, the apartment was always inundated with people and that made studying at home impossible. And so, when there were major exams, Eli would pack his small, battered suitcase, leave his brother sleeping alone on their "L" shaped shared sofa, and move in with his Aunt Lola, a place where he could have peace and quiet.

In his second year at the University, twenty-two-year-old Eli became active in the Student Union. One of their volunteer projects was to teach for half a year at a prison for young offenders. Eli and four other students joined the program. Eli always liked history and decided to teach that rather than science.

"So, what's it like at the prison?" Meir asked as they readied themselves for bed, the hour nearing midnight.

"It's a really strange experience," Eli said into the darkness, the only light coming from the nightlight in the bathroom down the hallway. "I'm a free man. I volunteer to walk into that prison. But when you go behind those heavy metal doors and they close behind you, it is a very uneasy feeling! I'm having trouble getting used to it."

"Do you think you feel that way because of the Holocaust?" Sixteen-year-old Meir asked. Frustrated that his parents refused to speak about the war, he never missed an opportunity to try and glean information from his big brother, even though Eli remembered very little.

"All I can tell you is I don't like the feeling of being locked in."

"Then why go?" Meir asked, a typical question coming from a self-centered teenager.

"Maybe because these boys remind me of you. Maybe because I know they are hungry to learn. Or maybe it's just because helping them makes me feel better."

Chapter 18

———— ••• ————

Eli graduated from the University of Tel Aviv in 1964 with a master's degree in Microbiology. His investigative research during his master's program was on a group of viruses that caused epidemics in Israel known as adenoviruses—viruses that gave people colds. He also worked on adenovirus strains that caused tumors in experimental animals.

This period in Eli's young life was a very difficult time. He had no choice but to accept that even if he were to be given a place in medical school, his parents could not afford housing and living expenses in Jerusalem. And so, using his master's degree research as a basis for acceptance, Eli decided to apply to the Weizmann Institute of Science located in Rehovot, only nine miles from his home in Bat Yam. The Weizmann was then and is still considered one of the leading research institutions in the world, offering graduate and postgraduate degrees in the exact and natural sciences: chemistry, astronomy, earth science, physics, biology and mathematics. Being accepted to the Weizmann would eliminate all his financial worries since PhD students were given a monthly stipend, and he could live at home.

Eli applied in the fall of 1965. His aspiration was to be accepted as a graduate student by Professor Leo Sachs, the founder of the Department of Genetics at the Weizmann. Specializing in cellular biology and cancer research, the professor was German-born and British educated with a PhD from Cambridge University. He was famous for his study of fetal cells within the human amniotic fluid that surrounds a baby while in its mother's womb. His research proved that fetal cells could be used to determine the baby's gender and to explore other significant genetic markers. Sachs's unique research became the basis for amniocentesis, used for prenatal diagnosis of human diseases.

Sachs was an intuitive scientist; he had an uncanny ability to sense the right scientific direction needed to implement amazing discoveries. In 1963 he designed the first cell culture system for growing, cloning and developing blood cells. He also confirmed, for the very first time, that malignancy could be reversed. And despite a huge ego and a bad reputation for treating even the professors working in his department more like students than equals, Eli knew that to work with him was an unparalleled opportunity.

As inconceivable as it was to Eli, during their initial interview Sachs actually told Eli he was accepted into his department as a PhD student. Eli was so shocked and excited he thought his heart would stop. Knowing that he must look the fool, smiling so hard his face hurt, he forced himself to reign in his emotions and take on a thoughtful and serious expression.

Continuing in English, because his Hebrew was poor, Sachs said, "I want you to contact Yoheved Berwald, a student of mine who just got her PhD," Sachs said with the authority of a general. "From her you will obtain the protocol and pointers as to how she induced malignant transformation of hamster cells by the use of a carcinogenic chemical benzo (a) and pyrene (BP)." He then added, "Your project will involve quantitative studies." Eli nodded enthusiastically, thankful that Sachs could not read his mind, since he had not grasped most of the things Sachs was saying.

Feeling confident and ecstatic in his successful acceptance, whatever Eli's hesitations had been in the past about being a scientist, those feelings evaporated as he left the Ullmann building. His steps sure, he wandered the lush, tree-filled grounds of the Institute. He walked past impressive structures, the architecture replicating the spirit of Modernism, Minimalism, and Functionalism, each building a representation of the austerity embraced by the young State of Israel. Eli saw the campus as a mirror of what Israel was now—what she could become. Yet, in his wildest imagination, he never envisioned that by 2019, the Weizmann Institute would have a campus with 241 buildings that stretched across 280 acres.

●●●

On his first day in the Institute, Eli entered the elevator that would take him to the Department of Genetics located in the bowels of the new Ullmann building. Laid out in an "L" shape, the offices and labs were spread out over half of the basement. Eli stepped into the office of Sachs's two secretaries and introduced himself. He was told to take a seat in the already student-crowded room.

At precisely nine o'clock in the morning Sachs with his authoritative demeanor and 6' 7" presence strode into the anteroom of his office. Hands clasped behind his back, Sacks' eyes swept from face to face, appearing to be examining the new stable of brilliant minds at his disposal. "Welcome," Professor Sachs said in a low baritone voice. "Today you will be assigned your labs and your projects."

Twenty minutes later Eli was asked to enter Sachs's large office. Without any pleasantries, Sachs started in his low rumbling voice. "As I mentioned to you before, you will be studying benzo (a) pyrene induced malignant cell transformation with an emphasis on understanding the mode of action. Do not forget to get in touch with Yohevet Berwald for the protocol and for her advice. Good luck with your studies."

Eli trembled as he pushed open the door to his lab. Sachs's words had overwhelmed him and to a degree seemed impenetrable. For a moment, he questioned his decision to come to the Institute and to Sachs in particular. But then, looking around the lab, he regained his confidence, telling himself to at least try.

There were narrow windows set close to the ceiling. Eli knew that was necessary in order to avoid direct light, which would harm cultured cells, the main target of Professor Sachs's research. He took a mental inventory, categorizing everything in the room. There was a bench with two wooden boxes each with an angled framed glass window in front, which could be lifted upward; it was a contraption fashioned for use as a crude ventilation hood to keep the area where the cell cultures were being made as sterile as possible. On the other side of the lab were Israeli manufactured green painted copper incubators. The incubators were hooked to large metal carbon dioxide and nitrogen gas cylinders. There was hardware on top of the cylinders that controlled the flow of the required gases needed for his experiments. All the pipettes, Petri dishes and the rest of the glassware on the shelves were manufactured from scratch at the Weizmann. And that was why there was a sign pasted to the wall beside the shelf: STERILIZE AND REUSE!

Tissue culture media and blood components needed for experimentation also had to be generated from scratch at the Institute. Eli would grow to admire the technician at the department, whose job it was to obtain blood from the local animal farm/butchery. That technician would separate the blood into various needed components and then filter the serum to eliminate the remaining blood cells and infectious agents. It took intuition and expertise to identify the blood batches that would or would not fulfill the needs of the researchers. This process took days yet nothing could or would stand in the way of any of these young Israeli scientists. After all, many were the progeny of survivors from the Holocaust.

Chapter 19

————— ••• —————

In the early 1960s, the scientific community did not yet understand the mechanism that underlay the development of cancer. All they had were assumptions based on their imprecise human-exposure observations and their studies with animals. Still, they had come to the conclusion that certain chemicals, radiation, and viruses could cause or contribute to tumor development. On that basis, Eli's research was to focus on the *chemicals* that were believed to cause cancer.

There were new cell culture techniques in use and being studied in Sachs's lab at the Weizmann Institute. These studies brought about a surge of research dealing with converting normal cells into ones with malignant cancer characteristics. The focus of that research was on certain animal viruses, especially mouse polyomavirus, a component of mouse leukemia extract capable of causing tumors.

The research underway showed that colonies of normal cells grew as an organized single layer of cells. A colony is a visible mass of cells that each originates from a single *mother cell*. The result: the colony grows and multiplies, each progeny of the cloned cell an exact replica of the *mother cell*. Scientists made the amazing discovery that the cells in the colonies with malignant characteristics, termed "transformed colonies," grew in a disorganized pattern and that the cells would regularly pile up on each other.

Following Professor Sachs' instructions, Eli tried to make an appointment with the recent PhD graduate Yohevet Berwald, a young woman Eli heard was very beautiful. She refused to meet with him, professing she was leaving for France and was much too busy to talk. Eli continued to pursue her, and she finally agreed to meet. Unfortunately, her acquiescence was a lie, as she not only stood him up once but several times. Eli was upset and angry and he needed help.

That assistance came in the form of two department scientists, Drs. Dan Medina and David Gershon. Upon seeing Eli's distress, they comforted him by saying that Yohevet had a "unique" personality and that he should not take her rudeness personally. They added that they would make themselves available to assist him.

He spent untold hours studying the scientific literature, learning about new and important scientific methods that were critical for his research on cancer. These articles described how to grow, with relative ease, normal cells from animal embryos. Before he could begin his research, Eli needed the correct growth medium, a specific liquid with nutrients designed to support the growth of cells.

The technique to grow cells also required the ability to recreate appropriate temperatures along with a particular combination of gasses. When the steps were followed perfectly, cells could be cultured on the surface of a Petri dish, outside their normal environments. These Petri dishes could then put forth many separate colonies. To observe the colonies, he had to aspirate the growth medium, rinse the Petri dishes gently with a special salt solution, and then fix the cells onto the surface of the Petri dish with Methanol, a special alcohol, which was later aspirated as well.

At that point in the process, Eli would stain the surface of the Petri dishes with dyes commonly used by pathologists. This process completed, the colonies of cells could then be visualized as blue spots on the surface of the Petri dish, their numbers counted by using a simple dissecting microscope at low magnification. To actually study the appearance of the cells within the colonies was another matter entirely. That required a special microscope at a high magnification.

Eli's ultimate goal was to have quantities of these Petri dishes available for his research, as they could be stored for long periods of time. Preparing the Petri dishes was a long and arduous process and even when he followed the instructions perfectly, he was more times than not unsuccessful. In a fortuitous and unexpected event, Eli was presented with a gift. With Yohevet in France Sachs gave Eli access to her workbench and her laboratory cabinets. Inside these cabinets he found a significant quantity of Petri dishes with their stained colonies. A number of the colonies were marked by circles around them, which Eli realized were the transformed colonies used for the photographs in her papers. By examining these colonies under a microscope, and comparing the results with normal colonies, and then studying the matching pictures and explanations in Yohevet's papers, he was able to teach himself how to identify transformed colonies. It was a turning point in his career. He learned how to convert normal cells into cancer cells and to identify the two types of cells.

•••

Herr Professor Sachs saw himself as a God-like figure. A demanding and tyrannical taskmaster, he expected his students to arrive early and to stay late. When a student was late to arrive, Sachs would say sarcastically, "What is going on? You decided to be a member of the Histadrut?" The Histadrut was a labor union whose members worked a negotiated number of hours in a week.

Eli never needed prodding to work longer hours. What he needed was prodding to go home. He was enamored with the challenges that beckoned and in fact, he would awaken in the middle of the night wishing it were morning so he could go back to the lab to observe the outcome of his experiments. Every waking moment was precious, Eli realizing that being a scientist meant making the unknown known, and if he was lucky, being able to translate his discoveries into clinical applications that could improve the health and life of others. That very notion ignited a flame within Eli's soul that blazed throughout his life.

One day, Eli was summoned to Sachs's office. The professor's office resembled that of a CEO of a major corporation. A library ran along the back wall with an imposing desk in front of it. On the right of the entrance door was a small couch, a low chair, and a cocktail table in between. Students would sit on the couch to report the results of their experiments.

"You asked to see me, Professor?" Eli asked formally, as Sachs was one of the only senior institute staff members who insisted on being addressed as professor. Most were called by their first name.

"Come in Eli, I want you to meet Martin Trout. He is a German-trained chemist, and he will be working beside you," Professor Sachs said in English.

Eli was dressed in a lab coat, shorts and sandals, his hair in desperate need of a haircut. He nodded hello to the meticulously dressed man wearing a well-cut navy blazer and perfectly knotted tie. His eyes were the deep blue of the Mediterranean and his Germanic good looks Aryan enough to make Eli's skin crawl.

Reluctantly, Eli had to bring Martin Trout into his lab. They worked side by side, the always-sociable Eli not friendly, limiting his interaction with Martin to the work they were doing. At the end of their second week of working together, as they were cleaning up their workspaces, Martin approached Eli. "You don't like me." It was a statement rather than a question.

Not looking up from the Petri dish he was preparing to put away Eli said, "I don't know you." But Martin's words were true. To Eli he represented death, Nazis and Hitler. Still, Eli had to admit that Professor Sachs was right: in only two weeks Martin's suggestions and chemical techniques indicated that he was clearly a gifted chemist from whom Eli could glean precious insight.

"It is understandable that you detest me," Martin continued. "But I want you to know why I have come to work for the State of Israel. It is the only way I know how to atone for the horrendous and hideous actions of my county and my people. I do not ask for your forgiveness. I have no right. But I must tell you that I am trying to help Israel."

Eli looked at Martin Trout and saw him, really saw him, for the first time. He saw the sadness and the regret, and he sensed the sincerity. He reached out his hand to shake the German's hand. "Thank you for trying to help my people."

Eli and Martin worked closely together and became friends. At one point early in their friendship, Eli approached his mother about inviting Martin to dinner at home. "There is this German I work with who is trying to atone. He really wants to help Israel and I would like to invite him for dinner."

Mina's mouth dropped open and her face turned scarlet. "I don't care if he is the best thing under the sun! If you want me to get a heart attack on the spot, bring him! Because I am telling you, I will not be able to withstand a German in my home."

And so, Martin was never invited to the Huberman home.

Chapter 20

—— ••• ——

A number of months after Eli's arrival, Sachs went on a sabbatical. Eli was relieved, knowing that he would not have to withstand the humiliation of having Sachs see the failures and the struggles he was having acquiring Yohevet's techniques. Once Sachs was gone, Drs. Medina and Gershon came to Eli's rescue, helping him master the specific cell culture techniques needed for quantitative analysis of malignant cell transformation. As he moved forward in his experimentation, they gave him constructive criticism—never discouraging him when he put forth an occasional "crazy" idea.

Even with Sachs' absence, the routine continued at the Ullmann building. Between 10 and 11 in the morning, students and senior staff working in different disciplines went to the cafeteria on the main floor. Amid a grey haze of cigarette smoke, the smell of brewed coffee and freshly baked pastries, ideas were exchanged, and connections were established. Desperate to find someone who could help substantiate his theories, Eli reached out to a number of those colleagues. Sadly, the reaction was always the same; they either did not comprehend his ideas or begged off, telling him it was out of their domain. And worse yet, some of his own colleagues in Sachs' lab thought that his concepts were harebrained and bizarre.

During one of those hour-long coffee breaks, he was introduced to Professor Izchak Steinberg, a biophysicist with an extensive knowledge of statistics. "Come to my office and we'll talk," Izchak said, a handsome, relatively young man with kindly intelligent eyes. Eli felt elated that perhaps someone might actually understand what he was trying to accomplish. Sitting across from Izchak, in a tiny office cluttered with books and papers, Eli told him about his project. Izchak heard Eli out, his attention riveted on every word said. Eli was hopeful as he sat silently, waiting for a response. After thinking for just a few minutes, Izchak said, "What you are doing is actually consistent with a basic statistical concept. I can do the math, but I believe it will prove that what you are doing is straight forward and correct!" Eli was elated, feeling for the first time, that he was on the right track with one of his theories on cell transformation.

•••

For lunch, the students in Eli's department were often invited to Carmia Borek's nearby campus home. A great cook, Carmia was a second-year graduate student, married to a senior staff member. The lunches were a treat. It was an opportunity to gossip about the department and to talk about Herr Professor Sachs. Sitting at a dining table, the conversations were lively and stimulating. Because Carmia and Eli were both working on cell transformation, and because of the mutual respect they had for each other, a friendship flourished that would last throughout both of their varied careers.

Carmia's work was focused on the cause and effect of radiation on cancer. She was a forerunner: the first to show that x-rays transform single normal cells *in vitro* (cell culture) into cancer cells. Along with other discoveries, at Columbia University she showed that radiation could transform human cells and that the DNA from transformed cells can induce cancerous events in other normal cells. In 1988, she would be on the cover of the journal *Cancer Research*. She would go on to hold tenured professorships at both Columbia University and Tufts.

• • •

Professor Sachs returned from his sabbatical when Eli was in the first semester of his second year of studies. Upon seeing Eli's novel concepts in cancer research and realizing their importance, Sachs insisted that Eli immediately write up the results and the conclusion. Sachs' intention was to submit the paper, under his name and Eli's, to the prestigious American journal, *Proceedings of the National Academy of Sciences*, in existence since 1915.

Eli was thrilled and excited and terrified. He not only had a limited knowledge of English, but he was completely inexperienced in writing scientific papers. The task was torturous. He would awaken in the morning with his head swirling, feeling as if he had never closed his eyes. Working non-stop, it took him two weeks just to get the first handwritten version completed.

Trembling with excitement, he handed that first draft to one of Sachs's secretaries. Once she had typed the paper, Eli set about inserting handwritten corrections. As a computer was still a distant dream, he crossed out some portions and rearranged others all with the aid of scissors and sellotape. With this "final" version in hand, he went to Sachs office.

Eli and the professor sat across from each other, Eli on the couch, the professor in the chair as Sachs read the paper. Eli was certain his heart would jump from his chest. After reading for about 10 minutes, Sachs began to dictate to Eli the changes he wanted to make. Bent over, using the small low table across from the couch as a writing desk, Eli wrote frantically. When Sachs finished dictating, almost everything other than the Materials and Methods portion and the list of publications had been changed. However, Eli's discussion points were left intact with the exception of language modifications.

Eli was elated that his first paper had been submitted for publication. He waited impatiently to hear the decision from the journal. Upon hearing that the paper was accepted, Eli felt for the first time that he was really a scientist and not just a struggling academia student.

During his PhD studies, he would go on to publish three more papers, but he was especially proud of that first paper entitled, "Cell Susceptibility to Transformation and Cytotoxicity, by the Carcinogenic Hydrocarbon Benzo[a]pyrene."

He told his family, "My paper involved cell culture studies. In it, I described that benzo[a]pyrene (BP). . ." Eli stopped and thought for a moment. From time to time he had shared his scientific thoughts with his brother and although Meir did not necessarily comprehend the science behind his experiments, he had come up with simple but interesting questions that occasionally forced Eli to rethink some of his scientific ideas. Noting the confused look on his parent's and Meir's faces, Eli said, "It's even hard for some of my colleagues to comprehend my thesis. It will therefore be hard for me to translate what it means. Let me just say that working with a mathematical concept, I have done something never done before. I have converted normal cells into cancer cells in a Petri dish. It is my belief that this work will advance cancer research and let's just leave it at that."

His parents and Meir smiled and nodded their heads with great enthusiasm, congratulating Eli on his amazing accomplishment. He knew they were proud and sincere, and he also knew they had no idea what he had actually done. And that was primarily because in Eli's universe, words that were simplistic and understandable to him were gibberish and foreign to a layman.

The publication of his first paper was significant and it gave Eli recognition in the eyes of Sachs and the cancer research community. Even though, in the second half of the 1960s, membership in the American Association for Cancer Research, which also included foreign members, only numbered in the hundreds— unlike today where there are tens of thousands of members. There were skeptics who questioned the concept that chemical carcinogens could induce malignant cell transformation in cultured cells. In fact, a few months after the publication, one of those skeptics, a renowned cancer virologist, visited the Weizmann Institute in order to meet Eli and discuss his results.

"I read that you have been able to distinguish between toxic effect and the ability to convert normal into malignant cells. So perhaps you can explain to me why a smart young man like you is wasting his time on malignant transformation by chemicals when the reason it works is probably due to viral contamination?" the virologist said.

"I can respectfully assure you sir, that the transformation is not due to viral contamination," Eli said, flattered by the visit but upset by the comment.

"No one has been able to duplicate your work. In fact, the results are being called into question as it seems that the transformation by chemicals can be achieved only with the help of the Holy Water of the Jordan."

"If your colleagues are intimating that my work cannot be replicated outside of the State of Israel, just give me the opportunity and I will prove that it can be replicated!"

Chapter 21

——— ••• ———

Grandmother Rachel frequently compared her two grandsons, Eli and Meir. Eli was sweet, studious, respectful, and he followed the rules. Meir was rebellious by nature, defied authority and had a lackadaisical attitude toward his education. "Nothing good will come out of this boy," Grandmother Rachel said of Meir. The parents disagreed having high expectations for both of their sons.

Meir was an average student but not because he had mediocre intelligence. In fact, he had a brilliant and inquisitive mind for the things he cared about. He studied military strategies and memorized the particulars for dozens of famous conflicts throughout history.

His big brother Eli shared his obsession with history. They would talk for hours about historical Jewish conflicts and world events. Meir was so well read there were times when Eli was actually speechless at the wealth of information his brother had memorized and digested.

Eighteen-year-old Meir Huberman grew up watching his father mesmerize a room full of men with his single-minded passion, devotion and aspirations for the State of Israel. That obsessive determination took hold of Meir from the time he was a little boy. He knew who and what he would be: a soldier in the IDF, a warrior who would one day join the Mossad, the Israeli Secret Service.

In order to matriculate in Israel, at the end of the last year of high school, students were obligated to pass final national exams in six subjects—*Tanach*, (Bible) Math, History, Hebrew literature, and

English. Meir knew that once he graduated, his parents would insist he attend the university, thereby raising the prospect of postponing his military service. That might make his family happy, but it would make Meir miserable. Deciding it was a perfect opportunity to declare his independence, he took his backpack and some shekels, left a note and went on a trip, skipping his final exam in English. There was hell to pay when he finally decided to come home, but it mattered not the least to Meir because he was finally going to be who he had always wanted to be: a soldier. Eventually his thirst for knowledge won out and Meir did sporadically attend university, where he studied painting and sculpture, but it was on his terms and in his timeframe.

Meir joined the IDF, the Israeli Defense Forces, in August of 1963. He volunteered for *Sayeret Mat'kal*, Israel's most secretive intelligence-gathering unit, believing that it would help him get a foot into the Mossad. Sadly, he was not accepted, the spots filled by *Sabras*, Israeli born sons of the founding families of the new State of Israel.

Detesting rejection, Meir then turned to the 35th Paratroopers Brigade, an Airborne Commando unit and an elite infantry arm, its specialization parachuting into areas under extreme and dangerous conditions. The Brigade's primary goals were to train an innovative and elite fighting unit that would be the leading force in any confrontation. It was clearly the right move for Meir, as another goal of the Brigade was to identify the next generation of military officers and commanders, and Meir believed that becoming an officer was a prerequisite for joining the Mossad.

Rising to the challenge, Meir partook in a two-day intensive selection process. There were physical fitness challenges, and he embraced the sweat and burning muscles as he might embrace a lover. Psychological tests were given to identify emotional preparedness, motivation, determination and persistence. Those tests were a reflection of his true self and he flew through the questions. Situations were simulated to test his ability to brainstorm with fellow soldiers and to be resourceful in finding ways to push ahead regardless of how physically and mentally exhausted he was. Meir passed that two-day testing with numerous stars next to his name, identifying him with leadership potential and an exceptionally high IQ.

He then spent the next seven and a half months in grueling training, so difficult that more than a quarter of his fellow soldiers dropped out. Meir had weapons training, his primary weapon the Israeli IMI Uzi submachine gun. He loved the way the lightweight Uzi felt in his hands. It was the perfect weapon for reconnaissance when he would be scouting in occupied territory.

To learn *Krav Maga*, close contact combat, he was taught the self-defense fighting art created by the IDF that was a combination of Karate, Judo, Aikido, wrestling and boxing. Meir stood only 5' 6" and had always detested being short. Yet, he realized that in close combat, being low to the ground gave him a greater center of balance. The excruciating pain was worth the exquisite reward of learning to use his fists and fingers, feet, body and brain as a weapon.

He participated in urban warfare training that taught him close-range street fighting and ruthless combat skills that he would use many times in the ensuing years. Meir was introduced to navigation techniques while partaking in miles-long marches carrying heavy equipment. There were weeks of survival training, where he learned camouflage techniques that taught him how to blend into mountain, desert and snow environments. How apropos that camouflage training was, as later in his life he would be known as the *King of Shadows*.

The last two weeks he spent learning how to jump out of an airplane without breaking a leg on landing. He would never forget that first jump, how his heart pounded, and his brain screamed danger. It was in that moment, when he was soaring through the ocean of clouds, that he knew he could do anything.

Meir (Huberman) Dagan

To complete his training, Meir participated in a twenty-four-hour, forty-two-mile march. Most of the trek was uphill, with him carrying equipment that weighed almost forty percent of his body weight. Stretchers were also introduced to simulate carrying a wounded soldier. It was grueling, exhilarating, and the perfect conditions in which Meir could see just how far he could push his body and his psyche.

At the completion of that challenge, in 1966, Meir was inducted into the Airborne Commando unit of the 35th Paratroopers Brigade. It was the proudest moment of his young life.

It would not take long for his leadership skills and intelligence to be noticed. He was tapped for promotion, becoming a reconnaissance unit officer within the Brigade. To celebrate that monumental achievement, Meir Huberman decided to change his name to the Hebrew surname Dagan, meaning earth or grains. It was Meir's way of identifying to the world that he was eternally connected to that area of the earth known as the Israeli homeland. Officially becoming Meir Dagan, it was a time that defined his character and it transformed him, turning the tough little kid into a warrior man.

Eli was in the second year of his PhD program when Meir came home from the army. Sharing their sofa beds once again brought the brothers close. Meir talked about his army experience, and they laughed at how very different Eli's cushy experience had been. Eli saw then as clearly as if Meir's life story had already been written, the gilded potential of a great man in his little brother. He knew then that regardless of what Eli might accomplish in his own life, Meir Dagan would be the one to change the world.

Chapter 22

————— ••• —————

In August of 1966, twenty-six-year-old Eli Huberman completed the second year of his PhD program. He was still single while all his friends had married, and his family began to worry that he might never settle down. His parents pestered and cajoled him unmercifully to go on a blind date with the daughter of an acquaintance of their friends, Lily Ginzburg. To get them off his back, he acquiesced.

He called Lily Ginzburg and made a date, arranged the time and place, and dressed in what he considered proper attire: a clean shirt and long pants. Lily stood him up. She called and apologized profusely the next day, claiming it was unintentional. Regardless, Eli felt insulted and decided he was never going out with her. But Lily was intent on meeting him. She called the Weizmann, got Eli's phone number, and then did the unthinkable at the time; she called him.

They met at a popular Middle Eastern Restaurant in Tel Aviv. Lily entered the restaurant dressed in a black skirt that fell right above her knees and a sleeveless white shirt. A bright red scarf was tied haphazardly around her neck, just what Eli was told to look for in order to recognize her. Eli was taken by how elegant she was, her presence making the restaurant suddenly seem shabby and an inappropriate place for them to meet. Moving toward him, her welcoming smile was disarming. Lily's porcelain white skin made her appear doll-like and fragile to Eli. The only contradiction to that assumption was the bold red lipstick she wore. Her hair was shoulder length and the color of café au lait. She had an oval face, high cheekbones, and arched brows that rested above almond-shaped light brown eyes. Slim and fit, at twenty years old, she was six years his junior. He took her hand in greeting, his dark skin contrasting hers. Sitting at a small round table, sipping coffee and getting to know each other, that first date was the best date Eli ever had.

But he just could not get past having been stood up. So even though he liked her, he decided not to call or contact Lily ever again. Not one to be dismissed, when a week had gone by with no contact from Eli, Lily took the initiative and called him. Eli was really flattered, as it was unheard of for a woman to call a man. Stepping all over his words, he apologized for not calling, telling a fib that he had been ill.

They began to date, sitting and talking for hours. Having to make an effort at conversation with someone who was not a scientist was a unique experience for Eli. It was because Lily was intellectually equal, her talents many, and her interests varied.

She had graduated from the Talma Yellin High School for Performing Arts and was now in her last year of a three-year B.A. program at Tel Aviv University. Her major was English literature and linguistics. She was also enrolled at the Academy of Music in a four-year program majoring in piano performance. As impossible as their busy schedules were, they managed to carve out time to be together. It did not take long for their friendship to turn into something much more.

• • •

Lily and Eli walked along Rothschild Boulevard after attending a concert by the Israeli Philharmonic Orchestra at the Mann Auditorium. The night was warm, the sweet breezes rustling the palms. Holding hands, they entered a crowded coffee house. As they waited, they noticed one of the waitresses kept staring at Eli. She was in her forties with messy bleached blond hair and wearing a bit too much make-up

Suddenly she pointed at him and screamed, "It's him! It's him!"

Eli was mortified. The woman was shrieking as if Eli had tried to rape or murder her. He was ready to bury himself alive. His hand trembled in Lily's as she squeezed it tighter and moved closer to him.

The woman approached them, but it took forever before she was calm enough to speak. By then the entire coffee house was involved.

"You don't remember me, do you?" the waitress finally asked, her chest heaving as she fought to stop crying and to catch her breath.

Eli shook his head, afraid to say a word.

"My name is Shoshana Sigalin. When I was fourteen, my job in the Soviet Union labor camp in the horrid frozen tundra was to take care of you." She reached over and gently touched Eli's shoulder as if to be sure that what she was seeing was not some apparition. "You were just a little boy so you wouldn't remember me, but I never forgot you." Her voice caught as she swiped tears from her red-rimmed eyes.

Eli felt frozen, the impossibility of such a coincidence so surreal he was having a hard time grasping it. "How did you recognize me?" he finally managed to blurt out.

"Your eyes. I recognized your eyes."

"Amazing," Eli replied.

"Unbelievable!" Lily added, watching this incredible coincidence, or was it a miracle, unfold?

"Come, sit," Shoshana said, leading them to the only empty table.

A half-hour later, in between serving her patrons, Shoshana found time to *kibitz* with Eli and Lily.

"Please tell your parents hello for me," Shoshana said, as Eli and Lily rose to leave.

"I will," Eli replied.

"Thank you," Lily said, embracing Shoshana. "Thank you for taking such good care of Eli."

•••

Eli and Lily spent every available moment they could together. And as their relationship grew stronger, Lily shared her story and the story of her family. She was conceived in a forest outside of Vilna, Poland during the war and was born on October 1, 1945, just after the Second World War ended. Lily's mother, Ada, unlike most survivors, talked about her experiences during the Holocaust. Lily hated when she did, horrified by the pain her mother had suffered.

Ada was the youngest of four siblings. The family had lived in Vilna for generations. In fact, her grandmother swore that her family was descended from the great Rabbi Eliyahu ben Shlomo Zalman, the *Gaon*, genius of Vilna who lived from 1720–1797. It was said that by the time the *Gaon* was nine years old, he had already studied the *Kabbalah,* the mystical interpretation of the Hebrew Bible. He went on to become one of Judaism's great Torah scholars and an expert in *Halakhah*, Jewish law. Lily had laughed, saying that half the population claimed him as their honored ancestor.

Before WWII, the family was well to do. Lily had learned about those years from family members. She knew her grandfather, Eliezer, dealt in lumber and traveled often to the woods of Poland and the forests of Lithuania. Her grandmother, Golda Rimdziun was head of the family, and before the War, she owned and rented apartments.

•••

Ada was an ardent Zionist and with her parents' blessing, when the rumblings of war began, she used her savings from work to purchase a ticket to Palestine. Family and friends gathered for a joyous going-away-party. Just before she was scheduled to leave, her grandmother's sister told her, "If you go, your parents will be all by themselves." Ada's two older brothers, Misha and Motia were both away at university. Her talented and beautiful older sister was studying at the Sorbonne in Paris. Guilt-ridden for even thinking of deserting her parents if war broke out, Ada canceled her trip. It was not long before Sonia also came home from Paris in order to be with the family. Sadly, she left behind her fiancé, a Jewish man who was destined to become a Professor of Philosophy at the Sorbonne. He was the great love of her life and consequently Sonia never married. As a result, Lily became the daughter Sonia never had.

In September of 1939, Hitler invaded Poland. In October, under the terms of the German-Soviet Pact, the Soviet Union reassigned Eastern Poland and the Vilna region to Lithuania. During this time Jews from occupied Poland found some refuge in Vilna, away from the murderous Nazis. Determined to fight rather than be slaughtered, Ada's two brothers decided to enlist in the Red Army. Vowing never to be at the mercy of the Nazis Sonia decided to follow the Russian army.

In the summer of 1940, the Soviet Union broke with Germany by claiming Vilna for Russia. Hitler's response to this land grab was to attack. The Germans were victorious, and Vilna was once again under the fist of the Nazi regime. In 1941, the Nazis turned the Jewish Quarter into the Vilna Ghetto. Allowed to take only what they could carry, every Jew, half-Jew, convert, and spouse of a Jew was forced from their home. Split into two sections, the Jewish Quarter became the Large Ghetto and the Small Ghetto. Niemiecka Street, a non-ghetto corridor, separated the two areas, making it easier for the Nazi guards to patrol.

The Nazis intentions were to dehumanize the Jews. Street executions in front of family members were daily occurrences. The SS would laugh as they tortured men, woman and even children for the tiniest infraction. Subjected to horrific living conditions and slave labor, hunger and disease became the war these Jews were forced to fight. Many did not survive and those that did were sent to the concentration death camps.

It was under these horrendous conditions that Ada met Elia Ginzburg again, the man who had been her mother's tenant. Elia was now a widower. He worked forced labor outside the compound during the day, as did all able-bodied men. Brave and daring, Elia snuck food for Ada and her family into the ghetto. Had he been caught with even a loaf of bread; he would have been shot. He also smuggled in arms for the Resistance. They were a group of strong-willed men and women living in the ghetto, who joined together in January of 1942. Their vow, to fight the Nazis! Their motto: *We will not go like sheep to the slaughter.*

One day, twenty-year-old Ada and her father, Eliezer, were arrested on the street inside the ghetto by the SS. Gun barrels shoved in their bellies, they were pushed into a crowd of terrified Jews being force-marched out of the city. Surrounded by armed Nazis, starving dogs nipping at their feet, there was little anyone could do to escape. And then out of nowhere, someone grabbed Ada's arm and yanked her out of the moving mass. By the time Ada realized what was happening, her beloved father was swept away in the throng. Dragged into an alley, heartbroken and hysterical, and with no hope of saving her father, she was inconsolable.

"We have to get you back into the Ghetto now!" the man who saved her life ordered. It was in that moment that Ada recognized him from her neighborhood: a collaborator, a Jew working with the Nazis! They were despicable and despised for their actions. But had it not been for him, Ada would not have lived another day, as all those captured that day were taken into the Ponary forest and massacred.

Its population nearing forty thousand, the Ghetto became so crowded it was uninhabitable. Desperate and determined, Ada and her mother Golda managed to escape. For a short time, Polish friends took them in, but if caught, the entire family would have been executed for their kindness. With no alternative, they hid in sewers below the city, living in filth, fecal matter and mud. German patrols would regularly search the sewers, capturing children and old people who could not run and hide fast enough. The results of those six months underground took a toll on Ada. For the rest of her life, she suffered horribly from a serious heart ailment, a persistent cough, trouble breathing, and rheumatism—her joints, bones and muscles always aching, a reminder of the horror she had endured. She would be dead by age seventy.

Chapter 23

— ••• —

With Elia's help, Golda and Ada escaped the sewers to join his partisan comrades in the Ponary forest. Hiding among the tall pines, Ada Rimdziun and Elia Ginzberg were married in an improvised wedding ceremony. The bride and groom were well aware that their wedding was one of the only moments of joy in that place of screaming souls. The Nazis had murdered seventy thousand Jews and twenty thousand Poles. Their remains lay forever in unmarked mass graves. It was also the final resting place for Golda's beloved husband Eliezer, the grandfather Lily would never meet.

Emerging from the forest at war's end, the family returned to Vilna, now under the control of the Soviet Union. Ada was pregnant and her mother, Golda, not knowing if her two sons Misha and Motia, and her daughter Sonia had survived was determined to protect her unborn grandchild. Petite as a ballerina, with the soul of a lioness Golda appointed herself the archival expert of the city. It was the only thing she knew to add meaning to her life to keep her from going mad. When survivors poured in from all over Europe, searching for their children, their mothers, fathers, sisters, brothers, grandparents, cousins and aunts, they were directed to Golda. She greeted them with hot soup, a hot shower, and clean used clothing to replace their lice-infested garments that would be burned. Once clean, rested and fed, Golda assisted them in looking for their family members.

Eventually, Misha and Motia made their way back from the Russian army. That they had lived was a miracle although Misha had lost an eye and Motia was left with a paralyzed arm. Sonia also returned, toothless and cadaver-like. All she would say was that she "walked after the Red Army." No one understood what that meant.

Life went on and that included moments of humor and laughter. One story told was the day Motia—by some miracle—found a chicken while he was serving in the Soviet army. He gave it to his older sister Sonia to cook. Sonia had never cooked in her life but was determined to prove she was capable. She had spent her life sheltered; her only responsibilities were to study and play the piano. Known for her beauty and knowledge but not for her common sense she asked for cooking directions from a comrade. *You put it in water and boil it.* So, she put the chicken in water to boil—complete with the feathers and the innards. Basically, the bird took a bath!

Motia thought about the chicken all day. When he came to eat he was greeted with the stink from three blocks away. They said my uncle wanted to kill her. "If a man wanted a woman who could serve him and do for him, Sonia was the wrong choice," Lily said remembering her with a loving mischievous smile. "But she taught me so much about living a good life."

When Lily was born, the Russians gave the family an apartment in the center of the city. It was Elia's reward for his service fighting the Nazis as a partisan. Still, living under the Communist regime was a strict and brutal life filled with danger. Even an unfounded suspicion of disloyalty to the authorities or a joke about the system or its leaders could send you to jail for weeks or months of interrogations. The best room in the apartment building that even included a balcony, had been given to a Russian woman whose sole job was to spy on them. As a result, if someone in the family wanted to say something deemed controversial, they would go out to the street to speak, or they would write it down and then burn the paper.

When Lily spoke to Eli about her life growing up, her eyes would glisten and the smile that so endeared her to him would shine. "I was the center of all the attention, the only child. After the war they wanted to fatten me up. They would feed me a concoction called *goggle mogel*: egg yolks, 3 or 4 sugar cubes, cocoa and milk. When you came from a war and there was no food, fat was good! But I was so fat that I had no neck. My mother was so worried she took me to the best Jewish pediatrician to ask him if I would ever have a neck. The doctor replied, "Don't worry you will have a giraffe living in your house."

The main mode of transportation was trains and thousands passed through Vilna on their way to Poland or to various Republics of the Soviet Union every month. Through ingenuity and intelligence, Ada was appointed head accountant at the Vilna train station. The position was very important and lucrative, allowing her to become a participant in the true philosophy of Communism: *I will give you: you will give me.* Determined to make a good life for her daughter Ada risked her life every day taking part in illegal activities.

In the train station restaurant, instead of having 100 grams of caviar on half a dozen sandwiches, they would use 80 grams. For sausage, smoked fish and other items they would do similar portion control. This way they would have food left over. It was really very simple: you give me what's left over from the food and I will do something for you. That was the only way to survive in Russia for many years. People would buy light bulbs that had already burned out so they could take the dead bulb to work. They would remove the good bulb and replace it with the bad bulb and then bring the good one home. Maybe it was cheating, but it was the only way to have a bulb.

Ada was never caught because while everything in the Soviet Union was supposedly regulated, in truth, nothing really was. Lily's uncle Misha, who lost one eye, and his wife, Sofia, a pediatrician, lived in a tiny room in the same apartment shared with Ada, Elia, Lily, Golda and Sonia. Even after Misha's wife had a son, Aaron, they wanted to live with the family because they had the luxury of a kitchen and a bathroom. Ada did so well working at the train station that they even hired a maid, a Russian village girl who lived with them and slept in the kitchen.

As an innocent child, Lily played every afternoon in the courtyard of her apartment building with her Russian and Jewish friends. In the morning she attended preschool. It was during that time that her father developed pemphigus, a horrific autoimmune skin disease that would cause his skin to fall off. He suffered horribly. Ada did everything she knew to do, including getting medication from Moscow, but nothing helped. He died at home when Lily was five.

Lily was sent to a Russian kindergarten with her friends. There she learned to speak Russian since Yiddish was the only language spoken in her home. But after her father's death, Lily had a very difficult time recovering. Aunt Sonia, who played piano, wanted Lily to play, believing it would soothe her sadness. But Lily could not sit still long enough to learn. However, she showed an uncanny ability to sound out by ear the melodies that Sonia played.

At six years old Lily took an examination given by the state-run music school. The competition was intense and to everyone's joy, Lily was selected. Her Aunt Sonia saw this as an incredible opportunity for her niece and decided that she would devote herself to practicing with Lily every day. Somehow during those early years of Lily's artistic development, Ada even managed to procure a baby grand piano. It was kept in the middle of the living room, despite all the people living in the crowded apartment.

Lily could read music before she could read words, the eighty-eight keys on the keyboard her unspoken vocabulary. By eight years old, beautiful little Lily with the magical fingers was deemed a child prodigy and began performing on stage. Appearing regularly by age twelve, her favorite pieces were compositions by Beethoven and Bach.

Yet, regardless of how well the family was doing under Communism and regardless of the future that lay before Lily, there was only one thing that Ada wanted for her daughter and that was to take her to the land of Israel.

Chapter 24

— ••• —

The Prime Minister of Poland Jozef Cyrankiewicz, announced that the Soviet Union would allow anyone with a Polish birth certificate to resettle back to their country of origin. For a short period between 1957 and 1958, just as they had done in 1945, the Jews were allowed to leave Vilna, Lithuania—then a part of the Soviet Union—and repatriate to Poland. Ada decided to take Lily and flee to Poland.

Ada had money but taking it out of Communist Lithuania was forbidden. The only solution was to exchange the currency for possessions that could be sold upon arrival in Poland. On advice of a friend, she took a trip to Moscow and bought a very expensive sable fur coat and jewelry that could be easily sold or traded. On the day she and Lily left, they bid Misha and his family and Golda and Sonia goodbye, knowing that their passage had been arranged and that they would all be joining them soon.

•••

Upon arrival in Wroclaw, Ada and Lily lived in a camp for immigrants, housed in a huge warehouse

Lily's Original Passport Picture

where hanging sheets offered their only privacy. Selling some jewelry, Ada was able to rent a room in the warehouse for Lily and herself. When the family was finally reunited, that room was transferred to Misha, his doctor wife, Sofia, and their young son, Aaron. Golda and Sonia moved to Warsaw where Golda stayed with a friend. Because Sonia spoke several languages, and no one knew that she was Jewish, she found a job at a Polish newspaper and lived in an apartment with a friend.

With no secure plan in place, a rabbi allowed Ada and Lily to sleep on a round table at the synagogue, on the table because there were rats. Sixty years later when Lily shared the story with Eli, that frightened twelve-year-old reemerged as she vividly recalled clinging to her mother all night, certain that she was falling off that table. Thankfully, a few days later a Polish woman rented them a tiny sofa in her living room that mother and daughter could share.

Ada was tired of waiting for their visas. By coincidence she met a single man who had a visa and was departing for Israel. Seeing this as a way to fulfill her dream, she offered him money to marry her, half now and the rest when she arrived in Israel. His only obligation was to write a letter, and have it notarized that he wanted his wife and her family to follow.

"It's crazy. How could you marry a complete stranger?!" Too young and innocent to understand her mother's motivation or explanation, Lily wept angry tears.

"Lily, you are getting upset for nothing," Ada said, stuffing a big pillow under her dress, molding it to look like she was pregnant. "It is not a real marriage. We will get divorced the moment I arrive in Israel. And what I am doing now, making myself look pregnant, is going to be our ticket out of here. Now come with me," she said, taking Lily's hand as they moved on to the crowded Warsaw sidewalk.

Keeping her arms tucked beneath the pillow to keep it from slipping, she and Lily strolled to the Warsaw government building that housed the offices of the Foreign Ministry. They found the office and were given a number, waiting in an interminable line that snaked its way down the long corridor. Hours later they were shown into the office of an underling. They were greeted with the smell of herring and onion and a curt nod of his balding head. Dark bags drooped beneath his bulging eyes; the suit he wore was wrinkled and stained. They were not offered chairs nor invited to sit so they stood while he flipped through papers.

When he finally looked up again Ada handed him the notarized letter. She knew that according to the Red Cross Treaty and the Polish Quota Agreement, families had to be reunited. He read it quickly. "I will see what can be done, but it will take time."

"A woman in my condition," Ada said, her eyes spilling tears, "and you don't let me join my husband immediately?"

With a disinterested look on his face, the man took a rubber stamp, pressed it on an inkpad and then stamped a document. He handed it to Ada, and then with a flip of his hand as if he were shooing away mosquitoes, he dismissed them.

A week later, Ada, Lily, and Golda boarded a train to Naples, Italy. From there they took a ship to the port of Haifa in Israel. For three horrific days they were all sicker than they had ever been in their lives. But the moment that land came into view, all else was forgotten. With tears that would not stop, they disembarked the ship. The moment Ada's feet touched land, she dropped her luggage and fell to her knees, kissing the sacred ground of the Jewish homeland. She stood slowly, trembling, as she inhaled air that seemed to smell sweeter, the light somehow clearer and brighter. To her great surprise, there were dozens of young Israelis waving flags as they waited to greet the *Olim Chadashim,* the new immigrants.

"Shalom," greeted a young man dressed in a t-shirt and khaki pants. "Please, let me help you," he said in Polish, reaching to help Golda with her luggage.

"Thank you," Golda said gratefully. After her knee injury in Vilna had left her with a permanent limp.

"My name is Dov and I am here to help get you settled." He smiled, his large cobalt eyes twinkling.

"I am Ada, this is my daughter Lily and my mother Golda," Ada said, handing him her papers.

"Nice to meet you," Dov replied as he led them to a long metal table and picked up a clipboard. "Do you have any relatives living in Israel?"

"We have a distant cousin, Fima Berkman, a lawyer from Poland who moved to Israel immediately after the War. I think he lives in Haifa, but we never told him we were coming," Ada said, trying to sound more assured than she felt.

"That being the case let me suggest that you go to *Kiryat Tiv'on*. It is only fifteen kilometers from here and sits in the hills between the Jezreel valley and Zvulun. People say it is as beautiful as Switzerland," Dov offered as he positioned the clipboard to begin writing.

"I know that Switzerland is beautiful, so if it is like Switzerland, then let's go," Ada said, smiling at the tanned and handsome young Dov.

"Ah, here comes Yael. She will show you to the bus. *Le'hitra'ot*, see you again, I hope."

The ride was surreal as they traversed the lush hills and moved toward the valley. When they arrived, they were taken to a small hut. There were beds and sheets, blankets and even food to cook. But there was a dirt floor.

"Just put a lot of water on the floor and it will become like cement," a neighbor in the hut next door offered, patting Ada's shoulder in welcome.

"A dirt floor?" Sitting on her suitcase outside by the front door, Lily refused to enter. "I want to go back to Vilna!" she whined, nuzzling next to her grandmother.

"They are giving us food so we will not starve, and we have a place to live and a bed to sleep," Ada said, disregarding her daughter as she brought water in from the outdoor spigot and began wetting the floor.

"Maybe we should help?" Golda suggested, taking her grand-daughter's hand.

"Absolutely not," Lily growled. "We need to go back to Vilna!"

An hour later, while Lily still stubbornly sat sitting outside, a car pulled up to the hut and a man and a woman got out. Contacted by Dov, they were Ada's distant cousins. Hugs and tears followed. And even though the Berkman's had three sons of their own crowded into a tiny apartment, they had come to take their relatives home.

They stayed with their cousins for over a month. Then more relatives of the Berkman's arrived and it was time for Ada and Lily to move out. Knowing that she had to find a way to support herself and her daughter, Ada decided to move into an *Ulpan,* a school for the intensive study of Hebrew. It was a six-month commitment and during that time Ada decided to change her name to the Hebrew name Hadassah. Going to the Ulpan was a fortuitous decision that enabled her to get a job when her studies were completed.

As a result, Lily was sent to *Aloney Yitzhak Youth Village* where she would live for the next six months. Founded the year Israel became a State, the boarding school was located in the center of the country, ten kilometers from Caesarea. Its purpose was to absorb children from all the various immigrations: first the children rescued from the Holocaust, and then throughout the years, children arriving from North Africa and Eastern Europe. It was at this school that the children learned Hebrew and the customs of their new home.

Being sent away from her family had a profound effect on thirteen-year-old Lily, an only child who had always been treated as special. She felt abandoned. Unable to speak Hebrew, not knowing one person, she found her only refuge when she was allowed to practice the piano at the boarding school. Overjoyed after hearing Lily play, Zalman Cohen, a noted piano teacher decided to teach her for free. Consequently, once every two weeks, she would board a bus and a train in order to take piano lessons from him. He remained her teacher all the way through to her graduation from the Tel Aviv Academy of Music.

As lonely and difficult as this transition was, Lily began to understand that it was in her power to attain happiness. She found girls that spoke Polish and made friends. With an uncanny ability to learn languages, a talent that would serve her well for the rest of her life, she quickly picked up Hebrew. And as happens so many times when faced with huge obstacles, Lily embraced the realization that she was strong and independent and able to adapt and that she was now and always would be a survivor.

•••

Lily attended Talma Yellin High School for the Performing Arts. Surrounded by fellow musicians, she found her footing, creating a social circle that included all the good-looking boys and the prettiest girls, many from Russia. Always bossy, Lily became their ringleader. Obsessed with style and fashion, Lily set the standard, giving pointers of how each girl should dress, wear their hair and put on make-up. But as smart and talented as she was, Lily was lazy when it came to her studies. That caused great conflict within the family. So much so, that Aunt Sonia would come in the mornings to check her homework, and Uncle Misha would come in the evenings to make sure she had learned her math.

Even with average grades, Lily was accepted into the three-year English Literature and Linguistics Bachelors program at Tel Aviv University after passing the entrance exam with flying colors. Obviously, being considered a piano prodigy had its benefits.

Parallel to her university studies, she was invited to study performance piano at the prestigious Academy of Music. That four-year program was demanding not just of her time but her abilities. She was an accomplished pianist, but these teachers were looking for greatness. Her days of being lazy were behind her forever. Those hours of practice were Lily's greatest joy, a time when all that existed in her world were the notes, the tones, and the music that embraced and fed her soul.

Chapter 25

May 1967

Eli was enchanted by Lily's courage, determination, love of the arts and sense of adventure. And while she had absolutely no interest in science, she thoroughly enjoyed hearing the stories about Sachs, the people who visited his labs and Eli's colleagues. She was strong and independent, and he knew that he had found his *bashert*, his destiny. Seven months after they met, on Eli's twenty-eighth birthday, February 8, 1967, he proposed to Lily Ginzburg. At the time, Eli was in his second year of graduate school at the Weizmann Institute. Lily was in her last year at Tel Aviv University, with another year remaining at the Academy of Music. And while she still loved the piano, her dream of becoming a concert pianist had diminished since arriving in Israel. She had quietly tucked away her dream of performing professionally and was content to be in love with a smart and accomplished man, a cancer scientist working in the famous Weizmann Institute.

The couple selected a wedding date, and both sets of parents took out loans in order to pay for a wedding that would include eight hundred guests. Even after inviting everyone that was anyone, Eli's father told him, "I can't even walk in the streets in Bat Yam, where I live because of all the people I am not inviting." Of the eight hundred guests, only fifty were the selected friends of the bride and groom.

With Eli and Lily saving every shekel earned from his Weizmann stipend and her part-time job, they thought all the fanfare was a waste of money, money that could be put to better use helping the newlyweds begin their lives together. Mustering his courage, Eli brought up the suggestion of having a small wedding. Shmuel was incredulous. "My first first-born son is getting married, and I should not have a great event? That will never happen!" In fact, Shmuel called in every favor to make sure that the Chief Rabbi of Tel Aviv would be officiating at his first-born son's wedding.

•••

When Lily was a small child in Vilna, there was a woman named Yocheved, who made children's clothing. Lily's father, Elia, had always teased her. "When my daughter will be a bride, you will do the dress." Sadly, Elia would not live to see his daughter married.

One day, Lily's mother, Hadassah, was at the central bus station in Israel when she spotted the seamstress. "It is so good to see you!" Hadassah said, holding Yocheved's calloused hands between hers. "I have often dreamt of finding you. As hard as it is to believe, my Lily is getting married. Will you hem the dress for us?"

"I would be honored," Yocheved said.

Lily had the perfect dress, a beautiful gown with Yemenite embroidery. On the morning Yocheved came to hem the gown, the sun filled the apartment with a magical golden light. Standing still as a statue as the seamstress worked, Lily drifted back to her childhood, remembering her father before he was ill. She pictured his handsome face, his wonderful smile, how he listened to her every word, laughed at her silly stories, insisted on tucking her in at night, even when she was too big to be treated like a baby.

Lily's mother, Hadassah, was also thinking of the past, Elia's courage and devotion during the war, how he made her feel safe and cared for even under the most horror-filled circumstances. And even though she had remarried Misha, a handsome engineer with a drinking problem, a mistake that she would forever regret, Elia was then, and would always be her everything. In the time it took to pin a hem, a husband and a father's wish was fulfilled.

During those fleeting moments, a silken cord surrounded Hadassah and Lily and Elia: a family once again.

•••

Although a bit theatrical in order to impress the guests, the highlight of the wedding feast came when the lights were switched off, and the waitresses came out carrying platters filled with flaming chickens, the birds having been doused with spirits.

Sitting with the bride and groom were Eli's parents and Lily's mother and her husband, Misha. Also at their table was Eli's famous professor and advisor, Leo Sacks. At 6' 7", when Professor Sachs asked Eli's mother, Mina, to dance, it was an awkward disaster. He was so tall, and she was so tiny, it was a conundrum where she should place her head. It was clear from the expression on Mina's face that she was suffering. Eli and Lily had to hold their breath to keep from laughing aloud.

Professor Sacks at Eli And Lily's Wedding

•••

Lily and Eli managed to scrape together enough money to buy an apartment. It was located in Bat Yam, the seashore town bordering to the south of Jaffa -Tel Aviv where Eli had lived most of his life. With windows facing north, west and south, there was always a gentle breeze wafting from the Mediterranean Sea. Although quite small, it had a living room with an exit to a large terrace on the west side, with a view of the roof on the floor below theirs and a view of the sea. Their bedroom faced south, and the tiny den was shared with the north-facing kitchen that had a window situated at the top of the wall.

The couple loved art and decorating, and Eli believed that he would have become an architect had he not gone into science. And so, they decorated the living room painstakingly with lovely pictures and simple furniture, which they ordered from a Jaffa cabinetmaker based on their own design.

The bedroom had a double bed and a built-in wall cabinet with many doors that Eli's father built by hand from heavy wood that he then covered in white Formica. It was so incredibly heavy they doubted it would ever be removed. Their kitchen had a noisy refrigerator that was always filled with leftovers and a simple stove where a soup concoction Lily dreamed up was always simmering. They ate their meals at a small table with four folding chairs. The dishes, pots and pans, cutlery and knickknacks came from wedding gifts.

Mornings settled into a routine for the newlyweds. Eli would wake before Lily. When he was ready to leave, he got Lily's toothbrush, put toothpaste on the brush and nudged it into her mouth to wake her up for the part time job Eli had found for her, teaching English at a secretarial school.

"I can't do it! I can't face another day around a bunch of obnoxious, loud seventeen and eighteen-year-old girls who don't listen to a word I say. Eli, if you really love me, you will tell them I'm sick," she mumbled one morning, heading toward the bathroom.

Eli knew that Lily had not established control over the girls at the secretarial school, but he dared not say that to her. Instead, he said, "I'm fine with you quitting. We will manage."

She came out of the bathroom with an incredulous look on her face. "I would never do that! It's a good job and who else would ever hire me with my crazy school schedule?"

He smiled to himself. That was his Lily, kvetching one minute and digging in the next. Besides, it was good that she was so busy because routinely Eli spent ten to twelve hours a day in the lab, then a one-hour bus ride. He usually arrived late. Occasionally there would be a time-sensitive experiment that required his hourly presence, and when that occurred, he would stay in the lab all night. And as it was with most scientists, even when he did get home, his mind was always occupied with thoughts about the experiments.

A phone in Israel was a luxury that could take up to five years to obtain, so most of their conversations took place when Lily used the public phone outside the nearby fish store. She would call to check on Eli and to tell him her news from the day. Eli would tell her that he was busy in the lab and did not have time for a long phone conversation, but his request fell on deaf ears. When Lily had something to say, it got said. She would ignore his protests and would talk until she had said everything she had to say. Over fifty years later, it was still the same. When Lily has something to say, Eli had no choice but to listen.

For Lily those early years foreshadowed what lay ahead: many lonely nights spent knowing that even though Eli loved her, he was married first to his career.

Chapter 26

―――――――――― ••• ――――――――――

Weeks after the wedding, Eli and Lily were lying on the bed looking at wedding proofs. Unable to afford many, they were trying to select their favorites when they were interrupted by a knock on the door. Shmuel had come to deliver a disturbing message to his son. Standing in the entranceway, his face ashen, he said, "All army reservists have been called into active duty!" He handed Eli his orders, delivered to his parents' home because the army did not have Eli's new address. Eli was ordered to immediately report for active duty at the central Israel base camp in Tzrifin. It was Sunday, May 21, 1967.

For months there had been violent clashes with Jordanian, Syrian, and Palestinian guerrillas along Israel's border. Eli and Lily had spent hours discussing the horror and the inevitability of this moment. It was all anyone talked about. Surrounded by a hundred million Arabs all calling for the destruction of Israel, the media was predicting a blood bath, daring to even use the horrific term: "Second Holocaust." Every bomb shelter had been stocked with food and medicine and bunkers were dug all across the country.

Israel would learn after the fact that the Soviet Union, in an attempt to further destabilize the region, had fed false information to the Syrian president Nureddin al-Atassi warning that Israel was mobilizing for an attack. Atassi then passed that false information on to President Nasser of Egypt. Nasser activated his army and also ordered the United Nations forces out of the Sinai. Sending his troops into the Sinai, he then announced a blockade of the Strait of Tiran.

Israel, in an attempt to stabilize the region, reached out to King Hussein of Jordan, asking him to restrain from joining the conflict. But Hussein felt compelled to fall in beside the Arab coalition. This decision created a noose around the State of Israel's borders.

As Lily processed this in her mind, she began to weep and reached for Eli's hand. "I don't want you to go!"

"I'll be okay. Please, just pack your things. We will drop you at your mother's. I don't want you to be alone."

• • •

As a scientist, Eli was stationed in the Sinai in a medical unit under the command of Major General Ariel Sharon—the man destined to become the Prime Minister of Israel. Eli's equipment consisted of a portable lab, which was nothing more than a suitcase outfitted with a small incubator and ready Petri dishes with agar containing medium for growing bacteria. It was Eli's job to check for E-coli in the water supply of the rivers, canals and reservoirs they would encounter. Although the Israeli soldiers carried their own water supply, they would need it to be replenished.

Constantly on the move, Sharon's troops arrived at the banks of the Nile River. Scrutinizing the water, Eli immediately went in search of his superior officer, a man he knew to be arrogant and difficult.

"Absolutely no drinking or bathing in this water," Eli announced, knowing that the water would sicken the troops.

"You make such a proclamation five minutes after we arrive? You could not have possibly tested the water!"

"When you see dead cows and dead bodies in the water, there is no need to check for e-coli! You simply do not drink, and you do not bathe. Period!" Eli said, biting back his sarcastic tone. He would later learn that the affiliated medical officer supported his decision.

"I have come up with a solution for our freshwater problems," his commanding officer said.

Eli remained silent as the man showed him a cockamamie gizmo that he assured Eli would clean the water and make it drinkable.

"Test it! You will see that it works."

Having no recourse but to follow orders, Eli tested the device. "Regretfully, this water is still contaminated," he said, when it became obvious it just reduced to a limited degree did nothing to quell the contamination.

"Are you refusing to approve it?"

"Respectfully so," Eli replied.

"I will court martial you if you don't approve my invention."

"I will not take responsibility for infecting soldiers," Eli replied stoically.

In the Israeli army, being a professor, an engineer, doctor or lawyer, being rich or poor meant nothing as to how you were treated. And so, in retaliation for refusing to certify the invention, Sergeant Eli Huberman and the couple of men under his command were assigned menial jobs such as moving military equipment and working in the kitchen cleaning pots.

By the third day of the war, Israeli forces had taken control of much of the West Bank and the Sinai Peninsula all the way to the Suez Canal. Eli and five of his fellow soldiers were deployed to a huge Egyptian reservoir in the Sinai near the front, to test the water for drinkability. Again, there was no need for lab results, as two bloated dead cows were floating in the water. Yet something was very strange. Those cows could not have gotten into the reservoir by themselves. Consequently, that meant someone had intentionally tainted the water supply. Whether the Israelis had done this or the Egyptians had, would be a question never answered. But the result was the same.

Upon leaving the reservoir, Eli and his men found themselves surrounded by Egyptian soldiers. As the highest-ranking soldier, Eli had to make the decision whether to engage in combat or not. Low on ammunition, he ordered his men to hide and not to fire unless their lives were in imminent danger. Feeling more like a spectator than a participant, Eli was not sure if what was transpiring around him was even real. The sound of enemy soldiers firing was deafening. It took only moments for him to realize that the Egyptians were not trying to engage but were in fact running away. When it was over, and the danger passed Eli berated himself: *With a little bit of common sense, I would have been very afraid.*

On the morning of June 5, fourteen days after Eli was deployed, two hundred Israeli Air Force planes took to the air. Flying below radar they headed toward the Egyptian airbases. Jordanian radar detected the IDF planes heading out to sea. But due to coding frequencies being changed the day before by Egypt, the message sent by Jordan warning Egypt of the impending attack was not received. Even without advanced warning, Egypt had enough time, firepower and missiles to shoot down every Israeli airplane entering their air space that morning. Yet, for some unknown reason, they did not issue the order to attack. As a result, on day one of the war, Israel obliterated half of the Egyptian Air Force, two-thirds of the Syrian Air Force, and most of the Royal Jordanian Air Force.

•••

Unbeknownst to Eli, two hundred air miles away the Israeli army had infiltrated the Old City of Jerusalem. Under Jordanian control since 1948, during that nineteen-year period the Jewish people had been denied any access to their holy sites. On June 7, the Israel Defense Forces (IDF) had reached the Western Wall, the retaining wall of the ancient Jewish Temple where Jews had prayed for thousands of years. In that moment of triumph, the Jewish soldiers approached the Wall. Placing their hands, their lips, their cheeks against the cool Jerusalem stone, they reclaimed what had belonged to their people since the time of Solomon. The soldiers wept and prayed as the Israeli flag was raised. Jerusalem would once again be the capital of the Jewish people.

Two days later, on June 9, after intense aerial bombardment, the Israeli infantry and its tanks advanced toward the Golan Heights in Syria, located northeast of Israel. The Syrians had spent eighteen years constructing an intricate network of fortifications, concrete bunkers, trenches, and minefields. At the ready, seventy-five thousand heavily armed and entrenched Syrian soldiers were amassed, waiting to anni-hilate the tiny Israeli army. Despite those odds in what could only be described as a miracle, the IDF, in twenty hours of vicious fighting managed to capture a wide strip of the Golan Heights.

On day six, a ceasefire was brokered, and the war came to an abrupt end. Israel was victorious. Among its many conquests were Judea, Jericho, Gaza and Ramallah. The victory tripled the size of the country. The Six-Day War was over.

•••

The war was over, but the Israeli soldiers remained. Eli was among thirty men who were sent to set up camp in the Sinai desert near the Suez Canal. Their orders: guard the temporary bridge. That meant that their only responsibility was the rotation of guards, making sure that when a soldier left his location overlooking the bridge, another took his place. Eli didn't have a clue why that bridge had to be guarded since no enemy had even tried to cross.

Living in tents, their food delivered by convoy, they were a slovenly looking bunch—the ambiance and attitude more like a day camp than an army camp. They had uniforms but no sizes to choose from. With Eli's small stature, he had to refashion his shirt and pants to keep from drowning in khaki cotton. Their biggest obstacle was the weather. During those long and tedious summer months of June through September it was windy and dry, the sun scorching hot. Temperatures during the day hovered near 100 degrees. Always perspiring, the men looked like drowned rats. It was not unusual to see a soldier, in the middle of the day, drop his shirt into a pail of water and put it back on dripping wet. Yet, at night, it was freezing, the temperatures often dropping to thirty and forty degrees Fahrenheit.

During the six months that Eli was stationed in the desert, he made friends, but friendships in Israel were often strange. The philosophy was as long as we are together, we are friends. Eli would say later in his life that his greatest accomplishment during his stint in the desert was learning to play a great game of bridge.

One afternoon, as if struck by an earthquake, the ground shuddered in reaction to an Israeli convoy of twelve Centurion and Patton tanks advancing toward Eli's G-d forsaken outpost. The roaring noise of six hundred plus tons of mobile steel was deafening as the tanks scared the sand with tracks and kicked up a blinding cloud of dust on their approach. When the tanks stopped only one hatch popped. A soldier emerged, found his footing, and climbed down.

Eli, standing amongst his fellow soldiers was awestruck by the man. It was his brother, Meir, whom he had not seen in months. Now a major of a Tank platoon stationed on the Sinai front, he was a reservist just like Eli.

"I heard you were here, in this cushy day camp," Meir said, striding towards Eli with a mischievous smirk as he eyeballed the unimpressive outpost and his brother's ridiculously too large uniform.

"Looks to me like you're the one having all the fun," Eli laughed, as the brothers hugged.

"Listen, although it is on my way, I'm breaking all protocol by being here, and I only have a couple of minutes."

"Then maybe you can tell me what's going on? Because we are totally in the dark here and any information we get is days old." Eli asked.

"Negotiations are underway with Egypt. We'll be withdrawing from the Sinai in exchange for peace and free navigation through the Straits of Tiran. You'll be going back to your bride soon."

"That's great news!" Eli said.

"Is it? We fight, we win, our soldiers die and then we give it all back?!"

Eli was about to respond when Meir held up his hands, palms facing forward. "I have to go. See you soon and take care of yourself."

"You too," Eli said, his heart bursting with pride at the confidence and strength emanating from his brother as he climbed back into the belly of the tank.

Chapter 27

————— ••• —————

1968

Eli picked at a ragged cuticle as he sat on the sofa in Sachs' office waiting for the professor to put down his pen. Sachs had a reputation for raising his voice and scolding his graduate students. They were all terrified of him. So far, Eli had successfully escaped his wrath until the horrific moment when Sachs unjustly yelled at him.

Eli did not hear the exact words coming out of the professor's mouth but rather his tone. It was completely unjustified. Mortified and with no forethought of the consequences, Eli closed his notebook to signal that the meeting was over. "I have a headache," Eli said. He stood, turned his back on the professor and without another word or a backward glance, walked out of Sachs' office.

During the two bus rides to Bat Yam, Eli could not stop shaking. He had walked out on the famous Professor Sachs, his doctoral Advisor! Entering the apartment, Lily took one look at her husband and cried, "Oh my G-d! What's happened? Are you sick? Come. Sit."

"It's over! I am going to be thrown out of the PhD program," he said, telling his four-month pregnant wife that he had been berated for an inconsequential oversight. He had barely finished telling Lily his story when their newly installed telephone rang.

"Hello," Eli said, expecting to hear the voice of his or Lily's mother.

"How do you feel?" It was Leo Sachs. "I hope your headache is better."

"I am better," Eli replied, disbelieving that the man had actually called, incredulous over Sachs apparent concern. While it appeared to be an innocuous gesture, Eli's actions that day caused a subtle shift in their relationship. The famous Leo Sachs never raised his voice to him again.

...

Months later Eli was summoned to his mentor's office. "I have great news!" Sachs said smiling. "The National Cancer Institute (NCI) in Bethesda, Maryland, will issue us a grant provided that we teach them how to convert normal cells into cancer cells without the use of the Holy Water of Jordan." His smile widened, "I want you to come along!"

Eli was flattered and thrilled for the opportunity to work at the National Cancer Institute, the preeminent cancer research agency in the world. He had read recently that the NCI was given a supplemental appropriation of over twenty million dollars for research, an inconceivable sum that had turned him green with envy. The very idea that a research paper written by him and Sachs in Israel and published in an American journal could actually come to the attention of the NCI seemed unimaginable. Yet here he was, a beneficiary of that funding.

Eli and Sachs had the perfect symbiotic relationship: the professor understood the conversion process in theory, but only Eli knew how to actually set up the experiment and then make it work. Turning noncancerous cells into cancerous cells required the use of environmentally hazardous chemicals, the process a harbinger for change that would allow scientists throughout the world to explore new avenues in cancer research.

Eli's research and eventual success on this project had happened while Professor Leo Sachs was away on sabbatical. Eli often fantasized that he would be recognized for his accomplishments, but he knew it was a foolish pipedream. Eli was nothing more than a lowly graduate student. Sachs would take all the credit. That was the way it worked in the scientific community.

March 1968

It was not easy for him to leave his pregnant wife for three months, but they both knew this was a career opportunity that could not be passed up.

"Take care of yourself and miss me," Lily quipped as she gave him one last kiss.

"I already do," Eli replied, before boarding his TWA flight to New York City. His contagious smile and twinkling eyes shone with anticipation. Surrounded by every member of his and Lily's family, he waved goodbye.

Upon arriving in New York, Eli planned to spend the night with his parents' good friends from Poland. From there he would go on to Bethesda. He looked at the address and directions he had written down: *take a bus to the Port Authority's 33rd street station, then board the subway to the Lower East Side.*

Luggage in hand, he stopped a man outside the JFK terminal. "Where can I get a bus to the Thirty-Third street station?" Eli asked in English heavily accented Hebrew.

"*Da Toity-Toid* street station?" the man asked.

Eli had a good grasp of the English language. He could hold his own in scientific and literary discussions, but his knowledge had huge practical deficiencies. For instance, he had never even learned the English word for fork. So standing in the street, the temperature hovering around forty, his short-sleeve shirt offering little protection, he was totally confused.

"No. I want the Thirty -Third Street station," Eli repeated.

"Right! *Toity-toid.*"

It was one of the weirdest accents he had ever heard. He surmised that the man was Jewish, and he asked his question again in Yiddish. Thankfully he was then given directions he could understand.

Later that evening, sitting at the supper table with Mr. and Mrs. Czerniak, Eli boasted by showing them the letter of invitation he had received from the director of the NCI.

"You mean you are not going to be a *real* doctor, but just one of those?" Mrs. Czerniak asked, disappointment etched on her raisin-like expression.

Her comment found its mark on Eli's psyche, that hidden place where he harbored regret for not becoming a medical doctor. He would come to learn that his sensitivity was accurate because in the United States medical doctors were revered while PhDs were not.

•••

In Bethesda, Eli was assigned to Dr. Joseph DiPaolo, the group leader at the NCI whose specialty was with chemicals that cause cancer. Filled with trepidation and excitement, he entered the Auburn building located just outside the NIH campus. He was immediately disappointed. Rather than being specifically built as a laboratory, it was nothing more than a converted office building. It looked dilapidated, a sharp contrast to the Weizmann where everything was clean and neat and beautiful.

He was shown to the tissue culture lab. To his consternation, it was a tiny room that had air conditioning and some fancy hoods and fancy incubators. But the room looked dirty and disorganized. He quickly learned that DiPaolo group grew their cell cultures in closed flasks rather than in Petri dishes—something Eli thought a huge mistake.

"We use closed flasks because our Petri dishes are often contaminated," DiPaolo said, noting the disapproval on Eli's face.

Examining his surroundings, Eli said, "The air conditioning is blowing too close to the hoods. That unsterile blowing air will surely cause contamination."

He then examined the incubators that required constant humidity. The water bath was located in the lower part of the incubator. He opened it and thought he would be sick. It was full of fungi and bacteria. Eli couldn't believe how poorly the lab technicians had been trained. DiPaolo looked at him in obvious embarrassment. By weeks' end, Eli and the technicians were cleaning and scrubbing the incubator and the room. He also personally redirected the airflow away from the hoods by placing cardboard in the appropriate places. The result was the ability to grow cells in Petri dishes.

Eli was thrilled to see that the rest of the labs had the most up-to-date equipment, but much of it was unused and neglected. And so, he spent the next two weeks having everything cleaned and put into workable condition.

The technicians and scientists in DiPaolo's lab, whom Eli taught the *Transformation Assay,* without the need for the Holy Water of the Jordan, were always dressed in jackets and ties. It was the legacy of the NIH physicians since they used to see patients in between their research studies in the laboratories. Eli hinted that for comfort and ease during lab work they should remove their jackets and ties under their lab coats. At first DiPaolo's staff were resistant and disgruntled that a foreign graduate student in a short-sleeved shirt and sandals had the nerve to come into their lab making too many changes and telling them what to do. Eli knew they thought of him as the barbarian Israeli.

Late one afternoon Eli was demonstrating a complicated technique. He then instructed the team to duplicate what he had just done. Watching the technicians struggling with their jacket sleeves he blurted, "You must be nuts! How can you work with ties and jackets? It's less cumbersome and easier to work with your damn jackets and ties off!!" Within a short time, the jackets came off and then so did the ties. Eli's influence changed the whole culture and before long, short sleeves became the dress code in the DiPaolo group.

•••

On Joe DiPaolo's invitation and urging Eli initially lived with him and his family. Joe had a nice home, a lovely wife and two cute kids. The problem was the house was in a quiet suburb of Bethesda. With no place to explore and with nothing to do in the evenings, Eli began to feel like a prisoner. To make matters worse, Joe was constantly querying him for information on his research; questions Eli did not particularly care to answer as his work was his private domain.

A colleague told him about a room for rent in a house that was within walking distance of work. It was a small two-story home owned by the elderly widow of an American general. The room was on the second floor and Eli did not hesitate for even a moment to move in. Bethesda, named after Jerusalem's Pool of Bethesda, was a sleepy town, where the restaurants he could afford closed by 9 pm. But Eli was happy, free now to be on his own. He could now take buses, go to the movies, eat what he liked.

After being warned to stay out of the city of Washington after dark, on the weekends Eli explored the city and visited the museums on the Mall. His landlady, Mrs. Emerson, was happy for the company and she would sometimes make him dinner. But that dinner included him listening to her badmouth Richard Nixon, a man Eli knew very little about. She had a mantra: Nixon is a crook! I'm telling you Nixon is a no-good crook!!!

He wrote to Lily almost every day. Occasionally they even spoke on the phone even though it was expensive. In school and enduring a growing belly, Lily was never alone. Her girlfriends and mother took turns sleeping over each night. Still Eli was lonely and missed her, wishing that she could be with him to share every new adventure.

Eli befriended two women scientists who worked together and were pioneers in cell culture techniques. Interested in the work he was doing and impressed with his knowledge, Dr. Katherine Sanford and Dr. Virginia Evens invited him to their lab in another building on the campus of NIH. It was like entering a different world. Their lab was made of stainless steel and it was meticulously clean. But then, that should not have been a surprise. In her late fifties, Katherine Sanford was famous. Shortly after arriving at the tissue culture section of the NCI Laboratory of Biology, she made an amazing discovery that made her name a household word in the scientific community. Katherine Sanford cloned mammalian cancer cells in vitro, outside of a living organism.

•••

Leo Sachs invited Eli to join him for dinner one evening at the expensive Bish Thompson's seafood restaurant on Wisconsin Avenue in Bethesda. He invited Eli to show his appreciation for teaching DiPaolo's staff how to transform normal cells into malignant cells by the use of chemical carcinogens. Eli knew that Sachs' wife was Orthodox and that their home was kosher. He also knew that Sacks ate *treif,* non-kosher when not with his wife. Filling the belly of a 6' 7" man meant ordering massive amounts of food, especially because Leo liked to eat. There was lobster, shrimp, crab cakes, escargot and all kinds of sides. Suddenly he said, "Eliezer, I don't feel so good. You stay. I will pay on the way out!"

Eli ate as much as he could eat, but still there was seventy percent left on the table. The waiter approached. "Would you like to take the food home in doggie bags?"

Eli looked around to make sure that no one had heard the waiter's despicable offer. *He thinks I am so poor and miserable that I need to take food home?* He felt insulted, humiliated and sorry for himself. Who even went to restaurants in Israel? But if so, no one *ever* took food home. Only later did he learn how stupid he was. This American custom would have given him food for two or three days, if not more. It was a lesson well learned.

By the time Eli left NCI, his reputation as a researcher and instructor had flourished. DiPaolo's staff was now able to perform the transformations assay using American river distilled water, proving that there was no need to use the holy distilled water of the Jordan River for the experiment to work. Leaving behind admirers, friends and a legacy, no one doubted that they would see and hear about this young and talented Israeli in the years to come.

Chapter 28

Eli returned to Israel when Lily was in her eighth month of pregnancy. Loaded down with purchases from the long list Lily had given him, his stipend was almost completely depleted. Sitting against the headboard on their bed Lily went through every item, cooing and awing, especially at the non-maternity clothing that she would hopefully be wearing one day soon. Ripping the tissue paper from a rather large package, she was shocked to see a stack of baby clothes.

"What's this?" She lifted an adorable sleeper in the neutral color yellow. "This is not for a newborn." She picked up another and said, "Eli, these look used!"

"Joseph DiPaolo gave them to me. They belonged to one of his children."

"Who gives a gift of used clothing?" Lily asked stupefied.

"I couldn't refuse," Eli said, scrunching his shoulders. "This is another one of those crazy American customs, like taking left-over food home from restaurants."

Lily wrinkled her nose as she shifted to find a more comfortable position. It was not an easy feat with her enormous belly.

"I didn't even tell you about another crazy custom. Like the time DiPaolo invited me to a birthday party for one of the guys in the lab. He told me to bring a drink and I did. I brought what I like—prune juice. I was the laughingstock! Who knew he meant alcohol?" Reliving the moment Eli's cheeks turned red.

Lily put a hand over her mouth to keep from laughing, not wanting to further hurt Eli's wounded pride. It was a wasted effort and once she began to giggle, she could not stop. Insulted for a moment, Eli was soon laughing with her.

Later that evening, when the family came to visit and Lily told her mother and mother-in-law about the baby clothes. They were both aghast and had the same comments: *it's bad manners, criminal and insulting*. But still, Lily saved the clothing in a box on a shelf.

...

On July 24, 1968 Lily gave birth to a beautiful baby boy they named Ilan Huberman. A nurse came to the house, the custom in Israel, to teach Lily how to care for her newborn son and how to nurse. Still reeling from a forty-eight-hour labor and trembling with anxiety, Lily was reticent to hold Ilan for fear of harming him.

Worried and anxious himself, Eli turned to Lily's aunt the pediatrician. She came to the house and after speaking with her niece told Eli that he would need to care for the baby until Lily regained her strength and confidence back. She then told the nurse to talk only to Eli until further notice. Thankfully, with her mother's help, it was only a matter of days before Lily was able to take over Ilan's care.

As the first grandchild born since the Holocaust, at the *brit milah*, the ritual circumcision eight days later, Ilan was greeted as if he were the messiah. Surrounded by family and friends, Eli's grandmother, Rachel, stood guard over her great-grandson, refusing to let anyone touch the baby for fear he might get germs.

Meir managed to get leave from the army for the circumcision. His presence was a wonderful surprise and Eli was thrilled to have him there. It also served as a sad reminder that they now had so little in common. Marriage and the six-year age difference were partly responsible. But the overriding reason was how they were spending their lives. Eli worked in a protected intellectual cocoon while Meir spent his days learning how not to get killed.

During the time Eli was in Bethesda, Meir and Lily had become good friends. Meir was a student at a senior army officer's training program and Lily was studying at Tel Aviv University in Ramat Aviv. Meir had a car and Lily did not, and so he would pick her and drop her off on his way to class. Their conversations during that forty-minute drive became the highlight of her day.

But many of Meir's views frightened Lily. He saw the future in terms of survival: the need to stay ever vigilant, to trust no one, to believe no one. Lily understood that people like Meir were indispensable if Israel was to survive. And knowing that her brother-in-law was tough and would never turn aside from fear made her feel protected and proud. Yet there was another side to this complicated man. He loved books and many of their conversations included critiques of what they were reading. His insight, intellect and self-taught knowledge fascinated her. He was also a gifted artist with a passion for copying the works of the great masters. They talked endlessly about the artists they admired and the museums they hoped to visit one day. They were both crazy about music and Lily was delighted to have someone to discuss the intricacies of the piano pieces she was learning.

Women found Meir irresistible, drawn to his self-confidence, bravado and mischievous smile—he never missed a chance to take full advantage. Yet beneath that welcoming facade a very different Meir Dagan lurked. Danger emanated reflecting a young man who had come to the realization that he was willing and capable to do *whatever* was necessary to protect his country and its inhabitants.

• • •

As newlyweds Lily and Eli had spent Friday night Shabbat with Eli's parents. Now that there was a grandson, to Lily's consternation they expected the ritual to continue.

"I'm done! I don't want to go!" Lily hissed, stamping her foot. "Call and tell them I am too tired." She wanted to go out with Eli on Friday nights, and she had no intention of having anyone in the family organizing her life or her schedule.

"Lily, they just want to see the baby. We have to go," Eli pleaded, even though he didn't really want to go either. Unlike Lily's mother who was a terrible cook, his mother was actually a decent cook. The problem was that the menu was always the same and it began with the gefilte fish she made from scratch. An appetizer neither Eli nor Lily liked. Yet, if you asked him today, Eli would tell you he still dreams about his mother's wonderful cooking.

Tired of having the same argument every week, Eli finally told his parents that it was too difficult with a new child and that they would only be able to come occasionally.

Lily was unhappy that Eli was spending so much time in his lab. Lonely and tired, she returned to her old routine of calling him daily. Horrified that—G-d forbid—Sachs would see him on the phone and embarrassed to be kibitzing in front of his colleagues, Eli would do what he had always done in the past: insist he had to go. The difference now was that Lily would get angry. Thankfully there was a neighbor who had a baby the same age as Ilan, and the women became friends. That friendship resulted in arrangements being made to babysit for each other one night every weekend. That enabled Eli and Lily to have grown-up time where they could attend the symphony, the theater or a movie.

Arriving back at midnight or later, they raided the refrigerator. Lily's mothers always dropped by to fill the refrigerator with goodies: herring, sausage, cheese, onions and hard-boiled eggs. Being totally decadent, they giggled their way through everything in sight. It was what kept them together, what reminded them of their love and the connection they had then and would always have.

When their son turned six months, having outgrown all his clothes, those used outfits Eli brought back from America were taken out of the box and washed. No longer perceived as an insult, they were now seen as a money-saving and brilliant idea.

Chapter 29

T hanks to Eli, Sachs returned to the Weizmann with a grant from the National Cancer Institute, funds earmarked for Eli's research. In the ensuing year he would publish four more scientific papers, a huge and unique accomplishment for a PhD student.

One of those papers was published in collaboration with Marian Fogel, a tenured associate professor from Poland. He recruited Eli to collaborate with him on *polyomavirus*, a virus present in some animals and humans, which in mice causes tumors in different organs. When their findings were submitted for publication, Marian intentionally omitted Leo Sachs's name from the list of authors. Sachs was furious, maintaining that any projects Eli was involved with fell under his tutelage. He insisted his name appear. Professor Fogel was secure in his position at the Weitzman and not a man to be bullied. He overruled Sachs and it became a huge and embarrassing scandal that secretly gave Eli great pleasure, as one rarely, if ever, got the *best* of the great Leo Sachs.

As renowned as Sachs was, there was another scientist just as eminent, an American Jew named Charles Heidelberger. Heidelberger, among other important achievements, had developed and patented an anticancer drug in 1957 known as 5-Fluorouracil. The drug was used to treat cancers of the stomach, colon and breast and in 2020, 5-Fluorouracil was still one of the treatments widely utilized. Fueled by jealousy and their competitive natures, the two men were enemies. And then to Sachs' great disdain, Heidelberger was invited to visit the Weitzman.

As unlikely as it seemed, meeting face to face in Sachs's office the two great scientists forged a friendship. That new relationship included a peace offering from Sachs to Heidelberger. He offered as a gift his most promising and brilliant student, Eli Huberman. When Eli was told that he had been selected for a two-year postdoctoral appointment with Charles Heidelberger at the University of Wisconsin in Madison he was overjoyed. Lily agreed it was an opportunity not to be missed and the decision to go was made.

The Huberman family left Israel and traveled via Paris and Montreal, arriving in Madison, Wisconsin, at the end of September 1969. They had been warned about the frigid winter weather but hearing about it and then experiencing it was very different. On the day they arrived, the high was 60 degrees Fahrenheit and by night it had dropped to 37. Add the bone chilling wind to the equation and the result was misery. Lily was in a state of shock trying to comprehend a life with a one-year-old child, no friends, and having to find a place to live in a city she knew nothing about. Conversely, Eli was too ecstatic at the prospect of working with Heidelberger to care about something as mundane as the weather.

At a party to honor Lily and Eli's arrival, Lily met an Israeli couple that she immediately befriended. The husband, Ilan Chet, would go on to become one of the presidents of the Weitzman Institutes. Determined to help with the transition so that Eli would be able to give his complete attention to their work, Charlie Heidelberger showed them various places to live. Lily went to look but her mind was closed. She intended to live near her new friends and on her own, she found a two-bedroom apartment near the Israelis. Located on Badger Road, it was close to the highway on the west side of town. Never mind that it was all carpeted, including the kitchen: not a great idea with a small child.

"You know this is not really a good neighborhood. It is a bit run down and there is no lawn for the boy to play," Charlie offered trying to dissuade her. It was good advice but at age twenty-three, Lily wanted what she wanted and would not listen. As for Eli, he knew that once Lily made up her mind, conversation was futile. They signed the lease and two weeks later they got furniture from the Salvation Army. Among their acquisitions was a three-legged couch that Eli jerry rigged using three bricks as a fourth leg. Lily, the creative creature that she was raided Kmart. When she was done, their drab little apartment was drab no more. As for the kitchen carpet, Lily would say that the spilled milk juice and smooshed baby food gave the carpet character.

•••

Eli's life was now all about his work, and he had never been happier. Being selected to do his postdoctoral training in Madison at the University of Wisconsin McArdle Laboratory for Cancer Research made him feel honored beyond his wildest imaginings. The McArdle was a world-renowned center for basic cancer research, with its senior staff being the leaders in diverse modern biological disciplines. And the fact that he had not even had to apply for the position made it even more special, as there were specific standards set by all scientific institutions throughout the world before offers were made.

The process of applying for a coveted postdoctoral appointment in a top research laboratory began six to twelve months before a candidate had completed their thesis. In order to even be considered the applicant had to have a postdoctoral period highlighted by publications and excellent recommendations from their mentor. The requirements for a fellowship were succinct: as scientific investigators, they could only do their training in a laboratory different from the one where they had done research for their thesis.

When accepted, support for living expenses and occasional travel was supplied by grants called fellowships. Eli had been offered grants from several international organizations and decided to accept the most prestigious from the International Agency for Research on Cancer, an arm of the World Health Organization.

Eli had completed all dissertation requirements needed for his PhD before leaving Israel. But it would not be official as the Weizmann Institute of Science granted their doctorate degrees only once a year. Eli would not receive official notice until January 1970 when his diploma arrived by mail. Enclosed were two versions, each written on thick parchment paper. One was in Hebrew and the other in English: both signed by Albert Sabin, President of the Weizmann. Sabin was the internationally acclaimed scientist who had developed an effective live polio vaccine that later replaced the one developed by Jonas Salk. It was a huge moment in Eli's life, as he could now be officially known by the honorific title, Doctor Eliezer Huberman, PhD.

Eli's postdoc salary was $7,800 a year, plus transportation from Israel to Wisconsin and back for him and his family, paid for by the World Health Organization. After his first year, when Charlie Heidelberg asked, "How much money would you like?" Eli replied, "What do you mean? I have a fellowship, continue the fellowship." Eli's response was predictable, as he had not a clue that he could negotiate his salary. In Israel it just was not done. "Fine," Charlie said, and not saying another word, left it like that. Eli would discover years later that a postdoc, whom he was mentoring in the technique of cell transformation and mutagenesis was getting twice his salary. Yet, another hard-learned lesson.

•••

From 1969 through 1971, Eli served as a postdoctoral fellow with Charlie. His studies focused on identifying the cancer-causing products generated by our cells from exposure to polycyclic aromatic hydrocarbons (PAH). These hydrocarbons are the byproducts generated during the incomplete burning of wood, coal, petroleum and natural gas. Cancer causing PAH are also generated in small amounts during the grilling of foods such as meats, fish and vegetables.

Identifying PAH products involved in causing cancers entailed hard work. It required discerning them from a myriad of other cellular products generated by our cells from PAH. Seeing the effect these PAH products had on cells was one of the highlights of cancer research at that time. It was important because among other elements it showed a relationship between mutagenesis and cancer causation. In textbooks today, that research is accepted as the way PAH induces cancer.

Working with Charlie was a great privilege for Eli. Not just because the man was an outstanding scientist, but because he was a *mensch* who valued and showed appreciation for the work of others. When they would go to scientific meetings Charlie would get up and say, "Wait, don't go yet. Dr. Huberman has something very important to say, and I know you will want to listen to his talk." Once, he even wrote in a cancer research review: "I am fortunate to have Toshio Kuroki from Japan and Eli Huberman from Israel in my lab. And I am proud of their achievements and proud to announce that I have promoted them both." Eli was overwhelmed when he first read those words of praise, knowing that Leo Sachs would never have said something like that.

Working under Charlie, Eli and his colleagues published twelve papers on cancer research, which was very unusual, as normally post-docs published one or two papers. To have a paper published entailed a substantial amount of technical work. The scientific data had to be arranged into tables, graphs, charts, diagrams and illustrations. They were all sketched by hand and occasionally included photographs. Each required a written explanation, called figure legends. Unlike today, there were no computers. To cut and paste meant to actually cut and paste, and only when this process was finished did the work get sent out to be professionally drawn.

The scientific papers had to be organized into specific sections: a Summary, Introduction, Material and Methods, Results, Discussion and References. The latter involved a list of publications quoted in the paper. Intellectually for Eli, the hardest part was the discussion section. Having to describe the real meaning of the presented data in the context of associated studies in the scientific field while writing in English was a challenge. Then it was his job to tell what made this study and its findings unique and to explain the data and come up with groundbreaking conclusions. When all of that was completed, the team would come up with a relevant title and agree on the order of the authors. The first author was usually the graduate student, postdoctoral fellow or junior scientist who was the main contributor to the study, while the last author was the mentor or group leader. At the end of the paper, there were the acknowledgments, which indicated who funded the study along with thanking the individuals who had contributed unique materials or helpful comments.

Once these sections were compiled, the paper was typed by a secretary and given for review to the mentor; in Eli's case that was Charlie Heidelberger. Charlie always had comments and criticism and without computers, those changes required painstaking cutting and pasting. The hard part was that Eli knew there would always be corrections, and at times he wondered if he would ever get it right. But in the end, he learned how to write a paper in a clear and logical way.

Sadly, Charles Heidelberg eventually fell victim to the nonprecautionary experimentations he had worked on as a young PhD fellow with a famous organic chemist. Having no idea they were endangering their health, they would actually taste and smell the chemicals they were using in their experiments. Sadly, the results of their actions were devastating. Charlie's discovery of 5-Fluorouracil would go on to save untold lives, but Charlie would not be saved. He died from cancer at the age of sixty-one.

Chapter 30

———— ••• ————

Lily was determined to find a job. With her degree in linguistics and English Literature, she interviewed as a teaching assistant at the University of Wisconsin. At the interview, Professor Menachem Mansoor, the head of the Hebrew and Semitic studies program was so impressed with Lily's resume and her engaging personality that he hired her on the spot. Little did she know that many of the scientists' wives had applied for this same position and were still waiting to hear. The result, Lily, the new girl in town immediately became *persona non grata*.

She did not care. For her it was a dream-come-true. She would not only get paid but she could go to school at the in-state tuition rate and that would enable her to get a master's degree. She and Eli bought an old clunker of a car for transportation and then she took driving lessons. Finding reliable babysitters became an on-going problem but somehow it always seemed to work out. Perhaps it was because being young and idealistic, Lily never doubted she would find a solution, truly believing there was nothing she could not do.

She began her master's degree program in Russian music and worked as a teacher's assistant and taught a class to priests at the university who wanted to learn to read Hebrew. Only days into the curriculum, the priests asked that she teach them the Hebrew Bible.

Lily freaked out. She could not say no but she had no background, barely passing Bible Studies in high school. She turned to Eli. The night before her class Eli would teach Lily from the text, enjoying every moment and smirking through it all. The next day she would teach the priests. Weaving her words into captivating portrayals within the context of the Bible, her sense of humor and charming demeanor captivated her class. Finding her confidence, Lily eventually turned back to a mantra that worked for her: *If you don't know what you don't know you make it up.*

Eli had learned first-hand about Lily's mantra. When he was a student in Israel, he needed to read scientific literature for his research, but his English was poor. He would ask Lily for the translation. When it became obvious that her translations made no sense, Eli became suspicious. So, he asked her for the translations of a few words that he knew. It was then that he discovered her sneaky little secret: if she didn't know, she would make up the answer. That was the end of him asking his wife for help with his work.

During their second year in Wisconsin their lives shifted and settled down. Because Lily was attending graduate school they were offered and accepted university housing. Gathering their meager belongings and their second-hand furniture, they moved to much nicer accommodations. And best of all, the husband of the couple who lived upstairs was a PhD student. Needing extra income, the wife, a mother of three boys, became Ilan's babysitter. From the very first day, Ilan and the boys became inseparable. Thought of as the youngest brother, he now had friends to play with who protected Ilan when a belligerent boy in the neighborhood accosted him. It was a great gift for Lily as she no longer had to worry about her son.

Lily collected friendships, friendships she would cultivate for the rest of her life. And to be one of Lily's chosen friends was to be invited into her world of glamour, laughter, music and stimulating conversation. She loved parties and once a month she and Heide Pleskin, the girlfriend of Hans Marquardt, a postdoc in Charlie's lab, would organize an eclectic dinner party for a number of postdocs.

The cooking menu was to reflect the country of origin of the postdoc. Toshio Kuroki prepared a Japanese diner, Heidi made German food, Sukdeb Mondal prepared an Indian dinner and Carol Selkirk prepared an American dish. When it was Lily's turn, she obviously was supposed to cook Israeli food. Cooking not being a priority, Lily decided to prepare something foolproof. Called *cholent*, the dish consisted of potatoes, fatty brisket, onions, beans, barley, brown sugar, prunes and hard-boiled eggs. It simmered all night. The postdocs liked to eat and they loved it. It was so good that whenever it was Lily's turn, they all insisted she make it again.

•••

It was a difficult time on college campuses across America. Protests against the Vietnam War raged. It was particularly apparent at the University of Wisconsin where every Monday and Tuesday there were huge demonstrations. Having grown up in a land where every breath revolved around patriotism and survival, Eli had a judgmental and cynical view of those student protests. "Have you noticed?" he asked Lily over dinner one night. "They come to protest as long as it doesn't rain. I guess when there is rain, there are no revolutions."

But people got killed at the University of Wisconsin in the late summer of 1970. After a call to the University police warning of a bomb, four men drove a van filled with barrels of ammonium nitrate and fuel, along with sticks of dynamite to Sterling Hall. Sterling Hall housed three floors of the Army Mathematics Research Center. The center was funded by a contract with the U.S. Army and the students believed the center was responsible for the mathematics behind the sophisticated computer warfare being used in Vietnam.

For years the students had demanded the research be moved off campus, but their demands were ignored. The ultimate result, at 3:45

a.m. a bomb exploded in Sterling Hall. Floors of the building were obliterated, and the explosion could be heard for miles. Five people were injured, and a thirty-three-year-old postdoc researcher was killed. The astronomy and physics departments were also badly damaged, destroying the research of many of the physicists on campus.

When Lily agreed to come to America she never once considered that her husband would ever be in danger. Now she was living in fear once again and had trouble sleeping. Eli did not know what to do. When he told Charlie Heidelberger what was going on, his mentor suggested Eli take his family on an extended vacation.

· · ·

In October of 1970, they headed toward Yellowstone National Park, twelve hundred miles away. Eli had purchased their old car from a salesman who told him it had been owned by a little old lady. When Eli had asked why it was rusted on one side, the salesman said, "Because she kept it on one side of her house." Before the trip Eli decided to bring the car to a garage to have it checked out. The mechanic looked at the numbers on the odometer in astonishment. "Do you know if the odometer has gone one cycle or two?"

Resolute that nothing was going to deter his plans, he had the oil changed, the wheels rotated, and the brakes checked. Then they loaded the car with Ilan in the back and took off for a three-week vacation.

Eli took hundreds of slides. When they were developed, Lily had one of her dinner parties. Eli showed the waterfalls, the rivers, the flowers and the green—a feast for their eyes, having lived in Israel where planting trees and turning the country green was a national passion. For Lily and Eli, Yellowstone had been a magical place that it reminded them of home.

A young postdoc from Pakistan had taken that same trip and brought his own slides. The pictures were naked mountainsides, dry barren land and rock formations, with not one photo of anything green. He said he had taken those photographs because it reminded him of the region in Pakistan that was his home.

Chapter 31

— ••• —

In 1971, Eli's two-year postdoctoral fellowship with the Department of Oncology at the University of Wisconsin was at an end. Under normal circumstances, the Huberman family would have headed directly back to Israel, where Eli would have begun his appointment as a scientist for the Weizmann Institute.

But back in 1968, while on a three-month engagement at the National Cancer Institute in Bethesda, Maryland, Eli made a commitment to his then host Joseph DiPaolo. Eli had promised to return to the NCI at some point during his postdoctoral fellowship to present studies in chemical carcinogenesis. Eli never would have made that promise if he had known that a year later, he would be leaving Israel yet again to do his postdoctoral training back in the States, under Charles Heidelberg.

DiPaolo knew well the value of Eli's knowledge and expertise and he was relentless, calling every couple of months, trying to secure a one-year commitment from Eli. In the end, Eli agreed to six months.

Lily was proud that her husband was being sought after and she readily agreed to remain in the States. Taking charge, she was in the middle of making all the complicated decisions and arrangements to move to Bethesda when an unexpected but joyous situation occurred. They discovered that Lily was two months pregnant. Because they both wanted their child to be born in Israel, Eli promised they would return home in time.

•••

No one in Bethesda would rent for half a year to a family that consisted of a pregnant woman and a three-year-old child. Eli managed to find a short-term rental apartment in Gaithersburg, Maryland. Only twenty-two miles from Washington, D.C., Gaithersburg was a rural farm town with only one movie theater and zero culture. For Lily, it might as well have been the end of the world. Eli felt bad but they had no other choice. So, he deposited his wife and son in their temporary housing and went off to work.

In addition to feeling sick and suffering with her pregnancy, Lily was bored and miserable. Cleaning the house, cooking and running after Ilan was simply not enough stimulation for her. Not after the life she had lived in Madison, managing to receive a master's degree in Music from the University of Wisconsin while working and caring for a toddler. She needed to be distracted and she needed a challenge, and neither was available in Gaithersburg. In the afternoons, trying to fill her day, Lily took walks with Ilan to the store for ice cream. More than once, while walking on the side of the road in places where there were no sidewalks, police officers would stop their cars to make sure she was not in distress.

Needing an obstetrician to follow her pregnancy, DiPaolo arranged for Lily to see a Jewish doctor considered one of the best in Washington. The doctor assured Lily that she was doing great and that the morning sickness would soon pass. In taking the history of her previous pregnancy, the doctor asked about the delivery.

"In Israel, when my son Ilan was born, I was not given so much as an aspirin! The pain was indescribable! I thought I would die!" she said, her hands trembling as she recounted the horrific memories, fighting back the tears.

"You know, it doesn't have to be that way," the doctor said, his voice gentle. "If you choose to remain my patient and have me deliver your baby, I can administer an epidural and you will deliver with no pain."

Lily shook her head. "No. I can't," she whispered. "I want my child born in Israel."

"I understand. Just know that if you change your mind, I am here for you."

•••

Eli was rarely home and while Lily did her best not to constantly complain about how miserable and lonely she was, in the end she just could not take another day. When she approached her sixth month of pregnancy, they decided that Lily should take Ilan and go back to Israel. With no other choice but to complete his fellowship, Eli stayed behind promising to be back in Israel before the birth.

It was a stressful two months for Eli. DiPaolo was back to his old tricks, pumping Eli for information and ideas and basically driving him crazy. Added to that, Eli was homesick for his family. Counting every day, it seemed that the end of his commitment would never come.

•••

One day, Eli opened an airmail package from Israel. It was from Lily and inside he found glass microscope slides encased in plastic sleeves. In the note, Lily explained that the slides were from Chana Shapira, Lily's friend from high school and that Chava's mother-in-law would be telephoning him. The call came at 6 a.m. the next morning.

After introducing herself, Chava's mother-in-law, a surgical nurse, said, "I am so sorry to impose, Dr. Huberman. But Lily thought you might be able to help me. My daughter-in-law has been diagnosed with cancer, lymphoma." After a moment of total silence, she continued. "I don't know what to do. They want to treat her with a mustard gas derivative which I understand is very toxic and terrible!"

"I am so sorry. I am not a clinician. I am doing basic research," Eli said, his stomach in knots, knowing the appalling side effects of the treatment being prescribed. "But I do know an eminent Jewish pathologist considered a cancer expert. I will ask him to take a look at your slides and I will get back to you."

Arriving at the lab with the slides in hand, Eli went to an upper floor in the building in search of Dr. Alan Rabson.

"Can you do me a favor? I am in an awkward situation. I don't know anything about pathology. Maybe you can help me and take a look at these?" he asked, handing his friend the slides as he went on to explain the phone call he had received.

"Don't worry. I'll take over and let you know."

And take over he did. He called another NCI pathologist whom he considered an expert and then he took the slides to yet another specialist in Building Ten, where the main clinical research was done. The very next day Allan called. "I have great news. Your friend does not have cancer! She has a unique and extremely rare case of mononucleosis."

"So, they goofed in Israel?" Eli asked, simultaneously shocked and happy.

"My colleagues believe every pathologist in this country and in Israel would have concurred with the diagnosis of lymphoma. Thank G-d I was able to show the slides to one of the top researchers in the world."

"Thank you so much," Eli said, gripping the telephone receiver so tightly his hand shook.

"I am happy I had the chance to help."

Eli immediately placed a call to Chava's mother-in-law even though it was the middle of the night in Israel. "Don't let them treat her! She does not have cancer!" he blurted before even saying hello.

In between laughing and crying, still groggy from sleep, Chava's mother-in-law said, "Thank you, thank you, thank you! And thank G-d they haven't started because they said that once she began the treatments, she would never be able to have children."

For Eli, saving that young woman's life was one of the most momentous events in his life. Sending those slides to Eli was *beshert*, meant to be. Because it was Lily who had introduced Chava to the young man she had married. And because a young Israeli researcher living in Bethesda, Maryland, took the time and effort to help, Chava Shapiro survived and became a mother.

Chapter 32

———— ••• ————

Egypt 1968, Three Years Earlier

Having reenlisted after the Six-Day War, Meir Huberman Dagan was once again serving with General Ariel Sharon, Head of the Southern Command. Meir was stationed at El Arish, in the Sinai. In the midst of all the danger, at the mess hall one day, Meir met an army nurse, a lieutenant named Bina. She and her fellow nurses did not live on the base but at the El Arish police station, not far from the military camp. They began to date. Meir was not the ideal man to have for a boyfriend. He had a roving eye and more often than not he was off on some secret assignation. But over the following year, when he was in the area, they became a couple.

In the summer of 1969, Egypt, Jordan and the PLO launched attacks against Israel in a conflict that would be known as the War of Attrition. Their enemies' goal was to extricate the Israeli forces from the Sinai Peninsula. Israel's response and objective was to protect the Egyptian border and the Suez Canal.

While on patrol in the northern Sinai, Meir's battalion was forced to halt when they came face to face with an impossible situation. Egypt had placed Katyusha rockets with timed fuses in the center of a minefield. The rockets were aimed toward an Israeli Defense Force base and it was imperative that they be diffused. Of the hundreds of soldiers, none volunteered to enter the minefield. Only a young soldier named Meir Dagan strode ahead, eyes never leaving the ground as he moved into the field. Moving inches at a time, each footstep harboring the possibility of being blown-up, Meir made his way to the rockets. In an act impossible to comprehend, he managed to diffuse all the Katyusha rockets. General Sharon would never forget that moment and he would never forget Meir Dagan.

• • •

Sixty-five miles to the north the Gaza Strip was another region of unrest and conflict. Bordered by the Mediterranean Sea to the west, Egypt to the south and Israel to the north and east, the Gaza Strip was one of the most densely populated territories in the world. It had been captured by Israel in the Six-Day War in 1967. The Hebrew Bible cited Gaza as belonging to the Israelite nation since the reign of King David in the 11th century BCE. With that as their proof, the Jews believed that they had reclaimed land that was rightfully theirs and began construction of housing settlements.

The Gaza was already a hotbed for terrorist Palestinian Liberation Army (PLO) activities, and Jewish construction in the region served to further inflame the Palestinians. In 1970 alone, there were five-hundred terrorist attacks against Israeli civilians living in the area undermining the security and wellbeing of Israel. Something had to be done.

General Ariel Sharon took the lead, deciding to create a new unit to be known unofficially as *Sayeret Rimon*—the Grenade Rangers. Their emblem was a grenade, paratrooper wings and a knife. In contemplating who would lead this highly secretive undertaking, Sharon turned to that young recon officer named Meir Dagan. And even though Dagan was only in his mid-twenties, Sharon was certain he was the right man to lead this elite group.

• • •

Meir Dagan established his base of operations just south of Gaza City, in an abandoned villa once occupied by President Nasser of Egypt. The Grenade Rangers were a special-ops unit consisting of only one hundred and fifty men. Each soldier was handpicked by Meir and notified of the requirements: a willingness to follow orders and the willingness to hunt, pursue and eliminate the enemy.

With his beloved Doberman named Paco by his side, Meir would begin each morning shirtless and armed. He would charge into the yard shooting at the soda cans the soldiers had left strewn across the lawn. Establishing himself as a fearless rule breaker, Meir ran a freewheeling unit where his ultimate goal was to implement and carry out as many decisive operations as conceivably possible. General Sharon's directive to all his secret forces was concise as well: kill terrorists before they strike.

It took half a year before Meir felt his team was ready to engage the enemy. Before that deployment, he was presented with a list from Shin Bet, Israel's security agency, naming known terrorists involved in attacks originating from Gaza. It included four hundred names; some were minor operatives, but others were identified as immediate targets for elimination.

In January 1971, Meir led a patrol from the Jabalia refugee camp to Gaza City. As a taxi passed by Meir recognized two terrorists. He cut off the taxi, slammed on the brakes and jumped from the car. One of the terrorists pulled out a grenade. Screaming for his troops to run, he attacked the terrorist and disabled him, preventing him from pulling the pin and exploding the grenade. He would later be awarded the Medal of Courage for his actions, the highest honor awarded for bravery in the State of Israel. Working in conjunction with Shin Bet and the IDF, by 1972, only ten names now remained on that original elimination list.

•••

Meir never talked about his work—never. Books would later be written about Meir Dagan's feats. They would describe in detail the team he had led and what those men were trained to do. How they attacked from treetops and assassinated Palestinians in brothels. How his teams collaborated with Palestinians who sold booby-trapped grenades, shortening the ignition time on the fuses to half a second. Books described how Meir's men were taught 'dead-checking' after an attack, which meant another two bullets in the head to be sure the fallen terrorist was dead. Meir was never one to be left behind. Because of his dark skin and perfect Arabic, he often entered undetected into Palestinian enclaves. And as incongruous as it seemed to Meir's men and his family, Meir Dagan was against war. He did not believe it was the solution and he would often tell his men; *you always know how to start a war, but you don't always know how to finish.*

It would be years later after reading books and articles written about his brother that Eli would learn the hard truth about Meir's career.

•••

That career almost came to a halt only months after the unit's creation, when the jeep Meir was riding in hit a landmine. With all the tomes of words written about Meir Dagan and his life, this event was portrayed as merely a footnote, when in reality, it impacted the rest of his life.

Eli was alone, working at the NIH in Bethesda when he received a letter from his parents that Meir was in the hospital. He had been there for weeks, but the family had decided there was no point in telling their eldest son until they could report that Meir would recover.

Eli was beside himself with worry. Lily's letters from Israel and her constant reassurances that Meir would be okay was all that kept him from going crazy. Sadly, no matter how badly he wanted to be near his brother, the price of an airline ticket was beyond his means.

Meir remained hospitalized for six months. As a consequence of his injuries, he almost lost his feet. The nerves in one foot were irreparably damaged, and for the rest of his life, he had no feeling in that foot. Nerve damage also caused a loss of sensation in parts of his legs, resulting in frequent bruising and bleeding. He developed a limp, and from time to time, he was forced to use a cane, but the severity of his injuries did not deter the heroic warrior.

During Meir's stay in the hospital and later during his rehabilitation he was cared for by Bina, the nurse he had met in the military mess hall while stationed at El Arish. She was madly in love with Meir, and even while he was suffering excruciating pain, the debonair Meir continued to charm her. On the day he was preparing himself to return to his unit, albeit with one of his legs still in a cast, his father, Shmuel stopped by.

"Day and night Bina devoted half a year of her life to you and now you are just going to leave? You owe her your life. If you don't marry Bina you are a cruel man!" Shmuel said, incredulous and disappointed in his son's decision to leave Bina and return to the Army, despite his own cultural misgivings about the match.

The Huberman's were Ashkenazi Jews of German origin who eventually migrated to Eastern Europe. Bina was a Sephardic (Spanish) Jew. Born in Israel, her Sephardim origins were from Spain and Portugal. When the Jews were expelled from those countries in the fifteenth century, the Jews then resettled in the more tolerant countries of Morocco, Tunis, Algiers, Turkey and Greece. The cultural differences were varied and marked. The Sephardim named their children after living relatives, a tradition strictly forbidden by Ashkenazi Jews. They also pronounced some of the Hebrew vowels differently, and their prayer liturgy and tunes for chanting were different. For Passover, the Sephardim ate rice and legumes, while the Ashkenazi Jews would never consider such a thing. Perhaps worst of all, the Sephardim neither spoke nor understood Yiddish. Instead, they spoke Ladino, a combination of Hebrew and Spanish. Yet, regardless of all of that, Shmuel believed she had earned the right to become Meir's wife and join the family. Unbeknownst to Shmuel, Meir had already proposed to Bina.

They were married in 1972. Eli had finished his six-month tenure as a visiting scientist at the National Institute of Health and was able to attend the lavish wedding. Among the attendees were General Sharon and many other senior army officers.

In the years that followed, Bina would shy away from all official activities, leaving Meir to go unaccompanied to national and international receptions. Perhaps Meir needed that, someone to stay in the background. Always the caregiver when Meir was home, Bina could not do enough for him. But she was reticent and a loner, even when Lily and Eli would invite her to accompany them on some outing. "How can I go?" she would reply. "Maybe Meir will come back and there won't be dinner for him!" Lily would say, "So we will bring him something." But that was unacceptable to Bina, a woman who spent every waking moment in the hope that her husband would make an appearance. It had not been easy, but Bina had learned to accept what had become evident. On the day she married Meir she became his second wife. His first wife was the State of Israel.

Chapter 33

———— ••• ————

The Yom Kippur War: October 6–25, 1973

The Prime Minister of Israel Golda Meir was aggressive, strong-willed and tough. It was admiringly quipped that the reason she wore long skirts was to hide her balls, the only minister in her government with them. It was an apt portrayal. She was also wise enough to be worried about the rhetoric being spewed by the Egyptian president Anwar Sadat. Through all of 1972 and most of 1973 he had been threatening war against Israel—vowing an attack unless the United States stepped in and forced Israel to accept United Nations Resolution 242. The resolution demanded that Israel withdraw from all the territories they had captured following the Six-Day War in 1967.

On the day before Yom Kippur 1973, the holiest day of the Jewish calendar, Syrian forces began amassing their forces on the Golan Heights. In an emergency meeting, only hours before the outbreak, Israel's Minister of Defense, Moshe Dayan, asserted that war was highly unlikely. General David Elazar, the Chief of Staff, viewed the situation very differently. He believed Israel was going to be attacked and advocated for a full-scale military mobilization and a preemptive strike.

Determined not to have a reoccurrence of the Arab onslaught that started the Six-Day War, Golda, as she was known throughout the world, concurred that the troops should be mobilized. But she would not condone a preemptive strike, asserting that the United States would not come to Israel's aid if they were seen as the aggressor. Believing that

Israel had adequate intelligence to warn them if war seemed imminent, the emergency meeting was adjourned.

The next day Israel was attacked. The military might that was aimed at the tiny nation of Israel was incomprehensible. In the Golan Heights alone, 180 Israeli tanks faced 1,400 Syrian tanks. Along the Suez Canal a force of eighty thousand Egyptians faced-off against five hundred Israeli soldiers. Supported by nine Arab states and some non-Middle Eastern countries, the war against the Jews was fueled with money. Qaddafi contributed one billion dollars—Libya sent Mirage fighters, and the Saudis sent 3,000 troops.

By October 8, Israel finally managed to mobilize all its reserve soldiers. And then with the strength and determination of a people facing total annihilation, they were able to somehow push back the Arab armies, moving deep into Egyptian and Syrian territory. At that point, the Soviet Union stepped in to resupply the Arabs by sea and air. In response to the Russian engagement, the U.S. began its own airlift resupply to Israel. Only after the Israeli military had isolated the Egyptian Third Army and defeat was imminent did the U.N. Security Council call for a ceasefire. On October 25, 1973, that ceasefire went into effect.

Eli and Lily had returned to Israel two years earlier and moved back into their old apartment in Bat Yam. Their second child, Ronni Huberman was born November 26, 1971. Eli had a staff appointment at the Weizmann Institute in the department of genetics. When the war was declared, he was sent to the Sinai desert for six months. That left Lily and the two children alone in the apartment. Thankfully, her Aunt Sonia and Cousin Aaron with his future wife, Gali visited almost every day. When the alarms sounded throughout the city—which was often— Sonia carried baby Ronni and Lily held Ilan's hand as they ran to the shelter five stories below. But in the evenings, Lily was alone during those nineteen days of a mandatory blackout at night. That meant every window was closed and every shade or makeshift window cover was down. It was dark, lonely and terrifying. With no communication, she had no way of knowing if Eli was dead or alive.

As for Meir, he was a combat officer in the armored division stationed in the Sinai. Under the leadership of General Ariel Sharon, Meir was a participant when the Israeli army crossed the Suez Canal. But the victory was bittersweet, as Meir had witnessed the death of many friends, young soldiers who left behind grief-stricken parents, wives or husbands, and little children. By the end of the war, over 2,500 Israeli Jews had perished.

It was a horrific time for Eli, leaving his wife with two children in the midst of the war and not knowing if they were safe. In addition, he was suffering from bleeding hemorrhoids so severe he could barely sit. There were doctors available but, in the desert, there was nothing they could do to help him. Once the ceasefire held, he was allowed to go home once every two weeks for 24 hours. He could see his family and take a bath— the only thing that gave him any relief from pain.

A cancer symposium was scheduled in Brussels before Christmas of 1973, while Eli was still in the reserves. Thanks to his growing reputation Eli was slated to be a speaker at the meeting. Stuck in an encampment in the Sinai, it never even occurred to him that he would still be going. But behind the scenes phone calls and letters were crisscrossing the world. The World Health Organization was sponsoring the event and they contacted the United Nations, who then contacted the Foreign Ministry of Israel. The case they made was that the presence of Dr. Eliezer Huberman was imperative because without him as the keynote speaker, there could be no meeting. Eli was not the keynote speaker, but it was a clever ploy and it worked, and he was certainly flattered that they were going to so much trouble.

On the plane to Brussels, he tried to make sense of what was happening. How was it even possible that one day he was an Israeli soldier stationed in the desert, and twenty-four hours later he shaved, showered and dressed in civilian clothing on his way to Brussels?

Upon his arrival, Eli was overwhelmed by the normalcy of everyday life in Belgium. There were lights in every window and people were shopping, sitting in sidewalk cafes and laughing as if they did not have a care in the world. And as surreal as all of this was for Eli, he found himself blocking out what was happening In Israel as he walked the city streets, his passion for architecture ignited. The European capital was the home of Art Nouveau, Art Deco, Neoclassical, Gothic and Neo-Renaissance. Everywhere he looked became a feast for his eyes.

In the evening he would dine with scientists from the meeting. One night that group included Professor Sugimura, the director of the most important Japanese cancer research center in Tokyo. Behind his back, the professor's Japanese colleagues called him *emperor Sugimura*. Eli liked the man and was flattered when he showed interest in his research. During desert Professor Sugimura asked Eli what his duties were in the war. Unable to resist, Eli told the group the story about his time in the desert when he refused to certify the water purifier concocted by his commanding officer.

"So as a punishment, I became a porter of military equipment," he said. Everybody started to laugh as if he was telling a joke.

Professor Sugimura turned to Eli and again quietly said, "Tell me the truth. What were you doing?"

Eli repeated, "In Israel you can be a professor, a scientist—whatever— and *still* you can become a lowly porter in the army."

Later Eli learned that the scientists had spread a rumor stating he was involved in confidential war activity and would not divulge his secret.

•••

By the time Eli returned to Israel, opinion had begun to turn against Golda Meir. A special commission had been set up after the war to report on decisions made before the war. It cleared her of any wrongdoing, but she still decided to step down as Prime Minister. Regardless of how the Israeli population felt about her, one thing could never be disputed: Golda Meir was the one who established the close relationship with President Richard Nixon. And that relationship was Israel's lifeline during the Yom Kippur War. The American airlift flew 567 missions, dropping twenty-two tons of supplies. An additional 90,000 tons were brought in by sea.

Golda would stay in contact with Richard Nixon for the rest of her life, always referring to him as "my president." In Golda's own words: *For generations to come, all will be told of the miracle of the immense planes from the United States bringing in the materiel that meant life to our people.*

Chapter 34

———— ••• ————

From 1973–1975, Eli served as a senior scientist at the Weizmann Institute. At the end of those two years, his name was put forward for an associate professorship. With its staff of two thousand scientists, only five or six applicants were selected from the various scientific disciplines of biology, chemistry, physics, etc., and usually only one scientist per discipline. Awarded once a year, the professorship came with a salary increase, on-campus housing, and most importantly, a tenured status. If selected, Eli could remain at the Weizmann, one of the most revered scientific institutions in the world, until the day he retired.

The appointment as an associate professor necessitated the approval of a special promotion committee of full professors at Weizmann. In making their decisions, the professors requested confidential opinion letters from the world's most distinguished scientists who worked in the relevant field of the nominee. Sadly, there was a dark side to the nomination. If not selected that year, or the following year, then the rejected nominee had to leave the Institute.

Eli was worried. If he did not get the promotion, he had no other options. And the buzz going around was that Eli had *zero* chance of being selected mainly because he was up against world-renowned scientific geniuses. Supposedly his colleagues did not view Eli as a genius. Always a person who accepted the facts of life, Eli did not feel hopeful of being given the promotion. Rather than sit around and wait for disappointment to come knocking on his door he made an appointment to meet with the chairman of a biology department at Tel Aviv University. Sitting in the office of the professor, an immunologist, and after a bit of small talk, Eli asked if there were any positions available.

"There might have been," the Chairman taunted, "if you had not wasted all your time publishing and focusing on cancer-causing chemicals." As if he were making fun of Eli, he then said, "Too bad for you. Had you been doing research in immunology; I would hire you on the spot. But now, I guess you will be out looking for a job."

Eli left the university insulted and angry. Years later he would look back on that afternoon and smile, knowing that the arrogant professor never became anything more than an unrecognized, second-class scientist.

Weeks after that disastrous meeting, at the conclusion of an International Cancer Conference in France, a group of senior scientific officials from Oak Ridge National Laboratory (ORNL) approached Eli. I am Paul Nettesheim, the chairperson of the Oak Ridge National Laboratory search committee. Nettesheim was a handsome man with blond hair, blue eyes and a kindly smile. He introduced Eli to his colleagues. "As you may know," Nettesheim said, "our facility is recognized as a leader in nuclear reactor technology and environmental science as well as our research in biology, physics, chemistry, medicine and more. We are here," Nettesheim hesitated for a few heartbeats and then smiled, "to invite you to join our team."

The opportunity could not have been at a more opportune time and Eli was thrilled as he waited to hear the offer.

"Funding for your research would not be an issue. Your labs will be state of the art, equipped with everything you will ever need to further your research on the chemical causation of cancer. And I am honored to inform you that we are not the only ones who want you to come to the States." He handed Eli a letter. "It is from Dr. Umberto Saffiotti,

Chief of Experimental Pathology at the National Cancer Institute. In it you will find an offer of additional research funding if you accept our offer."

•••

Eli and Lily had been taking long walks along the Weismann Institute's lush green pathways in the evenings, often making their way to the tombstone of Chaim and Vera Weizmann, located on the campus grounds. During those treks they had spent hours discussing the same things over and over again. First, they talked about the *what ifs*: what if he became a professor and what if he did not? Then they looked into the future and discussed what other options they might have if Eli was forced to leave the Weizmann. But that night their talk was different.

"I have an offer," Eli said, as he tried his best to repeat word for word what had transpired at the international meeting. "They are willing to generously finance my research and will pay all our moving expenses if we agree to go. I am entitled to a sabbatical year from the institute, which could most likely be extended for a second year. And if by some miracle, I get the professorship, . . . then in two years I will come back as a professor. And if I don't get it, we can still come back because I will have stellar credentials and it will be easy to find a position. What do you think?" he asked, turning to face Lily.

The moonlight had turned the evening into a dusty golden hue, and the sound of rustling leaves filled the silence as Lily contemplated their future. "Will we really come back, Eli?"

"There is no chance we will stay in the States. Israel is our home. We will be back here in two years."

Lily had begun work on her PhD in music and was teaching a course in music history at Bar Ilan University in Tel Aviv. She loved her job, her schooling and her life. But she also knew that her doctorate could wait. "Take it," she said, squeezing Eli's hand. "It sounds like the opportunity of a lifetime."

• • •

Oak Ridge National Laboratory agreed to cover all the shipping expenses both from Israel to Tennessee and when the time came, all expenses back to Israel. They even offered to ship a car and Lily's piano. As the most important and valuable possession they owned, Lily feared her piano would arrive not only out of tune but possibly even damaged. And so she decided to leave it behind. As they were packing and preparing to leave, friends who been on sabbaticals told them a way to bypass taxes in order to bring back furniture from America. Deciding to take full advantage of the loophole, on a steaming hot day in August, Eli and Lily borrowed a truck and drove to a Druze village not far from Bat Yam. Citizens of Israel the Druze were a secretive monotheistic Arab sect with an eclectic set of principles. They believed that Jesus, Mohammad and Moses were prophets. Loyal and unified to one another, this distinctive faith had survived for centuries.

Once at the village, they bought inexpensive straw furniture to take with them to Oak Ridge—furniture they would throw out the moment they arrived. Anything Israeli citizens took with them out of the country was written down. If their passport said eight pieces of furniture, then they were allowed to bring back, tax-free, eight pieces of furniture. Eli and Lily wanted nice things, and that meant buying furniture in America. This would allow them to do just that.

Shortly before their departure in September 1976, the appointments for associate professorships were announced. Words could not begin to describe Eli's feelings when he was informed that he was one of the chosen few! For Eli, it was tantamount to reaching the summit of

Mt. Everest. To make the appointment even sweeter, one of the professors on the selection committee told Eli later in confidence that among the many recommendation letters were two from the most famous scientists in the world. And in each of those letters, they questioned why the application was only for an associate professorship when they were sure that Dr. Eliezer Huberman deserved a full professorship.

Eli's parents were elated. "Mother and I are so proud that our son is now an associate professor of Microbiology/Biochemistry at the Weizmann Institute," Shmuel said, at a family dinner to celebrate the good news. "And Meir, we are certainly proud of you as well, being an officer in the Israeli Army." Meir was not just an officer. He was a full colonel. Eli exchanged a glance with his brother and they both smiled. "Meir has never been just an officer and he never will be!" Eli interjected.

Having already been approved for a two-year sabbatical from the Weizmann, Eli sent a telegram to his administrative contact at Oak Ridge telling him that he would come, but only for two years. Eli was well aware that the Weizmann did not have the financial deep pockets that Oak Ridge National Laboratory or the National Institute of Health had. But the Weizmann had something even more important to Eli. They shared his vision that science should be for the benefit of humanity.

Chapter 35

———— ••• ————

1976

Before being issued a visa to work at Oak Ridge, Eli was put through extensive interviews in addition to a complete physical at the United States Embassy in Israel. Anxious and curious as to why there were so many interviews, he asked several members of the diplomatic team. No one would give him a straight answer. Eventually Eli came to the conclusion that it was because of Meir's high position in the military.

Eli and Lily decided that he should go ahead of her and the boys That would give him time to acquaint himself with the town, buy a car, find a house and purchase key pieces of furniture in order to be ready for his family when they arrived. It would also give him the opportunity to prepare his labs and begin hiring some key staff, that last task needing his complete attention.

When the airplane landed in New York, Eli followed his fellow passengers to immigration. He presented his visa a "J" non-immigrant Visa to the officer to be stamped. It was issued by the United States Department of State to promote cultural exchange for research scholars, professors, etc. But instead of having his passport stamped, Eli was then escorted to another immigration officer. He was astounded when that officer handed him a permanent residence green card, informing him that his wife would also receive hers when she arrived. Eli would later learn it was a ploy by Oak Ridge National Laboratory in the hopes of keeping him the States, but at the time, in his naiveté, he had not a clue that was the motivation.

Oak Ridge National Laboratory, ORNL was located in the foothills of the Great Smoky Mountains of Tennessee. During World War II, it had been a well-guarded secret city. With a population nearing fifty thousand, its designated mission was the Manhattan Project—the production and separation of plutonium for the building of an atomic bomb. Ever since its inception in 1943, it had remained a highly secure facility—entrance obtained only if you lived or worked in the city or had clearance.

By the time he arrived in the fall of 1976, Oak Ridge's population was down to about 20,000 people, half of whom worked at ORNL. The laboratory had greatly expanded its focus and without question its scientists and technologists were the best and brightest in the world. Pragmatic in nature, the majority of those scientists viewed technology and science as a quiet evolution of change, each increment of innovation a step forward building upon itself slowly and with care.

Housing in Oak Ridge was like a swinging door, with scientists always coming and going. Consequently, it did not take Eli long to find what he considered the perfect home, a palace in comparison to their tiny apartment in Israel. He could not wait to show it to Lily. As a surprise he greeted his wife and boys at the airport in New York. They flew together to Knoxville and then drove to Oak Ridge.

Lily was enchanted with their new split three-level home on Newel Lane. The front faced the street and was situated on a downhill incline. The backyard was a wooded area filled with lush, beautiful dogwood trees that had dangerously encroached on the house. Lily vowed the moment she saw the dogwoods that not a tree would be cut down.

Inside there were stairs leading to the upper and lower floors. The upper level had three bedrooms. The boys each had their own room and shared a bathroom situated across a wide hallway. The master bedroom had a private bathroom and a wonderful view of the forest. The middle level was elevated from the street with side stairs that led to the front door. Opposite the entrance door were two double glass doors facing the forest. The large kitchen was to the right of those double glass windows and it would become Lily's favorite area in the house. The lower level had a large, finished basement with a guest room and a powder room. It had sliding glass doors that led to the backyard and views to the front yard and the street. Social as Lily was, she could already imagine what a perfect party room it would be. But on site, she detested the musty red shag carpet in the basement.

It smelled because unbeknownst to them the house they now owned was a dump. It sat below a hill and when it rained, water came into the lower level. The very first week while Eli was showering, he placed his hand against the wall. It gave way!

Eli knew nothing about buying a house and he was angry with himself for trusting the opinion of a postdoctoral student and friend he knew from his time with Charlie Heidelberger. He could not help but wonder. Did his friend view him as competition? Did he encourage the purchase of a damaged house intentionally? It was a lesson hard learned as Eli reminded himself that scientists are not a holy group. They are simply a reflection of society: some good and some not.

Unfortunately, he had used all their money as a down payment on the house and to make matters worse, his first paycheck would not be issued until the end of the month. That meant they were left without a penny. Thankfully, a friend loaned them enough money to carry them through.

Eli wanted to do something to improve the exterior appearance of the house, so he decided to put in a garden. He planted bulbs and flowers and a red flowering dogwood tree. It looked lovely until the first rain when everything washed away. Determined to save the tree, he spent hours sulking, adding more dirt and patting down that dirt. But regardless of his devoted attention the tree was still circling toward demise. And then one morning to his utter surprise he went outside, and his tree was blooming. He called Lily and they both looked on with joy and amazement, unable to figure out how it was even possible. And in fact, it was not possible. The miracle had occurred with the help of their neighbor from across the street, Joe Lenhard, an ORNL official. Joe had watched Eli's unsuccessful effort to save the dying tree. In the dead of night, while Lily and Eli slept, he properly planted a new tree. It was then that Eli had to admit that he might be good at certain things, but gardening was not his forte. More importantly, it was also nice to learn that they had a friendly and helpful neighbor.

●●●

Eli was thrilled by the reception he received at ORNL. In preparation for his arrival, the old labs were being painted and major restoration work was underway. And as promised, in addition to the Department of Energy monies allocated by ORNL, Dr. Umberto Saffiotti had also secured funds for Eli's research from the National Cancer Institute. It seemed surreal and Eli was joyous. He had gone from having a technician and two graduate students at the Weizmann to a staff of twelve.

While inspecting the construction he noticed an unsightly and unnecessary rubber tube running between two of his labs. Eli went to the painter and handed him a pair of scissors.

"Do me a favor, cut this thing because it is unnecessary and needs to be removed."

The painter looked at Eli as if he were crazy. "Sorry, that is the job of the pipe fitters."

"You must be kidding!" Eli said, thinking that perhaps he misunderstood because his English was not that good when a deep Southern accent was involved. He shared the story with a coworker who said, "Just do it yourself after 5 o'clock, when these guys are not around."

That evening Eli told his neighbor Joe the story.

"You didn't cut it? Just tell me you didn't do that!" Joe said wide-eyed.

"I did," Eli replied with a subtle smile.

"Tomorrow the union people will come and make a whole inquiry about it. My suggestion: deny that you did it. Because if you don't, there is a good possibility all the union workers at Oak Ridge will go out on strike."

"You are telling me that because I did something that was the job of the pipe fitters I could get in trouble?"

"Unions. You will soon learn."

A delegation came to see Eli the next morning. "Did you do it?" a union representative asked, his face flushing purple as he spoke.

"Absolutely not," Eli said, the lie seemingly harmless but still something so out of character for him.

"So, who did it?"

"I certainly do not know."

The man walked off in a huff. Eli received a bill that very afternoon for four hundred dollars, funds that would be taken out of his laboratory budget because he cut a stupid rubber tube.

Chapter 36

―――――― ••• ――――――

Highly classified top-secret experiments were taking place in the area known as Y-12 located next to the biology complex where Eli had his lab. The buildings were secreted behind a high barbed wired fence. When walking past the facility, his mind would conjure images of the work being done. The facility was producing uranium for the United States nuclear arsenal but as to what else Y-12 was doing, he did not have a clue. Curious about the interior, he inquired about being permitted to have lunch in the Y-12 cafeteria. His request was denied. Eli knew it was because he was a foreign national, namely an Israeli. When a Russian delegation came to tour Y-12, Lily an Israeli as well, was asked to serve as the interpreter, and she spent the entire day touring with the delegation. The Russians could visit, Lily could visit, but Eli was refused to even have lunch in the Y-12 cafeteria. Instances of American inconsistencies never stopped amazing him.

He was not really surprised when he received a call at his lab from a very official-sounding man asking if he would be interested in participating in a very lucrative opportunity to collaborate on a weapon. As an Israeli, he had been raised to question every motive someone might have when offering him anything. After trying to obtain entrance into Y-12, he felt certain that it was the FBI trying to entrap him. *Do they really think I am such a dummy?*

"That sounds very interesting," Eli said. "May I suggest that you contact Herman Postman, the Director of ORNL, as all such interactions must go through him?" He never heard another word on the subject.

...

The wonder of it all was that he had free rein to do whatever was necessary to set up his lab. Eli hired his team of technicians and scientists. When Ziva Misulovin, Lily's friend and a technician with an outstanding reputation at the Weizmann Institute, heard that Eli was going to the States, she begged him to take her. Eli responded that he would have been happy to do so, but there was no time to arrange for the appropriate approvals or a working visa. Smirking when she bid him goodbye, Ziva said, "Rest assured that I will find a way to come to you!"

Months later, while Lily, Eli and the boys were having a late dinner there was a knock on the door. When Eli opened it, there stood Michael Fry, the Department Head of Cancer Research—and Ziva! "I understand she was your technician in Israel and that you have been expecting her."

"Absolutely," Eli responded, stretching the truth to save them both from embarrassment. "And thrilled she has finally arrived. Ziva is the missing link in my team!" Eli was incredulous she had arrived without warning and without even knowing if he would or could hire her. Regardless, there was no denying that Ziva was a very smart and feisty young woman. Her dedication, work ethic, and her ability to intuit his needs would make her assistance invaluable.

Ziva would go on to marry a graduate student from the University of Tennessee assigned to the Biology Division at ORNL. Seven years her junior and not Jewish, Ziva told Eli she would rather end up a divorcee with a child then remain unmarried. Eventually Ziva and her husband, Dale Dorset went to the Weitzman Institute in Israel, but he could not get a permanent position, so they returned to the states. Ziva's husband became a successful scientist and a professor at St. Louis University. Ziva was his technician. Dale and Ziva raised a beautiful family and forty years later, remained friends with Eli and Lily.

...

During his years at ORNL Eli would meet many fascinating people. Among them was Alexander Hollander (Alex), the man who had been the first Biology Division Director at ORNL. He was an assimilated German Jew who built the division and ran it for many years. After retiring from his position, he moved to Washington, D.C. In spite of being retired, Alexander Hollander still tended to see himself as the director. He would often summon ORNL scientists to appear before him in Washington, especially the promising new hires from the Biology Division. Shortly after arriving in Oak Ridge, Eli was summoned to Washington D.C. by Hollander. Eli was told that Hollander had knowledge and connections that would be invaluable. The two men spent an entire day talking science, exploring new ideas and getting to know each other. He liked Alex and knew the feeling was mutual. In the evening he was invited to join Alex and his wife for dinner at a swanky restaurant in Georgetown. They soon found they shared a passion for art. In fact, Henrietta was considered an art maven, presumably because of a degree in art from a prestigious European university.

After he returned from Washington one of the division heads told Eli a great story about Henrietta Hollander. Soon after the war ended a group of so-called sophisticated women decided that Oak Ridge needed an art museum. They collected money and delegated the task of purchasing the art to Henrietta, who would be accompanying

Alex during his business travels throughout Europe. Scavenging every art store in every city they visited, the works she found were amazing, including art by luminaries such as Picasso and Chagall. The pieces were each purchased for a few thousand dollars back then considered a huge sum in Europe.

After Henrietta's returned, the museum planners looked at her acquisitions and after a few days of deliberations they told her that the pieces of art she bought were not the kind of art they were looking to acquire. Henrietta could not have been more thrilled. Her greatest dream was that they would not want even one painting or sculpture so she could keep them all. Henrietta did not have the money to pay for the cost of all the purchases, but she was determined to make them her own. Meeting again with the investors, she convinced the condescending ladies to let her keep the art and pay them back monthly. They agreed.

Eli was unsettled as he listened to the story. He knew how over the years; a myriad of articles had appeared in Israeli publications lamenting the precious art confiscated from Jewish homes by the Nazis. Did Henrietta acquire stolen art that belonged to the Jews? He wanted to believe that she bought the paintings from legitimate galleries. But was there even such a thing as legitimate art establishments in Europe right after the War? Eli chose to believe that people like Henrietta and Alexander Hollander would never intentionally buy stolen art. Years later, when Alexander Hollander died, the valuable art Henrietta acquired was donated to the St. Louis Art Institute in the city of her birth. The work she had acquired was worth a fortune and was now being shared with the world.

Chapter 37

————————— ••• —————————

Eli was given the designation of Senior Scientist and group leader of the Carcinogenesis Program in the Biology Division at Oak Ridge. In his five-year tenure at ORNL he published more than 40 papers in scientific journals, including the prestigious *Proceedings of the National Academy of Science and Nature*. Because of these studies, Eli was invited to be a member of a National Academy of Sciences Committee on "Identifying and Estimating the Genetic Impact of Chemical Mutagens" and "Quantitative Relationship between Mutagenic and Carcinogenic Potencies." He co-wrote reports of this committee that were published by the National Academy Press in 1982 and 1983.

Eli's research at ORNL was focused on two major areas. One was causation: to identify what caused cancer. Specifically, he analyzed the role cellular metabolism had in converting inactive chemicals into mutagenic and cancer-causing agents. His team established that metabolism played a role in defining the ability of certain chemicals to induce cancer in a specific organ.

The second area of their research was the treatment of cancer. Eli and his team showed that particular chemicals could force tumor cells to undergo terminal differentiation, namely, to acquire mature functions and stop dividing. These and related studies resulted in a cancer treatment called differentiation therapy, which is used in the therapy of certain leukemias. Some of the postdocs who worked in Eli's group on these projects became professors, including Drs. Carol Jones at Connecticut State, Dina Revel at Ben Gurion and Berhard Ryffel at the University of Glasgow, as well as Dr. Robert Lagenbach, a visiting investigator who would go on to have an outstanding scientific career at the National Institute of Environmental Health Sciences.

Along with Eli's many successes for which he was forever thankful, there were some negative consequences as well. One in particular had him flummoxed. He was experiencing difficulty with the results of experiments using a cancer-causing chemical called dimethylnitrosamine (DMN). In his research he and his team used two conditions, one that involved using untreated DMN cells and the other using treated DMN cells, both in Petri dishes. Under those controlled conditions there was an air exchange with the incubator atmosphere. They also used untreated and DMN treated cells in capped flasks, which do not have the ability to have an air exchange. Eli could not understand why he had certain results in the flasks and did not have the same results in the Petri dishes.

Eli said to a chemist working with him, "Perhaps the DMN in these experiments evaporates and it gets into the untreated Petri dishes, and that is the reason why we see a difference in the open dishes relative to the capped flasks."

"Nonsense. DMN doesn't have significant vapor pressure," the chemist replied, stubbornly adamant that he was right.

Eli shook his head in disagreement. "Then why is there a difference when I compare between open and capped containers?" Eli replied, always ready to question assumptions and concepts that scientists assumed as facts. Following his instincts, it suddenly dawned on him. "Maybe when the chemicals evaporate, they are going everywhere, including into the water bath of the incubator. We should test for the presence of DMN."

"Impossible!" the chemist replied. "No way!" To prove Eli was wrong, the chemist took samples from the water bath of the incubator. When the chemical analysis was completed, the chemist came back to Eli, wide-eyed astonishment etched on his face. "You know, you were right. And because you were right, that has to mean that we are breathing DMN!"

To soothe his colleague's concerns, Eli responded, "It's a good thing this lab has excellent ventilation."

Little was known at the time about chemical exposure. In one incident at Oak Ridge Eli's hand was badly burned by a toxic chemical that dissolved part of one of his safety gloves.

Suffering from COPD later in his life, Eli would come to realize that performing such experiments without having certain facts available was a contributing factor to his medical problems and he would often say, "Hindsight is always 20/20."

• • •

The Huberman's stayed at Oak Ridge for five years extending the initial two-year sabbatical for different reasons. The first time Eli asked for an extension from the Weizmann was because his son Ronni was having trouble with his vision. Going from doctor to doctor, they were told that it was necessary for Ronni to stay in the States to be treated. The difficulty with having to remain was that Lily had already packed. They lived out of suitcases as they waited for their son to get better. Surely, they would be going home soon. After all, Eli had the professorship and a guaranteed position for life at the Weizmann. And furthermore, they were now and would always be Israelis, no matter how long they lived in America. But when Ronni was finished with his eye treatments, Eli was in the middle of an important research study and felt deeply conflicted about abandoning the project. He turned to Lily for her advice as to what they should do.

Lily was anything but helpful to Eli in making the decision to stay or go. Their conversations went something like this: Eli told her, "You know something, let's go back this summer."

Lily replied, "Are you crazy? You have twelve people working for you. You have a big lab, and you are enjoying yourself."

The next day Eli would say, "Okay I have decided. We are staying!"

Lily replied, "Are you nuts? We have our parents in Israel. We have our friends, our culture!"

That was Lily, trying to be helpful but just as confused as Eli. The result was that Eli had a six-month period of sleepless nights trying to make a decision. The decision was not then nor would it ever be uncomplicated. In 1981, at the end of the five years, Eli was given an ultimatum from Professor Sela, the President of the Weizmann: return or lose your appointment. This ultimatum forced Eli to decide whether to stay in the U.S. or go back. Would America ever feel like home? Could Eli live with himself for not returning to their Jewish homeland when his brother and father had both dedicated their lives to the country?

"We cannot be halfway here and halfway there," Eli said as he and Lily were lying in bed one evening, the boys asleep for hours. "I am being offered amazing opportunities in America. We have to decide if we stay or go."

Lily had sacrificed her own ambitions while living in Oak Ridge, a provincial town even though half of the people had a PhD. Devoid of a university, she had been unable to pursue her dream of a coveted doctoral degree, which she started at Tel Aviv University. Her thesis was supposed to involve music created for Israeli/Jewish theater. As part of this undertaking, she had interviewed famous Israeli composers.

Eli and Lily missed going to museums and concerts. To fill the void, Lily practiced for hours on the second-rate piano they had purchased. She also gave a few piano concerts at the Oak Ridge Cultural Center. The rest of her time was spent raising their two sons. That was undoubtedly a fulltime job, but it was not the life she had envisioned. To compound the problem, six-year-old Ronni was beginning to speak with a deep Southern drawl, at times making his conversations almost incomprehensible to his parents. So, whatever was decided, one thing was certain, it was time to leave the South!

Even in 1981, it was too expensive to travel to Israel and international phone calls were so costly they were prohibitive. Communication took place through letters. Lily, as an only child, was her mother's heart. And yet, Ada never complained, caring only that her daughter was happy. Lily ached for her mother and was overcome by guilt, a feeling that inhabited her soul and remained lodged there for the rest of her life.

But Eli's work was undeniably an imperative, especially when what was being offered in the way of scientific resources and compensation could not be replicated in Israel. Lily loved him too much to deny him this opportunity. Her own desires and needs could wait.

Chapter 38

—— ••• ——

Three Years Earlier (1978)

The United States government made an agreement with Israel: if Israel sent an expert to teach U.S. soldiers about special ops, the United States would allow that soldier to spend a year in training at the Armor Branch program of the US Army post located in Fort Knox, Kentucky. Known for being the depository holding the bulk of America's gold bullion, Fort Knox was considered the most secure facility in the world.

Meir Dagan was the man chosen for the specialized teaching and training. Given officer's housing, Meir was able to bring his wife Bina and their two young children. The base was only a four-hour drive from Oak Ridge so it would be an opportunity for a family reunion, a chance for the brothers, once so close, to reconnect. Since Meir absolutely refused to write letters, they had everything to talk about. Meir called upon his arrival and within weeks Eli and his family made the trip to Fort Knox.

Meir and Bina's children were younger than Ilan and Ronni but still they immediately bonded. As for the sisters-in-law Lily was outgoing, friendly, well versed and interested in everything. Bina, in contrast, was reserved and even though she always smiled, had little to add to most discussions. Still over the years, they had managed to forge a cordial familial relationship.

For the brothers, the reunion was bittersweet. Meir was now the link between their parents, and he filled Eli in on family life. They each bragged about their careers. Eli was so proud of Meir—his rising through the ranks, his single-mindedness and courage. But in the years to come, like a parent never admitting their child had done wrong, Eli would never fully accept what people said and wrote of Meir's exploits. He would never admit that his brother had ever killed anyone.

Meir listened to Eli's journey in a state of wonder. He was amazed at his patience and perseverance and his ability to not get discouraged. He saw Eli as a soldier, just like himself, but his villain was the disease of cancer. And just as Meir had to constantly deal with politics, so did his brother, fighting for recognition, for the freedom to think differently, to dare to dream, to trespass into areas never before explored.

But beneath all the admiration and praise, there remained an underlying current of a conversation that was never broached during their visit: would Eli return to Israel. Perhaps it was because Meir was afraid to ask for fear of the answer.

• • •

Being at Fort Knox was an eye-opening experience for Eli. It brought back into focus how unique and contrary his brother really was. As a high-ranking visiting Israeli officer in the IDF, he was expected to maintain a certain decorum, and that included driving a car that reflected his rank. Disregarding those expectations, Meir instead purchased a twenty-year-old powder blue Ford Fairlane convertible for his year in the States, going so far as to have the insignia of his rank as a lieutenant colonel in the Israeli Defense Forces painted on the outside of the cockamamie old car. To Eli's joy and amazement, every time that absurd car moved past a group of American soldiers, they would see the insignia and jump to salute.

It was no surprise that Meir purchased an old fixed-up clunker. His love of antiques and art was a passion he shared with Eli and Lily.

They learned that there were antique stores aplenty tucked along the roadways outside the base, so when Meir and Lily visited, the two couples would leave the children with a neighbor and head out for a treasure hunt. Bina was a good sport and came along without complaint, even though she did not have an eye or a proclivity for antiques. By day's end, they had filled the trunk with their finds. On one of those visits, their quest for antiques and art objects included an auction house in close-by Knoxville. To this day, pictures and rugs purchased still adorn Meir's beautiful Rosh Pina home in Israel and two antique chairs and a cabinet continue to adorn the Huberman condominium in Chicago.

As Meir became immersed in his training and teaching and their visits became more and more sporadic. Before the brothers knew it, the year had slipped away

●●●

Meir would be back in Israel when he learned of Eli's decision to stay in America. He said he understood why and professed to the family that he was not upset. True or not, from then on, Meir never talked about having a brother with anyone outside of the family. The reason, Meir knew he had too many enemies to even count, men and women who would have happily taken their revenge by murdering an unprotected member of his family living in America. He could have protected him in Israel, but in the States Eli was too easy a target.

During his years as the head of Mossad, the national intelligence agency of Israel tasked with covert operations, counterterrorism and collecting intelligence, Meir would come to the United States often for meetings with high level officials in Washington. Making excuses, he did not arrange to see his brother. Not understanding why Meir did not make time for him, Eli spent years feeling hurt and at times even angry.

...

In the 1970's Meir spearheaded the defeat of terrorism in Gaza. By 1980, Meir was deemed the IDF's top authority in special ops. As a result of that success, he was promoted to full colonel and designated to head a new unit: the SLR (South Lebanon Region). In a quote taken from *Rise and Kill First* by Ronen Bergman, Major General Avigdor (Yanush) Ben-Gal, head of the IDF Northern Command, told Meir, "From now on, you are emperor here. Do whatever you want." Given free rein to coerce, to dissuade, and to make it apparent that Israel would be assertive, instead of waiting to be victimized, Meir took full advantage. He and his team covertly struck PLO bases throughout southern Lebanon and destroyed the homes of people who aided the terrorists. In southern Lebanon, at the SLR base in Marjayoun, Meir set up a clandestine organization that reported directly to him. Under cover of darkness, Meir had bombs manufactured in a kibbutz. He used Lebanese irregulars to keep his unsanctioned attacks secret not only from the PLO but also from the Israeli government.

Meir Dagan was regarded as a wild man. With little choice, the Major General's attitude was to just let things flow and to back Meir if things went wrong. Those rogue attacks were seen by some as one of the most dreadful periods in the history of Israel. In fact, once their activities became known, the Deputy Defense Minister insisted that both Major General Avigdor Ben-Gal and Colonel Meir Dagan be thrown out of the army.

But nothing deterred Ben-Gal's high opinion of Meir. Another quote from *Rise and Kill First* reads, "It was what Meir loved best, being involved in secret, small-scale warfare in the shadows and dark places, in espionage activities and in weaving conspiracies, small or big that was his forte. He's a very brave guy, very creative, very opinionated, who's ready to take huge risks. I knew what he was doing but ignored it. Sometimes you have to turn a blind eye."

•••

Meir spoke Arabic like an Arab, and with his dark complexion and the proper clothing, he even looked like an Arab. In the early 1980s, disregarding his high rank and the regulations that forbade him from putting himself in a position to be captured, tortured and broken, Meir crossed the Lebanon border and successfully infiltrated a terrorist camp. Regardless of the valuable information he gleaned from his time as a bogus terrorist, his actions caused a huge scandal, and he was again sanctioned. But no matter how extreme Meir Dagan acted, Israel needed his bravado and inventiveness. And he was always forgiven.

Chapter 39

———— ••• ————

Making the choice to remain in the United States had taken a huge toll on Eli. Feeling restless and in need of a change he made the decision to leave ORNL. After making some circuitous inquires to people he knew and respected, numerous offers for employment had been offered, and it was time for him to decide what his next position would be.

Glancing at the bedside clock, hating that the hands were hugging 4 a.m., he slipped quietly from the bed, trying not to disturb Lily. Putting on his bathrobe and slippers he wandered the house for a while before stopping at the doorway of his boys' bedroom. Ilan, his teenager, had the covers pulled over his head as if hiding from the world. Ronni, ten years old, was sleeping sideways on the bed, the covers half off, as if ever ready to dash into the next moment of his life. The passage of time assailed Eli as he tried to make peace with how quickly the years had flown. How many nights had he come home late? How often had he missed dinner with his boys? And all the trips he had taken., all necessary, but still …

Pulling his thoughts from negativity and guilt to tender memories, Eli focused on the love he had for his sons. Maybe he could not be a traditional father, home by 5 o'clock, but no father ever loved his children more than Eli loved his. He envisioned the boys when they were little, cuddling up to him before bed, listening intently as he told them Bible stories about King Saul, David, Jonah and the whale, and more.

Eli's reputation and exuberant personality stood out amongst his august colleagues with their dour expressions and dry dialogue. As a result, he was often invited to international symposiums, asked to speak at various cities throughout the States and was often in Washington D.C. at the National Institute of Health. When he was going to be on an extended trip for a week or more, Eli would make tapes of his stories. While he was away, Lily would play the tapes so his sons could listen and hear his voice. Eli chose Bible stories to instill a love of Judaism into his children. He did not see these stories as religious but rather as cultural. To him, culture was a presence and religion was a belief, and he did not believe in religion. Eli was the product of his father Shmuel's lack of religious conviction. Shmuel had been a leader in a major Labor Zionist Movement, a speaker at Zionist gatherings and had attended Jewish memorial events. Being a Jew was important to him, but the religion was not. Consequently, he did not deem it necessary to have a Bar Mitzvah for either Eli or Meir. And yet, as incongruous as it seemed, Shmuel insisted that his sons always celebrate with him and the family every major Jewish holiday. Eli would do the same with his sons and when he became a grandfather, he would repeat this tradition of telling Bible stories to his grandchildren.

Perhaps because Eli did not have a Bar Mitzvah, he and Lily made sure their sons would have extraordinary events. To celebrate, when each son reached the age of thirteen, they were taken to Jerusalem. At the Wailing Wall, Judaism's holiest place, they read the Torah and the prayers in Hebrew guided by a rabbi. Both Bar Mitzvahs were attended by the extended family, and its proudest attendee was Grandfather Shmuel.

Eli had no idea exactly who or what this entity called G-d was, and most of the time it did not bother him. He believed he would live on in the minds of his sons and that when he was dead, he was simply dead. But sometimes he did think it would be comforting to believe in reincarnation and he was envious of people who did accept that as truth.

That ruminations continued as he moved into the living room, the moon casting a mellowed light as he stood at the window reflecting about the people he had worked with and would now leave. Those people who had been more than employees, more like partners in his quest to conquer cancer.

Dina Raveh came to mind. She had been a graduate student with Professor Ezra Galun at the Weizmann's Plant Science Department. When Eli moved to ORNL, Dina wrote to him asking if there were any post-doctoral positions available. Eli had called her immediately and told her to come. Divorced, she arrived with her mother and three daughters. Of course, Lily being Lily, she had embraced her five guests, housing them, feeding them, looking after them and sending Dina off to work with a packed lunch for two weeks until a rental home became available.

One day at a coffee break in the Ullmann building cafeteria, Dina had come up to Eli to ask for help. She was having trouble trying to regenerate a plant from a single cell, hoping that it would be a way of speeding up plant breeding. Eli had experience in this type of work with normal animal cells. He suggested she use a technique known as a feeder layer and he offered to help. That first experiment worked and six months later a paper describing the procedures to create a plant from a single cell was published. It was a first and Dina and her PhD mentor were elated and insisted that Eli be a coauthor. As a result, he was credited with an important paper in plant biology, memorable because it was so distinct from his life work in cancer research.

Eli found himself smiling as he thought about his daily routine. Curious and always interested, he would walk through his lab with a large cup of coffee. The young scientists worked hard, and Eli would stop at each workstation and ask: "what's new?" He listened intently to each answer, offering suggestions and when there was a breakthrough, regardless of how small, he complimented and shared the excitement. When out of town, he called every day, remembering the details of every experiment and he always asked for updates. When a paper was published in Eli's department, credit was always given to the scientists that worked on the project. It was a vow he had made to himself, after toiling under the oppressive Professor Sachs at the Weizmann in Israel. He would always give credit where credit was due.

The dawning light that beckoned a new day seemed to be calling Eli to make a decision. Of all the offers he had received, Argonne National Laboratory managed by the University of Chicago, and under the auspices of the United States Department of Energy, seemed to be his best choice. He would have the prestigious position as head of biological medical research at a national laboratory, a job that would give him open access to a global network platform that included other national laboratories, institutions, industries, and universities in America and around the world. Located in Lemont, Illinois, it was about a forty-five-minute drive from Chicago. Lily would have proximity to the university, and they could again go to the opera, theater, and concerts. And his sons would live in a vital, thriving community where they would get a first-rate education. Argonne National Laboratory would be his next right move.

Chapter 40

———————— ••• ————————

Before accepting the job at Argonne National Laboratory (ANL), Eli researched its history and discovered some of its issues. Named after a battle in France, Argonne's initial priority at its inception in 1946 was to develop the world's first controlled, self-sustaining nuclear reactor for the United States military. The purpose was to compete with the Soviets, who had already achieved nuclear reactions.

In the 1950s, after the horror of Hiroshima and Nagasaki, the world was terrified of atomic energy. To stem those fears, President Dwight D. Eisenhower established Atoms for Peace. The president promised the world that the focus would now be to commercialize uranium reactor energy for peaceful use. During the Korean War and later with the launching of Sputnik by Russia, Argonne was seen as essential and was awarded funds to build a proton accelerator. That project put Argonne into rarified air as the leading research institute for high-energy physics.

Throughout Lyndon Johnson's presidency nuclear power was embraced. And then in 1967, the Clean Air Act brought environmentalism into the spotlight, giving Argonne a new mission: improve the environment. Under the presidency of Jimmy Carter in 1977, attention turned to conservation and coordinated energy programs. Carter was gravely concerned with the disposal of spent plutonium, reactor fuel that could only be disposed of in long-term storage. His outspoken concern brought national awareness to environmental issues.

Priorities would continue to shift and change and by 1981, when Eli was given his position as Head of Biological Medical Research Division (BMI), Argonne was in flux. Staff positions were being eliminated and programs throughout the national laboratory systems were being reevaluated. The perception at that time was that Argonne was directionless and in decline. Under President Reagan, it was even rumored that Argonne might close. But defeat was not an option for the scientists at ANL. They were explorers, researchers who fearlessly crossed into a world that was yet to be discovered. Facing one disappointment after another, they trekked on. They started over when necessary. Failure was inevitable but they saw failures much like open wounds that would heal painful memories that would pass.

Throughout its history, the University of Chicago was a collaborative partner with the United States Department of Energy (DOE) at Argonne National Laboratory. They shared research, some faculty, students, laboratory scientists, and engineers. In rare cases, a very select group of scientists from ANL would even hold joint University of Chicago professorships.

In 1984, three years after Eli's arrival, Walter Massey resigned as the director of ANL to become vice president of the University of Chicago. An intensive recruitment initiative followed, and the perfect replacement was lured from his position as the general manager of the Engineering Technology Department at Exxon. Alan Schriesheim had a succinct mission statement for Argonne. "The laboratory has reached its nadir in terms of both funding and morale. Capricious political winds have taken their toll on every aspect of the laboratory— its programs, its infrastructure, and especially, its people. Argonne must develop a fresh initiative; it must keep moving forward or die. Its programs have to anticipate and respond to the nation's long-term scientific and technological needs. Only by tuning the laboratory's work to meet national needs can we hope to enlist the political support required to ensure continued funding."

Under his leadership, Argonne would eventually employ five thousand people; fifteen hundred of them scientists and its budget would grow to several hundred million dollars.

•••

Before accepting the position as a department head, Eli knew that one of his responsibilities was to secure funding. For over half a century Argonne and the sixteen other national laboratories were impacted by the political leadership of the time, as well as the shifting societal needs. It would be Eli's job as a manager to look ahead, to question the significance of the research to be undertaken as it pertained to the future of a technological society and then to try to obtain funding from the government. He was honored and thrilled to be at ANL but of course, like every institution, once appointed to a senior position, he came face to face with the politics and intrigue among the management. In truth, they mostly despised and competed with each other. Those first years, before Alan Schriesheim took over as director, times were difficult. But as always, Eli persevered, becoming stronger and more confident as he built his team.

Eli interacted with the biological research division at the Department of Energy. He was frantic when he learned that the DOE intended to eliminate the one crystallographer employed in his division. By means of X-ray crystallography it had become possible to study the structure of proteins, the engines of life. Consequently, Eli believed that X-ray crystallography would hold an influential position in deciphering the secrets of life. He made an appointment at the DOE in Washington. By the time he was through making his case, he was promised the extra funds needed to maintain and modernize his Division and to keep his crystallographer.

ANL had a neutron reactor and through its radiation there were ongoing studies using beagles to identify the threshold of radiation risk. It was an area of research Eli agreed to participate in as part of his agreement with the DOE. Eli did not want to have dogs in his division for practical rather than emotional or scientific reasons. He saw the process of using big animals as overly expensive and inefficient. But he was given little choice and it would take a decade before he was able to divert the focus and the money back to basic research in radiation without using dogs in their experimentation.

During that time animal rights activists would occasionally come and angrily accuse him of cruelty to animals.

"You should do this testing on humans and not on animals! Humans can object, animals can't object!"

Eli would always give the same response, "To me, saving the life of a child is more important than saving the life of a mouse, a rat or even a dog."

They would leave infuriated but that was okay with Eli. He understood and accepted that there were different attitudes to science. He had his own very clear-cut convictions: science had to move at its own pace, with its own approaches, and should be given the freedom to do that. Finding a way to cure cancer should not be overseen or second-guessed by activists or politicians with no scientific expertise. However, he did remain convinced that large animal experimentation was unnecessary.

For him, an example that exemplified his beliefs could be seen in the discovery of DNA. There were three laboratories working on DNA and at the time the science of DNA was considered obscure to most politicians and to the public. Yet through this obscure science, Francis Crick and Maurice Wilkins from the UK, together with James Watson from the U.S. were awarded the Nobel Prize in 1962 as pioneers in DNA. Their discovery would be crucial for the future and the good of mankind. Their findings revolutionized science. Eli was then and would always remain convinced that science must be allowed to meander and flow by itself. He believed discoveries would occur when people were not afraid to dream and experiment and sometimes do trivial things because what looked trivial in the present often ended up a key element in the future development of science.

•••

Eli at his desk

It was not an easy equation, balancing between family and career at this point in Eli's life. He adored Lily and his sons but the quest for a cure for cancer often took precedence. Many nights Eli spent in his lab, especially if there was something scientifically interesting going on. It was his love.

There was a joke about scientists that Eli often told. "This scientist comes back home in the morning after being away all night. He tells his wife, 'I have a confession to make. I went out with friends and had a few drinks, and I met this beautiful woman. I forgot myself and we had sex. I fell asleep in her bed and woke up in the morning. Can you ever forgive me?' The wife replied: 'don't tell me, again you stayed the whole night in the lab!'"

For Eli science was not work; it was his passion. To be a scientist— that was his life.

Chapter 41

—————— ••• ——————

Within six months of Eli's arrival at Argonne, his reputation within the scientific community, coupled with important published papers to his credit, brought him to the attention of the University of Chicago. He was extended the honor of a full professorship appointment in a number of departments. To that end, he taught graduate students and found the experience fulfilling, the students holding on to his every word, their quest for knowledge invigorating. But the commute from ANL to the university consumed half his day and that, coupled with his responsibilities as a division head at Argonne, was exhausting. He had no choice but to limit the classes he taught. Over the years, a number of students asked him to become their PhD mentor but due to his overburdened commitments, Eli selected only one—David Glesne, who would pursue a PhD under his direction. Sadly, Eli would eventually find the extra responsibilities of teaching too burdensome and he would resign from the University in 1997.

•••

Lily remained connected to her mother regardless of the distance. They spoke every week and Lily wrote to her every day. On Yom Kippur 1988, Ada decided to walk to synagogue even though she was not feeling well, having had heart problems all her life from living in the sewers during the war. She wanted to pray that her brother Misha, who was gravely ill, would not suffer. Before she left, Ada called Lily in Chicago and left a message saying she would be back in an hour. On the way to the synagogue, she had a massive stroke. There were no cellular phones at that time and on Yom Kippur everything in Israel was shuttered and closed. By the time Ada was finally transported to a hospital, she was in critical condition and placed in intensive care. Lily was on the first flight out of Chicago. She spent every day at her mother's side and at night, she slept in her mother's apartment. Ada managed to hold on for weeks. But on October 31, 1988, Lily received a call from the hospital in the middle of the night that her mother had passed away. Ada was sixty-nine years old.

Exhausted and unable to comprehend that it was actually over, Lily fell fast asleep and did not awaken until dawn. As she opened her eyes the following morning, her first thought was that she was now an orphan. Ada had always insisted that when she died, she wanted her body to be donated to science. Jewish law forbade that. Regardless, wanting to fulfill her mother's wishes, Lily called her brother-in-law, knowing that if anyone in Israel could pull strings and make something happen, it was Meir. By the end of the day, all the arrangements were made, and Ada's body was picked up and delivered to the appropriate facility. Lily went back to the States and back to her family. She was inconsolable with grief and like a stone in her heart, Lily would always have a part of her that wished they had decided to live in Israel.

•••

As Director of the Center for Mechanistic Biology and Biotechnology, Eli was determined to upgrade his division into a modern biology arena. As part of that effort, he decided to launch a genome program. The genome is the organism's complete set of DNA that includes its genes. Eli believed that DNA research together with structural biology was the future and that it would have extensive effects on the diagnosis and treatment of human diseases, including genetic disorders. To that end, in Yugoslavia there were two scientists, Radomir Crkvenjakov and Radoje Drmanac, who were developing a new technique for sequencing DNA based on hybridization principle coupled with computer algorithms. Eli wanted these men to be the foundation for his program. In 1989, with the blessing and support of Schriesheim and Drucker, Eli was able to recruit them. It was the beginning.

By 1994, the Soviet Union had been realigned and a new Russia emerged under the leadership of President Boris Yeltsin. With America promising funding, Russia allowed a biotechnology delegation from the United States to inspect their weapons and biological warfare laboratories for the purpose of converting those facilities into laboratories that would be used for civilian purposes. To his great surprise, Eli along with one other scientist was invited to join the delegation as advisors. Early in the trip Eli started to suspect that the CIA was embedded in their group in order to get access into the Russian facilities. But that did not matter to Eli because, just like the other delegation members, he also had an ulterior motive. He was interested in meeting Russian scientists working in the genome arena.

After days of touring labs, the delegation was moving from Moscow to Novosibirsk. It was originally a closed city involved in military weaponry research, uranium enrichment and centrifuge technology. Eli was tired and needed a break. He decided to disengage from the group and stay in Moscow, knowing that the purpose of visiting Novosibirsk was purely to gain insight into Russian military objectives.

In Moscow he was allowed to visit several different institutes. At one institute, the woman in charge of over two hundred people showed him a concoction of plants that she vowed cured everything including cancer. Upon asking questions, Eli came to the conclusion that she must be a relative or mistress to an important person in Russia because in his estimation she was scientifically incompetent and ignorant.

Eli asked to be taken to the Engelhardt Institute of Molecular Biology, the premier Russian Academy of Science institute. He was familiar with their excellent work, in particular with their genome program led by its director, Andrei Mirzabekov, a member of the Russian Academy of Sciences. In fact, Eli had had the pleasure of meeting him a year earlier at a conference. At that time, he had tried to recruit Andrei for Argonne. The conversation was very polite, but it had gone no further than that. He hoped this visit would give him another opportunity to convince Andrei to come.

Touring the Engelhardt Institute, Eli noted the obviously impoverished facilities but his interactions with the various scientists were enlightening and interesting. Andrei Mirzabekov greeted him warmly and an immediate camaraderie was established. Eli was thrilled when Andrei invited him to his dacha, his summer home two hours outside of Moscow.

The hospitality shown to Eli by Andrei and his wife, Natasha, was very welcoming. After being served delicious Russian food, and an overabundance of vodka, the two men sat in front of the fireplace. Listening for the first time to the classical music of the Soviet and German composer Alfred Schnittke, Eli slowly sipped yet another glass of vodka as the two men talked. Feeling a bit inebriated, even though he had tried to moderate his consumption, Eli, perhaps a bit recklessly, made Andrei an offer to come to Argonne. After a lengthy discussion, they came to an agreement. Andrei and an élite team of his choosing would spend six months at the Engelhardt Institute, and six months at Argonne. "But will the Russians let you go?" Eli asked hopefully. "Yes," Andrei replied, "it is different now with *detente*, things have changed."

Thankfully that was true. It was a time of innovative and creative initiative that lasted several years.

...

Eli maintained a philosophy that winning was always possible. And to him this arrangement was a win for Russia and the United States. All he had to do now was convince the management of Argonne. Upon his return, he went to his supervisor, Harvey Drucker. Unfortunately, Drucker was not crazy about the idea. Refusing to let such an amazing opportunity slip away, Eli waited until Drucker was out of town and then made an appointment with Alan Schriesheim.

Eli knew that he would be seen promptly as Lily and Bea (Beatrice) Schriesheim had become close friends. As a result, the two couples occasionally dined together. Bea was an intelligent lady with a strong and dynamic personality. She worked tirelessly to improve the physical appearance of Argonne and to ensure the well-being of its ANL employees. She was also instrumental in renovating the laboratory's central cafeteria, setting up a children's nursery on the property and arranging numerous musical events. Unfortunately, Bea would later die prematurely of ovarian cancer.

Eli was shown into the Director's office. Alan stood and extended his hand warmly. He had a receding hairline and wore glasses that magnified his dark brown eyes that crinkled mischievously when he smiled. With thin lips and a nose that was in perfect proportion, Alan was a fine-looking man. Always dressed immaculately in a suit and tie, on first impression one might think him gentle. That persona was deceiving. He was hard-hitting and determined and took charge with aplomb. With very little small talk, he asked Eli what he needed.

Relating all the information about his trip and the offer made to the Russian scientists, Eli concluded and then remained silent. He knew that Alan was brilliant and that he would appreciate the amazing opportunity being offered: having a world-class advanced genome program at ANL.

Alan stared off into the distance for only a few heartbeats before smiling. "Just tell me what you need."

It took a while to arrange for the visas and to set up housing for the Russian scientists. When all was said and done, Eli had established an unprecedented team of researchers in his division. The Department of Energy came on board, as did the Defense Advanced Research Projects Agency (DARPA). DARPA's singular mission was to make pivotal investments in breakthrough technologies for national security. They viewed the genome and DNA research as a useful component in the development of biological warfare. Eli viewed DARPA as nothing more than a funding source. In his mind, the work being done by the research team, using sequencing by hybridization was for peaceful purposes. It was a way to quickly decipher a person's genetic code, thereby changing the future of medicine. Eli thought it was an intriguing approach, choosing to remain in the dark as to how it might be used in the military.

•••

Andrei Mirzabekov was a loyal Russian, but he enjoyed poking fun at his country with his close friends. "Let me ask you a question," he said, one afternoon over a cup of coffee. "What's the difference between the U.S. and Russia?"

Eli smiled and shrugged his shoulders.

"In Russia it is very simple, the government of the Soviet Union pretends to pay its people a salary and the people, in turn pretend to work."

Eli laughed encouraging his friend further.

"During the former Soviet Union being an academician was like being next to G-d, after the leadership of the Communist Party. So, when the police use to stop me, I would show my identification card and they would salute and apologize and let me go. Now," he said, "when a policeman stops me and I show him my card he says, 'Oh, you are an academician, please go, we are sorry for you!"

Eli scowled. "It's not funny because it is true. That is why you should stay in the States," Eli responded, seeing it as an opening to try again to convince his friend not to go back to Russia when his six months were over. "You live in a nice house and have a good life, why not just stay here permanently?"

Eyeing Eli, Andrei whispered, "You are my good friend. But I am too lonely. I must be with my parents; they are growing old. And I love my country, the good and the bad." At his home, Andrei kept birch next to his fireplace because that is what was used as firewood in Russia and it always reminded him of home.

Eli understood about missing family and about missing one's country. But he had made the difficult decision to stay in America and he wanted his friend to do the same, knowing that together they would do great things. But Andrei Mirzabekov could not be cajoled. And so, year after year, Andrei would come back with his team for six months at a time.

The arrangement worked for many years until the day Harvey Drucker came to Eli and said, "We cannot have it. Either Andrei stays one hundred percent at Argonne, or he goes! If he doesn't want to stay the whole time, we are going to fire him."

Incredulous Eli asked, "Why? What are you gaining?"

"If he stays, he will become an American citizen. Either he is here or there!" Drucker said, convinced that Andrei would decide to stay.

But Drucker was wrong. Andrei was a sophisticated gentleman and a good Russian who was devoted to his country. He refused to remain full-time in the States. Because he was a very proud man, he resigned before Drucker would force Eli to fire him. For Eli, this decision was nothing more than an ego exercise on the part of his supervisor.

In 1995, Eli was appointed to the International (Scientific) Advisory Board of the Engelhardt Institute of Molecular Biology, Andrei's lab in Moscow. That honorific designation gave him justification to accept what would become a recurring invitation to visit Moscow and to see his friend. Lily usually went with Eli and together they would visit the Mirzabekovs. It was a friendship that distance could not diminish. But living in Russia was not easy. Alcoholism and pollution were conditions of life and men often died in their fifties and sixties. Sadly, his dear friend Andrei would die very young as well from the cancer he had spent his life trying to cure. It was a sad truth that throughout Eli's career, many of the cancer research scientists who spent their lives searching for a cure would themselves succumb to the disease.

Chapter 42

————————— ••• —————————

Eli published dozens of papers while at Argonne during the 1980s and 1990s, each one moving the science of cancer small steps forward. He remained at ANL for twenty-five years. Eighteen of those years were spent as the Division Director overseeing a myriad of programs. With a staff of nearly one hundred and fifty people under his tutelage, over time he eliminated the antiquated thinking that had become an outgrowth of lackadaisical leadership. The results were that his division advanced on the cutting-edge of science. Yet, regardless of the responsibilities he had as an administrator, Eli still made time to check on the progress of all his teams. He stepped down as Director and spent his last seven years at ANL focusing on his own research group.

Never losing sight of the future, he continued to recruit top scientists from around the world. One of those scientists was Debora Tonetti. She was a young woman who responded to an advertisement for the Enrico Fermi Postdoctoral Fellowship. The fellowship program was set up to identify and recruit exemplary young researchers to Argonne—scientists who were expected to become leaders in their fields. Debra was finishing her PhD at Loyola University. Eli was impressed with her submission and an appointment was made for her to present to him.

Debra knew little about ANL but the idea of working at a national laboratory thrilled her. She was breathless with excitement on the day of her appointment. She drove to the gate, showed her identification and was handed a badge. Driving up to the ultra-modern administration building, gleaming silver and green, she entered a room filled with little cubicles and presented herself to Human Resources. From there she was sent to the biology building. An older facility and much less impressive, she was met with the disconcerting and unfortunate sound of barking dogs that she knew were being used for experimentation.

Debra entered the small conference room and introduced herself to Dr. Eli Huberman and his laboratory group. Unconcerned and perhaps even unaware of how beautiful she was, with her highly arched brows over wise gentle eyes, full lips, and thick brown hair. But to these men of science, her looks were of passing relevance. They were more interested in her intellect.

Eli smiled and said, "Don't be nervous. Just relax and tell us about your project at Loyola."

"I'm working on a bacterium known as *pseudomonas aeruginosa* that has developed resistance to an antibiotic."

As she placed her slides in the carousel Eli saw that she was trembling. He understood why she would be intimidated; it was not easy to be young and inexperienced and to stand before the Director of the Division of Biological Sciences. Debra visibly calmed as she found her confidence. Eli was thrilled with her presentation and at its completion he asked her to write a proposal applying for the Enrico Fermi Fellowship.

Debra was awarded that fellowship and she came to ANL in October of 1989. She had not yet finished writing her dissertation for her PhD and decided to shift her paper and her focus to leukemia. It was a monumental decision that meant starting all over.

ANL had primitive computers but Eli refused to use them, insisting that Debra bring him typed drafts of her dissertation. Days later, after careful perusal, Eli would hand Debra back what looked like a ransom note: her rearranged sentences cut and pasted together. As laborious and frustrating as it was, she quickly learned how to organize and write—Eli's way. It was a juggling act that she finally accomplished, defending her dissertation in April of 1990. From that moment on, she was able to concentrate completely on her research.

Debra worked in a specialized lab where they analyzed human leukemia cells cultured in incubators. Her assignment was to identify vital steps in a process whereby certain chemicals could convert leukemia cells into normal behaving blood cells. She loved listening to NPR on her headphones while working. But she always knew when Eli was approaching because the exhaust system for the hoods would bring in all the smells from the hallway, and she would recognize the fragrance from his cologne. Eli always showed interest in her research projects, looking into the microscope to see what she was working on, and offering his thoughts and ideas. It was a very exciting time with Eli as her mentor. She felt important and appreciated, her name appearing on the two papers they published together. His selflessness and willingness to share his success was a lesson Debra would take with her and always try to emulate in all her future endeavors. She would never marry, her life focused on all that she ever wanted to be: a scientist.

...

Eli was always busy and that left Lily in charge. Into the minutia of everyday life, she made sure her husband had a beautiful home in which to rest and rejuvenate. She filled their lives with the laughter of children, the fragrance of flowers, the sounds of music and most important of all, love. But love would not take care of the badly needed repairs for their fifty-year-old prairie-style house in LaGrange, a suburb of Chicago.

When they first moved in, Lily insisted that they update their home, but it had to be done on a budget. At a hardware store she met a policeman who was a professed handyman. He assured Lily he could handle her projects. Lily hired him never expecting that sub-contractors needed for the job would all be members of the policeman's family, from children to grandparents.

The house had stained glass windows and the interior walls were finished with wood, but sadly the previous owners had painted over the wood. Lily wanted it restored and had it all stripped back to its original grain. There was a myriad of rooms, including a basement and a guest apartment over the garage. The job stretched into months and months. Lily felt it was worth all the aggravation because once the house was finished it was a treasure. Over the ensuing years she filled their home with art and antiques.

It was not long before their house became a gathering place for Eli's students and postdocs. Lily, who considered herself only an adequate cook, opened her heart and her home to these underpaid aspiring scientists, who usually had families and could barely afford decent housing and meals at McDonald's. The dinner conversations were always lively, and Eli enjoyed being surrounded by people who shared his interests. During the summer, meals were served outside on the patio and on the deck. When visiting scientists came from the U.S. and other countries, the good china came out and the dinners Lily prepared were exceptional.

Eli saw his students as family, not employees. And one of his favorite students was Debra, believing she was indeed unique and destined for a great future. He recognized her attributes, not just because she was brilliant but because she took joy in her work and dared to be different. They would occasionally carpool since she had to drive past his neighborhood anyway. On one occasion in February of 1990, there was a huge snowstorm in Chicago. It was snowing so badly they could not get Debra's car out of the parking lot. Removing a shovel from her trunk, Eli insisted on shoveling.

"Let me do it," Debra begged, not wanting to tell him she was afraid he would have a heart attack."

Eli refused, insulted and aware that she thought of him as old. When they finally got on the Stevenson Expressway, it was covered in ice. Going five miles an hour, it was snowing so hard the windshield wipers were freezing on the windshield. It was almost impossible to see and Eli could sense that Debra was figuratively melting down. Certain a crash was imminent; he grabbed the wheel.

"You drive," he said, meaning she would handle the accelerator and the brake. "I will steer!"

The words Eli said that night, *you drive, I'll steer* were a subtle reminder to Debra that if she were ever going off course, he would grab that wheel and help her steer. Debra would remain at ANL until 1994. She then joined Northwestern University to work beside Gregory Jordan, the scientist who developed the breakthrough breast cancer drug tamoxifen.

...

Debra became the interim department head at the University of Illinois in Chicago. She started her own company and in 2019 received FDA approval for a phase 1 clinical trial for a therapeutic breast cancer drug termed TTC-352 that mimics estrogen. The expression of the enzyme PKC Alpha is a predictive biomarker that can foretell whether a particular drug is going to work or not. It may thus be a life-saving treatment tailored for the individual patient by eliminating the wrong drug. The clinical trial will hopefully move into phase 2.

"It is surreal," she said to Eli on one of their occasional telephone conversations. "At first, we thought we would just do this and go through the motions, trying not to expect a whole lot out of it. But it has really turned out to be quite exciting. We only have a few patients and so far and there is no toxicity associated with this drug. In fact, even when going up in dose, which is what you do in a phase one trial, there is still no toxicity and the disease is stable."

Eli was happy to hear about her progress and said, "People can go through their entire careers and never have the opportunity you are having. You are doing something very special and you must savor every moment. I am proud of you."

Chapter 43

———— ••• ————

Eli's devotion to work had its downside. In his heart Eli was a devoted husband and father but there was a limit as to how many ways one could split oneself. He would vow to work less and spend more time with his family, but the days turned into weeks and weeks into months and the months into years. That meant that Lily had to shoulder the responsibility for everything that occurred in the family's daily life. She served as the chief engineer, housekeeper, cook, mother, nurse, and social director for her husband and her sons. Needing her own identity outside of the home, she taught music appreciation at a local college and gave piano lessons in her home to adults. She also spent over twenty years teaching Russian language and culture to the scientists at ANL.

Ilan their eldest was a gifted student and athlete. He was nice looking, his features a combination of both parents. Focused and responsible, things seemed to come easily to Ilan. At the University of Chicago, when his fellow students were busy studying for exams, Ilan was sitting in front of the TV watching sports. He excelled on the soccer field, and with his sense of fairness and skill he was selected as the university soccer team's MVP and captain. But sport was not seen as a priority at the university, and soccer, regardless of how good the team was, was not highly regarded. When Ilan's team made it to the state and national tournaments, they were given no special treatment. In fact, they were forced to share hotel rooms with two or three other players, whereas when the football players traveled, they were each given their own room.

Ilan graduated from the University of Chicago in 1989 with a bachelor's degree in Economics and a master's degree in International Relations. He was accepted into the Law School and attended for one year. On track in his career, Ilan felt unfulfilled and decided to take a sabbatical and enlist in the Israeli army. It was a requirement for his dual citizenship and as a huge admirer of his Uncle Meir, he could not think of a better way to spend a year. After basic training, Ilan was offered an assignment working in public relations where he could use his perfect English and Hebrew.

"That is not the reason I joined," Ilan announced. His refusal resulted in re-assignment to a tank unit stationed in northern Israel close to the Lebanese border. When given leave, Ilan would spend time with the Dagan family, moments he would remember and cherish.

Ilan returned to Chicago and in 1994 he received a Doctor of Jurisprudence degree. He married Dr. Jennifer Shlaes, a clinical psychologist and a champion of woman's rights. Upon her encouragement, Ilan added her last name to his, a decision that displeased his parents, especially Lily. Ilan Huberman-Schlaes is the father of two sons and a daughter and a successful portfolio manager.

Ron (Ronni) was much like his Uncle Meir. He did not excel in school, but he loved adventure. He started working at age twelve delivering newspapers. His parents were not thrilled because it was a huge hassle. Ron would jump on his bike at the crack of dawn and ride to the neighborhood pickup location. Loading his bike-basket to overflowing, he would speed past each home throwing the newspapers. Unfortunately, Ron's job became Eli's job, as it was necessary to follow his son in the car to make sure he was okay. Ron was talented, athletic, macho and handsome, with his warm smile, dark complexion and sparkling eyes. In high school, he played football until a serious injury at a practice collapsed his lung and put a permanent end to his participation.

Ron got a job at a pizzeria while still in high school. Starting out as a bus boy he was soon promoted to evening manager. That entailed closing the pizzeria at night. Eli and Lily would begin watching the clock as closing time neared and if their son was even five minutes late arriving home, one of them would jump in the car to go and check on him. As a favor, Ron hired his brother to work for him as a waiter. Ilan's first night on the job, he dropped water on two men. At that same table, the pizza slipped and careened toward the floor. Catching the pizza before it landed, the men thought it hysterical and could not stop laughing. They gave Ilan a large tip—the last he would receive in his very short career as a waiter. Ron fired him saying *as much as I love you, you can't work for me.*

One evening Ron came to speak with his parents. With his brother standing by his side, in what must have taken great courage, Ron announced that he was gay. It was an earth-shattering moment for Lily and Eli. But this was their beloved son, and they would never be anything but supportive. That love and understanding helped Ron Huberman move through his life never ashamed of who he was.

After graduating from the University of Wisconsin-Madison in 1994, Ron joined the Chicago Police Department and soon became a bike-riding beat officer, looking like a kinder, gentler version of the action star Vin Diesel. While working for the police department, he attended night classes at the University of Chicago, earning two master's degrees, one in Social Work from the School of Social Services and the other from the Graduate School of Business.

After graduation Ron began his Chicago government career. He modernized the city's emergency-response center, served as Mayor Daley's Chief of Staff, headed the Chicago Transit Authority, and was chief executive of the Chicago Public schools, a five-billion-dollar bureaucracy with almost forty-four thousand employees and more than four hundred thousand students. In 2011, he retired from the

Eli and his sons Ron on the left and Ilan on the right.

public sector and joined a private equity firm. In 2019, Ron married his long-time partner Darren DeJong. They are the fathers of a son and a daughter. As Lily's boys grew and passed the milestones in their lives, she marked those years off as accomplishments of her own life's work. Her beloved sons had turned out pretty terrific.

• • •

The rule in Eli's research group was that normal human cells were never to be wasted. Cells grow and reproduce in cultures, basically as they do in the human body, and the medium used to grow those cells need to be replaced and refreshed with nutrients frequently. Eli's lab group was predominantly staffed with postdoctoral fellows and a few technicians, all of whom knew to follow this protocol.

Eli had a Chinese post-doctorate fellow who was working in his lab at Argonne in 2001. The postdoc was working on blood cells known as monocytes. Those monocytes could be induced to mature into different blood cell types. But they were not known to have the ability to mature into cells belonging to other tissues. The young man became ill and did not come to work for days. He broke protocol by not calling in to ensure that one of his colleagues would tend to the monocytes he was cultivating.

Eli had been at a conference and when he returned and learned what had happened, he was not happy. "Let's look at your monocyte cultures and see what's going on. Maybe we be can revive them somehow," he said to his distraught postdoc who had been the cause of the problem. Looking under the microscope, at first Eli did not see anything. Adjusting the scope, he unexpectedly saw elongated cells, which looked like fibroblasts, cells found in between various tissues. In addition, he saw cells that appeared to come from tissues other than blood. Some were twitching like heart cells.

"How long have they been incubated?" Eli asked

"Ten days," the postdoc replied.

"Let's see if we can repeat it!" Eli said, heart pounding and every fiber of his being bursting with excitement as he tried to comprehend what he was observing. Could it be possible that monocytes had the ability to mature not only into different blood cells but also into cells from various other tissues? Eli wondered.

Scientists knew that different cells acted as if they talked to one another by sending out chemicals called cytokines. Cytokines could induce immature (stem) cells to replicate and then to mature into cells with a specific function: to become mature functioning cells of the liver, heart, kidney or skin. With that knowledge in mind, Eli decided to treat these newly discovered monocytic stem cells with different cytokines. The result: the monocytes were able to convert into cells from distinct tissues that included liver cells. Eli was awestruck, never expecting to make such a momentous discovery emanating from a misstep. As was his belief, through serendipity *multipotent stem cells were discovered.*

...

Eli and Meir's father, Shmuel Huberman was never fully recognized by the Israeli leaders for the contributions he had made to Zionism while living in Poland. The result of being overlooked planted a stone in his heart and he lived in an endless state of frustration and disappointment, his demeanor turning intense and serious. Yet despite being snubbed, Shmuel never turned his back on Zionism and continued to give inspiring speeches for the cause.

By the time he reached his late 60's, Shmuel's personality and behavior changed. He became extremely distressed and angry for no apparent reason. Although always loving towards his wife Mina, Shmuel became verbally abusive to others, even to Lola, the sister he adored.

Eli was aware that something was amiss. Riddled with guilt for being so far away, he wrote letters often and called. But regardless of his attempts to be a loving son, his father was always upset with him. The arguments made no sense. Eli's mother and Lily's mother were friends. And if Lily wrote a letter to her mother that was three pages long, and Eli only wrote two pages to his parents, on their next phone call, his father would fly into a tirade for Eli's writing such a short letter. He would hang up on Eli.

Ultimately a horrific diagnosis was revealed. Shmuel Huberman had Alzheimer's disease. As his illness progressed, he became more and more belligerent. When Eli visited, it tore his heart out to see what his father had become and to witness what it was doing to his precious mother. But Mina remained determined to care for her husband, regardless of Shmuel's escalating violent behaviors. Eventually Shmuel lost total grasp of reality as the disease worsened. He had hallucinations and became a danger to himself and to Mina, even going so far as threatening to kill her.

Eli was deeply involved with his research on stem cells at the time, and as happened so often, he was living in his mind, isolated and distracted. When Meir told him how hopeless the situation had become and that their mother refused any assistance, Eli was overcome with guilt. He knew he had a great influence over his mother. Had he intervened sooner; she would not have been left so long at his father's mercy. With no other choice, the brothers made the unbearable decision to put their father into a nursing facility.

...

Shmuel became gravely ill and was hospitalized in critical condition. Eli was sad and distraught upon arriving in Israel, knowing that he would be saying goodbye to his father. His mother met him at the doorway to the hospital room, embracing him, her body trembling. Walking into his father's room, whatever he had imagined or expected to find was not even close to the horror that he actually did find. His father was lying in bed blankly staring into space. He was unable to close his eyelids because he had lost the ability to blink. There was a feeding tube in his nose that snaked into his stomach because he could no longer even swallow. It was like stepping into a nightmare. Eli could not comprehend the end-of-life care being given since there was absolutely no hope for recovery. Mina moved to a chair beside the bed and took her husband's hand. She looked at her beloved oldest child and shrugged her shoulders as tears filled her eyes. Meir called for updates and the hours slipped by. Eli became more and more incensed as he watched the hopelessness of his father's situation. When the doctor finally came into the room, Eli could no longer hold his tongue.

"You must stop feeding him! You are just extending his torture," Eli demanded, his voice tremulous with anger.

"If only we could," the doctor said sadly. "It is by Jewish law that we must do everything we can to extend a patient's life."

For Eli, those next days were some of the darkest days of his life. He drifted back to his childhood, imagining the timbre of his father's voice, the passion and the light in his eyes whenever he stood in front of an audience. Helpless and heartbroken, Eli prayed that his father was not aware of what was happening to him. Shmuel held on and did not pass until a few weeks after Eli arrived back at Argonne. He was only seventy-four years old. Eli did not go back for the funeral. He had already said goodbye.

Chapter 44

————— ••• —————

Before Eli could hope to publish his paper on stem cells, he needed fulfillment of two accomplishments: to establish conditions for replicating the stem cells and to identify natural compounds, which could trigger the stem cells to acquire properties of distinct tissues. The work was arduous and took over his life. In a seemingly endless loop of trial and error he finally had success. Planning to submit the paper for publication, Eli had to accept the realization that the very suggestion of adult stem cells would be unfathomable to the scientific community—a population still accepting the assumption stem cells could only be harvested from embryos, a practice that was extremely controversial.

In 2002, Eli submitted his paper to the prestigious Proceedings of the National Academy of Sciences (PNAS), a peer-reviewed multidisciplinary scientific journal. To be considered for publication, the most straightforward way was to ask a member of the National Academy of Sciences to read and then recommend your paper to the Journal. Eli reached out to people he knew and admired. They were respectful in their responses, but the outcome was the same, each one turned him down, refusing to believe that what he had done was even a possibility.

Discouraged and nearly giving up, Eli decided to submit his paper directly to PNAS. Hearing back could take half a year since the journal was the intermediary between the author of the paper, the assigned academy member and the selected reviewers. After months of anticipation, he got a response that the journal would consider publication only if his work could be replicated in cultures derived from single cells.

Eli knew what a monumental task it would be to create an entire population of stem cells from single cells. He and his team worked ten to twelve-hour days, seven days a week, for months. They had failure upon failure and moved through incalculable attempts until they finally managed to succeed in obtaining stem cell cultures from about half a dozen distinct single cells. They were able to show that the cells from these cultures could be triggered to acquire characteristics of distinct tissues. The paper was accepted and published on February 26, 2003.

The publication caused vast controversy in the scientific community. Articles were written in newspapers and periodicals throughout the world. From the moment the paper was published, work was begun by his peers to validate the research. Two fellow scientists reported to Eli that they had tried to replicate his experiment and could not. He was flummoxed and finally realized that the difficulty his colleagues were experiencing was due to the serum batch being used. Replicating his outcome was indeed difficult and there was no doubt in his mind that he had been fortunate to find a serum batch that served his purposes.

Behind the scenes, his discovery had far-reaching consequences that Eli did not unearth until much later. There were members of Congress citing his work and putting forth the premise that his paper showed evidence there was no further need for the use of embryonic stem cells. Those remarks did not reflect what Eli thought or believed.

Soon after his paper was published, a wealthy entrepreneur who owned a small airline contacted Eli, offering him a million dollars to fund his research. In return the man wanted rights to the project. Unfortunately, the airline executive had been sued twenty years earlier by one of his partners. Because of that stain on the man's reputation, the University of Chicago, the contractor for government-contracted research at Argonne, turned down the offer. Eli did not believe that was the only reason they refused. He was convinced that the technology transfer group at the University of Chicago did not consider his stem cell discovery of consequence.

Frustrated, disappointed and angry, he arranged a meeting to make his case with the technology transfer group. Their response to his presentation was to send a young economist to prove to Eli that there was no economic value to his work. Insulted, Eli decided to circumvent the normal channels and submit a patent through Argonne, with the idea to apply later for international patents. That pipedream came to an abrupt demise once Eli realized it would cost a small fortune to pursue. It could have been applied for inexpensively in Canada, but again the University stepped in and stopped the process.

Two men with no track record in anything scientific contacted the University, offering to fund the patents and buy the rights. Eli could not believe that these people were even being considered. Infuriated and experiencing untold anxiety he was beside himself, not understanding why the university would even consider giving his discovery away to inexperienced men. It mattered little to him that the deal included the university getting a percentage and Eli also getting a percentage. The company would be given exclusive worldwide licensing from the University of Chicago through its contractor relationship with ANL for all patents relating to the use of adult pluripotent stem cells derived from a patients' own circulating blood.

The unconscionable and inexplicable end-result was that these men never even applied for the patent, instead deciding to do research for multiple sclerosis. Without a patent pending, the information shared in his paper was now totally unencumbered. Eli believed then and still believes to this day that there were powers opposing everything surrounding his stem cell discovery.

Unbeknownst to Eli at the time, his Chinese post-doctoral fellow at Argonne went behind his back to work part-time for the entrepreneurs given the rights to the patent. He found this out years later and indirectly, after that company combined with another company and became PharmaFrontiers. After the merger, Eli was invited by David B. McWilliams to be Chairman of their Advisory Board. Upon Eli's appointment McWilliams commented, "We are very honored to have Dr. Huberman, a pioneer in the field of adult pluripotent stem cell technology. This technology holds tremendous promise for new medical therapies and because these stem cells can be produced from a patient's own blood cells and it may negate both donor rejection issues and the controversy surrounding embryonic stem cell research."

Once Eli was in his new board position, he learned the entire story surrounding the postdoctoral student who had worked beside Eli and betrayed him. The postdoc had attended the University of Illinois for a second postdoctoral period. It was during that posting that he took blood from a placenta and eventually published a paper where he took total credit for the stem cell discovery. Always a highly ethical man, who trusted that the people working beside him were also ethical, it was a huge blow to Eli. Eventually this man wrote to Eli wanting to meet in New York to have a conversation and make peace, but Eli never responded.

Despite all the heartbreak, Argonne was still the focus of Eli's life. Knowing that they, unlike the University of Chicago, valued him and were supportive was the bridge that carried him across this dark and difficult time in his career. Still, there were many days when he contemplated leaving science forever.

•••

Eli and Lily's grandson had diabetes. Convinced he could find and determined to look for insulin-producing stem cells, Eli and his team worked tirelessly for over two years, coming up with promising concepts. Even though the amounts of insulin produced were small, the concept was there. The idea was to eventually generate cells for people like his grandson, the end-result to find a cure for diabetes or at least to mitigate it. A paper was prepared. To his utter disbelief, every scientific journal rejected it. This was exceedingly personal for Eli and he was devastated. He just could not understand how his fellow scientists could be so narrow-minded. For the first time in his scientific life, Eli gave up. The paper on insulin-producing stem cells was never published.

· · ·

In his youth Eli had not appreciated or seen the bigger picture. He would focus on a specific subject and see what he was working on as the center of the universe. That was the reason he would get so excited whenever a paper was published. As director of the Biological and Medical Research Division at Argonne, focusing on a myriad of different disciplines, he began to embrace the bigger picture.

Seventeen years after his insulin producing stem cell paper was rejected, he read in the very journal that had refused to publish his work, an article on insulin being generated from stem cells. Eli was thrilled that other scientists had improved on his initial work. It was not about ego or recognition; it was about reading that a cure might be near for his beloved grandson. Still, there were times when he would think about his original work, imagining it filed away in the journal archives. It brought him satisfaction—and a tiny smile—to know that he had been first and he had been right.

Chapter 45

—————— ••• ——————

Meir Dagan retired from the army after thirty-two years of service with the rank of Major General. He then served as a National Security Advisor to Prime Minister Ariel Sharon. In August of 2002, in what was the culmination of everything Meir had ever dreamed of, Sharon appointed him Director-General of the Mossad, the national intelligence agency of Israel. Sharon had been unhappy with his Mossad Director, Efraim Halevy, due to the man's wordy reports giving his analysis of situations rather than acting upon them.

Meir's new responsibilities included gathering intelligence, counterterrorism, and counterintelligence. In their first meeting the Prime Minister made it very clear that he did not want analysis: he wanted accomplishments. That was all Meir needed to hear. In the ensuing years, his operatives covered the globe gathering intelligence and taking action.

In Meir's office, a photograph was hung on the wall positioned so that everyone who ever entered his office would see it. It was a picture of Meir and Eli's maternal grandfather, Berl Slushni being forced to ride a man as if he were a horse. A lot of fictitious stories surrounded how Meir obtained the photo. In truth, his father had it, given to him by an author who placed it in a historical book he wrote in the 1940s.

To the uninitiated the photo was a repulsive shock. But the pictorial records kept by the Nazis and their co-conspirators could never accurately reflect the horror. A picture could not bleed, or hurt, or portray the agony of starvation or what it was like to not wash for a half a year.

That image of his grandfather being humiliated was the first thing Meir saw each day when entering his office. While he had never known his grandfather, their bond was eternal, a touchstone that trumpeted the words "never again." That photograph was meant as a stark warning and reminder to all who entered his domain: the warriors of Israel are descendants of the Holocaust, men and women who will never again go silently to their graves.

During his tenure, recruitment was always a priority. Ever the innovator, Meir launched a secure website where applicants could actually apply online. Meir held the position of Director-General of the Mossad for eight years serving under three Prime Ministers: Ariel Sharon, Ehud Olmert, and Binyamin Netanyahu.

•••

As head of the Mossad, Meir came often to the States. He ached to visit or at least to speak with Eli on the telephone. But instead, he forced himself to disassociate completely. He knew Eli was angry and hurt.

Trying to make amends, on one of his trips, clandestine arrangements were made for them to meet at a restaurant in Georgetown, under the watchful eyes of an Israeli security detail. For that hour, the hurt and the estrangement melted away. Love had a way of making that possible.

Whenever Eli and his family came to Israel Meir would invite them to his home for dinners with his wife, Bina, and the extended family. Two of their three children had already married. Israeli security was present twenty-four hours a day. An electronic fence surrounded the residence and the street leading up to it was secured by the military. Even though there was always a detail not far behind, Meir planned outings to spend time alone with his brother. Riding in the jeep together, they would explore archaeological sites. Regardless of how old or how renowned he was, Meir still needed and wanted his older brother's approval. They would wander through the ruins as Meir expounded on the history, his voice excited and animated as the years of separation melted away. On one of these trips, Eli decided to broach the subject that had obviously bothered him for years.

"You come and you don't visit? What? You are too busy and important now to find time for my family and me?" Eli said, giving Meir hell before he could even get a word out.

"It's for your own protection. I don't want anybody to realize that you are my brother. I don't come because I don't want to endanger you or your family. With different surnames, my enemies will never make the familial connection. Whether you like it or not, we have to keep it that way!"

Meir had selected a Hebrew last name years earlier, as was the custom for army officers. Changing his name was not an option for Eli, as he was a known and published scientist. Meir knew that Eli was proud of him, and he could see that he was upset. But there was no way to disregard the reality that anyone related to Meir could be in danger from a terrorist's revenge.

•••

In 2007, while tracking one of Syrian President Bashar al-Assad's intelligence operatives in Europe, Mossad agents were able to search the operative's room and photograph his files. No one paid attention or even looked at the garnered information for days. When they finally did, the information seen was astonishing. There were images of a reactor being built in Syria, one much like the North Korean reactor. Meir was notified and went directly to Prime Minister Olmert.

Israel was never a country that underestimated danger. Consequently, arrangements were made for Meir to go to the States for a meeting at the Pentagon. At that encounter, one of the military men in attendance asked Meir, "Why are so many of the general's in Israel so short?" and Meir, known to have a terrific sense of humor, did not hesitate as he replied, "Some are tall like you, but the best generals need two things, brains and balls and a shorter distance between the two." After a good laugh, Meir made his case and showed the proof that Syria, with the help of North Korea, was constructing a nuclear reactor for the production of plutonium. While the timetable for activation varied, the worst-case scenario was that the reactor would be completed and activated within months.

A meeting was arranged with President George W. Bush, who had been fully briefed on the situation. President Bush was resolute that he would not under any circumstances attack a Muslim country for fear of provoking a war. Not to be dissuaded, Meir tried to explain to the President that if it was done quietly and not publicized, then Assad would brush it under the table, not wanting the world to know that his attempt to become a nuclear power had been defeated. Meir's words fell on deaf ears. In his 2010 memoir, *Decision Points,* President Bush actually admitted that he refused to give Israel a "green light" for the raid.

The State of Israel was unanimous in its commitment to never allow nuclear weaponry in the hands of its enemies. To that end, Prime Minister Olmert, Meir Dagan and Benjamin Netanyahu, Chairman of the Likud party and candidate for Prime Minister, understood: if the Syrian's were to be stopped it would be up to Israel. Despite Bush's refusal to get involved, a clandestine operation was carried out in two bombing raids on September 5h and 6h of 2007. F-15s and F-16s fighter jets took off from the Ramon and Hatzerim air bases. They flew to the Deir al-Zor region, just under four hundred miles away and dropped eighteen tons of armaments on the site. Not wanting to incite Syrian President Bashar al-Assad into a retaliatory response, it was decided that Israel would not claim responsibility. And so, for eleven years no one knew for certain who bombed the nuclear reactor.

In March of 2018, Israel announced that they had obliterated the Syrian reactor and that they would be releasing redacted top-secret documents and photos to prove it. The reason for the admission to the raid was two-fold: to warn Iran that Israel would not stand-by and allow them to become a nuclear power and because the memoirs of the former Prime Minister, Ehud Olmert, who ordered the attack, were about to be released.

Chapter 46

—————— ••• ——————

Meir was a complex man. He could be charming, amusing, gentle and kind. An accomplished artist, the walls of his home were filled with his paintings. Growing up he learned to play the accordion and had developed a great appreciation for music. He loved Mozart, Bach, Brahms, Haydn and Beethoven. Meir astounded both Eli and Lily, the expert who had majored and taught musicology, with his uncanny ability to listen and recognize the style and musical idiom of the composer within moments of the opening sections. A conversation with Meir about history or politics was like opening a *Google* search. A self-educated man, he knew the dates, the details and the background information on so many historical figures that it boggled the mind.

But there was another side of this Renaissance man. If his beloved Israel was ever threatened, he was ruthless, determined and ferocious, willing to do anything necessary to protect the State of Israel. Without a moment's hesitation, he would approve and coordinate killings to prevent a potentially horrific terrorist attack planned against Israeli civilians in Israel or abroad. When it came to Iran, he spearheaded covert assassinations, mystifying explosions and computer viruses: resulting in delays in the Iranian nuclear weapons program.

Knowing that terrorists could not survive without huge infusions of funds, Meir decided it was time to follow the money trail. It was not an easy task to unmask the shell corporations and covert bank accounts, but in the end that trail led to the doorsteps of who was financially backing the enemies of Israel. With sanctions against Iran in place, his greatest hope was that the Iranians would blame the regime rather than the international community for their economic woes. Meir foresaw the day when an uprising would result in a more open society.

By mutual agreement with Prime Minister Netanyahu, Meir resigned from the Mossad in June 2010 and the Prime Minister appointed Tamir Pardo. It was then that Meir went public with his concerns about Netanyahu's position on attacking Iran's nuclear facilities. At a conference in 2011, Meir was quoted as saying it was a "stupid idea." That brash remark resulted in Meir having his diplomatic passport revoked before its expiration date. Self-assured, a bit cocky, and not a man to ever bow to intimidation, he repeated that remark ten months later in an interview with Lesley Stahl on the CBS news telecast *60 Minutes*. He said an Israeli attack on Iran before all options were exhausted was "the stupidest idea." He added to the controversy by saying he regarded the Iranians as "a very rational regime." Meir had spent his life studying the enemies of Israel. His personal insights led him to believe that the Iranians in general were serious and clever people with an exceptional educational system.

Meir eventually toned down his remarks and actually acquiesced, admitting that the use of the word *stupid* was too harsh an expression. He said they were spoken in the heat of a discussion and that it was something he was not very proud of.

Regardless of that apology, Meir would continue to hold tightly to his beliefs. "The problem with military action is that it cannot disarm the core factor of the Iranian program—knowledge. Knowledge on the nuclear issue is something that you are not able to prevent because knowledge is something that remains in the brains of people." Meir put in place an operation that resulted in the assassinations of several Iranian nuclear scientists thereby eliminating some of the knowledge.

Meir wanted the Iranian situation put into "the hands of the international community, as an armed Iran with nuclear capability would be a menace to all the oil-producing countries of the region." There was no question that Israel had the capabilities to eliminate the Iranian infrastructure on the ground, but Meir felt a strike should never be the first option, but rather the last. It was his opinion that in a best-case scenario, all an attack would do was delay the production of Iran's nuclear capabilities, not stop it. He warned in no uncertain terms that an attack by Israel would result in a regional war that would unite "Tehran's proxies—Hezbollah, Hamas, Islamic Jihad and perhaps even Syria." He believed that uniting those factions would provide Iran with justification for going to a nuclear response. With all of that said, Meir never wanted the option of an attack taken off the table.

Loyal to his beloved country above all else, Meir never said anything that could ever impact or damage the security of Israel. In fact, he saw his comments about an attack as a warning to Iran, letting them know it was strongly considered and that if they wanted to avoid a conflict, they needed to find a way to comply with the wishes of the international community. Still, the very idea that he was speaking out as the retired Director-General of the Mossad was unprecedented. Government officials and some in the military were angry. Yet Meir refused to be silent, holding on to his conviction that if the retired generals could give interviews and put forth their opinions, then he could as well. Many of the retired senior officers agreed that Meir Dagan had a right to voice his opinions.

Upon leaving the Mossad, Meir became Director of the Israel Port Authority, a governmental agency that oversaw both the ports and the railway systems. He was also appointed Chairman of the Board for Gulliver Energy Ltd., a company focusing on the search for oil and natural gas. Onshore, Gulliver Energy had licenses in the southern Dead Sea region and in the Judean Desert. Offshore, they were licensed for exploration along the coast of Tel Aviv and Haifa. During his tenure, the company was awarded a uranium exploration license in the Negev. In 2011, a year after leaving the Mossad, Major General (ret.) Meir Dagan was awarded the Chaim Herzog Award for his unique contribution to the State of Israel. He was also awarded the Moskowitz Prize as a hero for Zionism.

Chapter 47

———— ••• ————

Eli knew that it was time to part ways with Argonne National Laboratory, a decision that had been lurking in the back of his mind ever since the fiasco surrounding his stem cell research and the lack of a patent. For twenty-five years, he had been living under the impressive and protected umbrella of two highly respected institutions. He had resigned from the University of Chicago in 1997. That association had opened untold doors and he had no way of knowing if walking away would close those doors. To be on his own for the first time in his professional life was a life altering and terrifying decision. Who would he be now?

He would miss his well-equipped lab, the availability of all the sophisticated Argonne facilities, the postdoctoral fellows, and the basic funding support. But win or lose, Eli was willing to take the risk because he had a new project in mind and he knew that before any new research could begin, he had to be out on his own. Before putting in his resignation, Eli turned to his son Ilan, who worked at a hedge fund, to help him secure funds to open a lab where he could do his research. Ilan arranged a meeting with a group of investors and Eli made his pitch, doing his very best to explain and simplify his objectives.

He wanted to find a less toxic alternative to ribavirin, the noxious and only available broad-spectrum antiviral drug. The creation of such a drug would treat the widespread hepatitis C virus (HCV) infections, which according to the *International Journal of Medical Sciences* affected one hundred and seventy million persons worldwide. Eli explained that HCV was the leading cause of chronic liver disease, cirrhosis and liver cancer. He mentioned again to his potential investors that the only drug available to treat HCV was ribavirin, a drug so toxic it was only administered as a last resort, as it often caused death.

The investors were so awed by Eli's presentation that they agreed, on the spot, to fund the entire project for three million dollars. In return, they would get the major portion of whatever proceeds came from any discoveries Eli made. The investment was considered small for these successful men, but to Eli it was a fortune. It represented the opportunity for him to control his destiny.

In 2006, Eli's company NovaDrug was incorporated, the name derived from the Latin word nova meaning new. Eli needed to establish an office and he found one not far from the University of Illinois at the Chicago Technology Park that rented incubator laboratories. Eli signed a lease for an inexpensive wet-lab and an adjacent small office.

Eli hired Philip Tokarz, a technician with a master's degree in Molecular Biology/Biotechnology from Northern Illinois University. Phil assisted him in purchasing the initial supplies used equipment needed to run Eli's laboratory. Later Eli hired Dr. Igor Gavin, one of his ex-postdocs and together they began searching for additionally needed used equipment. Once purchased, they repaired whatever needed repairing and within a relatively short time they had a fully functioning laboratory. A few years later, Igor left for another job in California. Eli hired Igor's wife, Anna Selezneva, a talented technician with a medical degree from Russia. Anna eventually divorced Gabin and as a result was a much happier and more productive member of Eli's team.

Soon after the creation of NovaDrug, Eli was offered an adjunct Professorship by Professor William Beach, head of the Department of Biopharmaceutical Sciences in the College of Pharmacy at the

University of Illinois in Chicago. Professor Beck's decision was championed by Debra Tonetti, the young woman Eli had hired at Argonne as an Enrico Fermi Postdoctoral Fellow, who was now working at the University. That appointment gave Eli a platform that was useful for speaking at academic seminars. He also taught occasional classes relating to his past cancer research.

•••

Eli had spent years searching for a drug that would have the ability to inhibit the replication of the hepatitis C virus in culture. To continue his research, he developed a unique bacterial system that mimicked cultured human cells with respect to the ribavirin target. This development was far less expensive than using cultured human cells. He then purchased a chemical library that contained hundreds of thousands of chemicals in small quantities that he could use to test with his systems. There was only one problem: all his experiments failed. He could not come up with a less toxic replacement for ribavirin.

Yet even in failure there are always unexpected opportunities. To his utter amazement, Eli noticed that some of the chemicals he had selected did not operate or react as he had expected. In fact, three of the chemicals amazingly appeared to inhibit hepatitis C. He immediately ordered smaller chemical libraries with a myriad of variations of each of those three chemicals. From those libraries he selected drugs that effectively inhibited HCV reproduction in human cell cultures. Driven and obsessed, he lost himself in the project, often forgetting when it was time to go home.

Eli felt triumphant, as he had in fact discovered a potential anti-HCV drug. He then began to ask himself if it was possible to create a multi-spectrum anti-virus drug that was not only safe but could treat viral epidemics that were spreading throughout the world: Ebola, AIDS and SARS (Severe Acute Respiratory Syndrome). But his research was still in its infancy and he needed to convince a drug company to take his work to the next levels, and that included human trials.

Having submitted patent applications since opening his lab in 2011, with data in hand, he turned to Merck, one of the largest pharmaceutical companies in the world. A meeting was arranged. Having spent an enormous amount of time and energy in preparation for his presentation, Eli explained to a group of mid-level executives the potential his drug had to treat HCV. With lukewarm enthusiasm, they asked to see his detailed research. Eli had a huge problem with divulging that information, feeling certain if Merck knew the exact structure of his discovery, they could easily take his information and come up with a fifth or sixth generation that they could claim as their own discovery.

Believing that the mid-level employees at Merck were short-sighted, he attempted to make an appointment with a senior-level executive. He was refused an appointment. After a lifetime of having access to government officials and the most brilliant minds in science, that snub was a blow to Eli and his self-esteem. It would be years before he was able to look at Merck's rejection from a different perspective. The people he was meeting with were businessmen and women and their viewpoint on scientific exploration was far removed from his. Eli did not see science as a business, and he had always looked down on the people who did. Only later in life did he understand that science in the hands of pharmaceutical companies was a business and that drug companies did not jump on an opportunity when a drug was only halfway to human clinical trials. It was simply not cost-effective.

•••

Refusing to give up on the idea of broad-spectrum antiviral drugs, Eli had a contract drawn up to work with Professor Lena Al Harthi from Rush University Medical School in Chicago to work on HIV. It was a disease that always needed new drugs in its drug treatment cocktail and Eli's compounds worked not only on HCV but also on HIV.

Working with highly infectious viruses that cause epidemics required the highest precaution levels. Those requirements were set in stone: multiple containment rooms with unique airflow systems, positive air pressure suits, extensive training and high levels of security to control access to the facility. Because of those exacting requirements and the expenses involved, there were a limited number of laboratories available with those facilities.

Eli knew that he would never get approval to work in his lab on viruses in general and especially those causing Ebola or SARS a serious and life-threatening form of pneumonia. The SARS virus belonged to the coronaviruses; members of that virus group caused a broad spectrum of human and animal diseases from the simple common cold to the deadly coronavirus that caused the worldwide pandemic of 2020. That pandemic virus is genetically related to the original SARS coronavirus, SAR-CoV-2.

Because of the danger involved in working with the Ebola virus, any testing had to be done by the Army at Fort Detrick, a medical command installation in Frederick, Maryland. Eli needed assistance in gaining access to Fort Detrick, so a friend introduced him to Dr. Gene Olinger, a scientist who had worked there. Dr. Olinger introduced Eli to a senior ranking officer at the medical command in Frederick. Because of Eli's past position at Argonne and his standing within the scientific community, an agreement was reached with the US Army lab to perform the tests.

During Eli's visit to inspect the laboratory, he saw technicians wearing what was tantamount to a spacesuit. The lab was completely enclosed and there was another glass perimeter in place to create double protection. The air had negative pressure to prevent the virus from escaping. The work was extremely dangerous, and Eli was not under any misconception as to the Army's motives. They did not care about finding a broad-spectrum antiviral product; their interest was in the creation of a drug that would work against Ebola. To Eli's enormous satisfaction, his drugs worked again.

Eli was unsuccessful in finding a lab that was willing and able to work with him on the SARS virus. He compromised by contacting a commercial company called BioScience Laboratories in Bozeman, Montana. They did a study for him using a surrogate of the SARS virus, namely the coronavirus that caused the common cold. To his delight, the drug worked. Again.

He now had proof that his drugs inhibited four different RNA viruses, each with its own distinct structure and dissimilar life cycles. He had in fact discovered drugs that inhibited, in cultured human cells, the replication of viruses that caused Ebola, the common cold, AIDS and HCV. It had taken twelve years of his life, but Eli could now declare victory. He had discovered broad-spectrum anti-virus drugs.

Up until this point, his research had been done in human culture cells along with occasional animal toxicity testing. Before moving forward, he would now have to prove that his new drugs would not cause cancer. Those experiments were painstakingly performed, and the result was that there were no mutations. That was not a guarantee, but the testing was a success and that meant that the probability of his drug causing cancer was very small.

Eli rushed to put patents in place on his discovery, his investors insisting that he use one of the top law firms in Chicago. The lawyers were astute, professional, and in the end, they managed to swallow almost three-quarters of a million dollars of the money he had raised. Having spent so much money on his research, Eli was running low on funds and feeling desperate. He had to find a large laboratory someplace in the world willing to take his discovery to the next trial level.

He turned to Technion Institute of Technology in Israel. They were more than willing to do the research if Eli was willing to pay.

Disenchanted and depressed, he was close to giving up. He felt horrible about letting his investors down, but there was a limit as to how much energy he had left to deal with disappointments. Still, how could he ever give up? He had an obligation to humanity to see this through. What he did not know then was that having no safe and effective broad-spectrum antiviral treatment in the twenty-first century would become the catastrophe that even he, in his most pessimistic times, had not envisioned: a pandemic that would bring the entire population of the world to its knees.

Chapter 48

————— ••• —————

Eli had another commitment that brought him untold satisfaction. That commitment was the result of his time spent as a Postdoctoral Fellow at the University of Wisconsin's McArdle Laboratory for Cancer Research. Under the tutelage of Charles Heidelberger, Eli had finally found the man of science that he wanted to emulate. Charlie, the name he preferred used by his students, colleagues and friends, was humble and appreciative, giving recognition to everyone who worked with him. He encouraged, complimented and listened, all attributes missing in Eli's previous posting with Leo Sachs at the Weitzman Institute. While working at McArdle in 1957, Charlie patented the drug he discovered known as 5-fluorouracil for the treatment of breast, colon and stomach cancer. That remarkable discovery was still being used in the 21st century for the treatment of cancer.

Charles Heidelberger left McArdle Laboratory after twenty-seven years to become a Professor of Biochemistry and Pathology and the Director for Basic Research at the University of Southern California's Comprehensive Cancer Center in Los Angeles. As fate appallingly intervened, after a lifetime of devotion to finding a cure for cancer, Charlie himself was diagnosed with the dreaded disease. He was treated with his own drug, 5-fluorouracil. Sadly, it did not help him, and Charles Heidelberger succumbed to the disease on January 18, 1983, at the age of sixty-two.

Two months after his death a memorial service was held in the Alumni Lounge at the University of Wisconsin. The Director of the McArdle Laboratory spoke, along with distinguished oncology professors and Eliezer Huberman, who was then Director, Division of Biological and Medical Research at Argonne National Laboratory. Eli felt the full force of this loss as he reminisced about a man who had changed and shaped his career. He hoped that his words were sufficient; his goal was to be the verbal reflection for the postdocs and students that Charles Heidelberger had taught and inspired.

Eli was determined to do something to memorialize his mentor and friend. Upon his return to Argonne, he decided to call some of Charlie's colleagues at McArdle, considered the top cancer research laboratory in America. Eli explained that he wanted to initiate a symposium in Charles Heidelberger's name. His suggestion was met with unbridled enthusiasm and offers of help.

Eli's intention was to arrange a manageable meeting of fifty to sixty attendees. When word got out, the phone calls and letters began to arrive requesting invitations. Of course, there could be no refusals. When the guest list hit two hundred, the meeting had to be moved to a hotel in Oak Brook, a western suburb of Chicago, because Argonne did not have the facilities to host such a large event. Eli, ever the innovator, managed to secure sponsorship to defer the cost by recruiting not just Argonne but also the University of Chicago, the U.S. Department of Energy, the U. S. Environmental Protection Agency, Hoffmann-La Roche, and Burroughs Wellcome.

The attendees were the *Who's Who* of the scientific community including members from the National Academy and at least one representative from almost every important cancer research center. From August 26–29, 1984, Argonne National Laboratory held an international symposium dedicated to Charles Heidelberger entitled, *The Role of Chemicals and Radiation in the Etiology of Cancer.*

Eli presented the opening remarks on Sunday evening, and for three successive days top experts in their fields lectured continuously from 9:00 a.m. to 6:00 p.m. The keynote speaker at the gala dinner was Howard Temin, a Nobel Prize Laurent and Charlie's close friend from the McArdle.

The final day included ten presentations and ended with an overview given by Leo Sachs, founder of the Department of Genetics at the Weizmann. He was the genius who had been Eli's least-favorite teacher. But he was also the man who had introduced and arranged for Eli to work with Charles Heidelberger. And for that Eli would always be grateful.

The lectures covered all that was currently known about the causation and treatments of cancer. For many of the attendees, it was their first opportunity to meet face to face with other scientists they had admired for years. Ideas were shared and friendships emerged. After the symposium, Eli was asked to compile all of the lectures into a book. Sent to each participant when completed, the book became a valuable compilation of scientific research. Twenty-four, and still counting, Charles Heidelberger Symposia and books would follow.

In the ensuing years, The Symposia—Eli's testament to his mentor—would be held in the U.S., Hawaii, Japan, Germany, Norway, Thailand, Israel, China, Portugal, Chile and Russia. As an international event, important dignitaries from the hosting country tended to open the symposiums. Eli's reputation always preceded him, and invitations were extended for him to speak to various universities and forums in whatever country the meeting was held. That gave Lily and him the opportunity to extend their stays and explore various countries. Consequently, their home was filled with mementos of every trip they took.

During the years of the Heidelberger Symposia there were some unexpected debacles. In 2008, a meeting was scheduled for Urumqi, the capital of the Xinjiang province of China. With its three million people, it was considered a small city. From Urumqi it was possible to take a short nonstop flight to Tashkent, the capital of Uzbekistan. Meir recommended they take the opportunity to visit the unique cities of Samarkand, Bukhara and Kiva. Eli and Lily planned the trip and were joined by their close friends, who often traveled with them to the Heidelberger symposia. Avi Shaked was an Israeli born Chicago businessman and his wife Babs Waldman was an American born physician. While in Uzbekistan, Eli received message that the Chinese government had ordered the meeting canceled a day before the opening. No explanation was given. The organizer had spent an entire year working on the event. It was a nightmare—many of the speakers and attendees had already arrived and some were still on their way. In response, Eli sent the organizer an e-mail telling him that he would be going home directly from Uzbekistan. Regretfully, the man never read the correspondence and hoping to host Lily and Eli, he went to the airport to await their arrival.

Another fiasco occurred in 2016 at the Marriot Hotel in downtown Moscow. The day the symposium was to begin at the hotel, Eli was notified that the Minister of Science, a sponsor of the meeting, decided to deliver a welcoming speech and insisted on arriving by helicopter. Since he could not land near the hotel in Moscow, he demanded that the entire gathering be moved to a physics and technology institute outside of the city. Buses arrived and the attendees boarded. Traffic in Moscow was beyond horrid and it was hours before the befuddled group was in place and the conference could begin.

During the Moscow symposium, Eli mentioned to his friends Avi and Babs that there was a very impressive cancer treatment study underway in Israel at the Technion Institute of Technology. Professor Israel Vlodavsky, a colleague of Eli's headed the study. Avi was immediately interested, having gifted the Technion Institute with a biology laboratory in memory of his parents. After hearing Eli's explanation of

Vlodavsky's research, he decided to fund a cancer treatment venture based on the professor's work. But there was a caveat attached to that decision—Eli would have to agree to direct the research. Eli concurred. Once established, the company invested in Vlodavsky's project. Eli then suggested that they invest in Zucero, an Australian cancer treatment company. The result of that investment was an invitation for Eli to join the board of Zucero.

On February 11, 2020, the World Health Organization declared the outbreak of COVID-19 an international public health emergency. What the world did not know was that a global nightmare, while in its infancy, was looming. Eli was alarmed and concerned. He had never forgotten the outbreaks in 2002 of Severe Acute Respiratory Syndrome (SARS) and in 2012 the Middle East Respiratory Syndrome (MERS), both caused by coronaviruses. Those epidemics were the reason he had been working on developing a broad-spectrum drug to work against hazardous viruses that included the coronaviruses.

That outbreak resulted in the 2020 symposium planned for either Ireland or Brazil to be canceled. Even though the symposium had to be put on pause, the roots of the conference were deep and true. Eli was confident there would be another and then another because the sharing of knowledge was the life force of a scientist.

No statistics exist on the scientific collaborations that resulted from the friendships birthed and forged between those who attended the Heidelberger Symposiums. One thing remains constant, Eli is still committed to never let the scientific community forget his friend and beloved mentor, Charles Heidelberger.

Chapter 49

————— ••• —————

M eir Dagan was diagnosed with liver cancer in 2012. His only hope for survival was a liver transplant. Israel, on the cutting edge in medicine and surgical procedures would have been the ideal place for Meir to have the surgery. But due to shortages of donated organs, the Israel National Transplant Center (INTC) had established policies in 1994 deeming that the maximum age for a liver transplant was sixty-seven years old. Meir was sixty-eight. Age-biased decisions for transplants would be lifted two years later in 2014.

In America, age was not the criteria and many seniors received transplants. But Meir was seen as a political time bomb due to his prior activities, and he was discouraged from coming to the States for the procedure. The Indian government had an airplane ready to take Meir, but they were afraid that if word got out that the ex-head of the Mossad was in India, there would be trouble with the Muslim population. So at the last minute they canceled the flight.

Luckily, the Israeli Defense Minister was a good friend of Alexander Lukashenko, the President and Dictator of Belarus. After just one phone call, arrangements were put in place, and in 2012, the Republic of Belarus in Eastern Europe greeted Meir with open arms. The country had an abundance of organs, as the population was "strongly encouraged" to register. As a favor to the Israeli government, Dr. Daniel Azoulay, a Jew originally from Morocco, traveled from the Paul Brousse Hospital in Paris to supervise the operation. Considered one of the top transplant surgeons in the world, Azoulay performed the surgery. It was said afterward that watching Dr. Azoulay operate was like witnessing a performance by Tchaikovsky—every move was absolute perfection. In August of 2018, Dr Azoulay would leave France and immigrate to Israel, where he joined the staff of Sheba Medical Center in Ramat Gan.

Eli wanted to be hopeful that Meir could survive, but he knew with the cancer his brother had, the only question was: *how much life could Meir borrow?* That realization tore Eli apart. He had worked a lifetime to find a cure and to what end, if he could not even save his only brother?

···

Not only was Meir ill with a fatal disease but their beloved mother was also sick, spending the last eight years of her life suffering from the same disease that took her husband; Alzheimer's. She was no longer able to live on her own so Meir had arranged for her to be moved into a nursing facility in Kfar Szold. It was a lovely kibbutz located in northern Israel nestled amongst the trees in the Hula Valley. Mina had excellent care and she seemed content, even in her vast confusion. Ever the thoughtful caregiver, Meir's wife Bina visited often, checking to be sure that Mina had whatever she needed.

Eli and Lily visited Israel at least once a year and while it was never often enough or long enough, it was all they could manage. On one of the visits, Meir and Eli went together to the kibbutz nursing home. Just as he had felt with his father, Eli was assailed with guilt and indescribable sorrow when he saw his brave and determined mother, who had survived the horrors of a Russian labor camp during WWII, sitting in front of a television set with a vacant stare. Eli waved his hands in front of her face trying to get her attention. In Polish Mina said, "I am waiting for my mommy." As the day progressed, she also told them, again in Polish, that she was waiting for her boys to come and visit. Realizing that she did not even recognize her own sons broke Eli's heart. Underlying all the sorrow, if there was a bright light, that bright light was that Mina never knew that her Meir was sick and suffering.

In 2014, Eli was at a conference in Buenos Aires, Argentina. He was walking on the street with Lily and his friend Martin Mozes, a retired transplantation surgeon and his wife Chava, a colleague and his spouse. They had been warned about robbers and specifically told that new Rolex watches were rarely stolen because there were so many fake copies. But an old Rolex was another story. The sophisticated thieves would know which Rolex was real and which was fake. In spite of this warning, Martin insisted on wearing his old Rolex, a gift from his father. Standing behind his friend when the attack occurred, Eli was violently shoved out of the way and fell to the ground, hitting his face. Eli was in the Emergency room, bloodied and bruised, sore and shaken when the call came that his precious mother had died. Due to his injuries, Eli was unable to travel. It became another layer of guilt that remained with him for the rest of his life. Mina was ninety-four.

•••

Meir never completely recovered from the transplant. It was not long before all the medications and treatments began to take their toll on him. Suffering silently but horribly, it was decided that Meir should go to a Chinese American doctor in California for treatments. After those visits, Meir would stop in Chicago for a few days to see Eli and to rest. It was during those visits that the brothers managed to reclaim their childhood affection and trust.

Meir's wife Bina had spent her life catering to Meir's every wish and whim. His illness shook her world and brought Bina to her knees.

Always shy and uncomfortable in unfamiliar surroundings, she was simply too fragile to accompany her husband on his trips. Meir's oldest daughter Noa did accompany him once. Already a mother of three, Noa was like her father—bright, competent and strong. Meir's son Dan, a father of four was more like his mother Bina, a bit timid, not particularly driven, but always kind and considerate. His youngest daughter, Nitzan was gifted with the best characteristics of both her parents. As yet unmarried in the last year or so of her father's life she was in a serious relationship.

•••

Eli and Lily lived in The Montgomery; an upscale converted twenty-eight story building that had once been the Montgomery Ward department store headquarters. With only three condominium units on their Penthouse floor, upon entering the front door, a view of downtown Chicago could be seen through an expanse of fourteen-foot ceiling-to-floor windows. The view made Lily's grand piano look small in the huge open space against the backdrop of the city. A reflection of a lifetime of exotic travels, art from those trips covered the walls. Seating areas were arranged for comfort and easy conversations. The kitchen was part of the main living area and a den was off to the right. The only walled-in spaces were an office and Lily and Eli's bedroom.

A private elevator within the unit went to a small apartment with a rooftop terrace, garden, and a panoramic view of the city. The tiny apartment had a fully stocked kitchen, a bedroom, and a bathroom—it would be Meir's accommodations when he visited.

Although Meir was no longer Director General of the Mossad, before each visit to Lily and Eli, an advance team would arrive to check security. The team insisted on full access to the roof, a vantage point that would allow a Mossad agent to keep watch while Meir was in residence. Thankfully their neighbor graciously agreed to loan their adjacent rooftop guest apartment. Security was found to be adequate in the lobby, as a doorman announced all visitors before they were allowed in the elevator. Even so, it was decided that another agent would be posted in the hallway outside the Huberman apartment.

•••

"I thought you might like to know that the CIA and the FBI have always been aware that we are brothers," Meir told Eli one day, a smirk on his sallow-tinged complexion as they sat on comfortable overstuffed chairs, with the city of Chicago their backdrop. "I was told they were watching you by the U.S. Secretary of Defense. He asked me if I had visited you in Oak Ridge lately," Meir smiled. "I told him perhaps it was time to update their files, as you had not been at Oak Ridge for a while! So now you know how well protected you would have been had anyone known we were related." The brothers had a good laugh but in truth it was far from funny.

When Meir was young, he was considered a thin, handsome devil with a charming smile that made women melt. Over the years, he had become extremely overweight and that had always worried Eli. But looking at his brother now, skeletal, drawn, and pale, he would have given anything to have those extra pounds come back.

The brothers spent countless hours just sitting together. There were times when Meir would lean over and put his head in his hands to hide his suffering. In those moments, Eli felt his heart would break but he could say nothing. For Meir to admit pain was to admit weakness and vulnerability: two character flaws he detested in others and would not tolerate in himself. And so, the brothers would pretend that Meir was fine as they reminisced about their growing-up years and talked about their parents, friends and families.

Meir never talked about his past activities in the Mossad and Eli never asked because he did not want to know. But inevitably their conversations would turn to politics. Meir did most of the talking. It seemed that he needed to unburden himself by rehashing his concerns about problems that he could no longer take an active role in.

"It is hard to understand how naive so many Israelis on the left really are. They talk with Western eyes and don't realize that tribal heritage and religion dominate everything in the Middle East! It was a big mistake when Obama visited the Middle East, refusing to stop in Israel. He will never know what a negative message that sent. And then going to Egypt instead!" Meir hesitated, reaching for a glass of water sitting on the coffee table in front of the sofa where he sat. Eli watched him closely as his brother shifted his position, a grimace momentarily crossing his face.

"Would you like to have a rest?" Eli asked softly.

Meir shook his head and continued. "This whole business with Obama giving speeches encouraging an Arab Spring—it was disastrous. His words incited and fueled the actions that followed. Those young Arabs assumed that if they acted, Obama would help them. Of course, he didn't do a thing! Not that Obama started this movement: it started in Tunis in 2010. But the Arab Spring anti-government protests and pro-democracy uprisings caught on and took place in North Africa and the Middle East. I don't know if Obama realized the animosity he created among most Israelis. What I do know is that, as president of the United States, it was a misstep to taint Israel. Yet he did castigate us and for what purpose? Did it endear him to the Muslims? Here are the facts: the Muslim world detests Obama!"

Regardless of what Eli agreed with or disagreed with, whenever his brother felt like talking about his concerns, Eli would sit quietly and let him vent. Meir felt that Benjamin Netanyahu was the perfect choice to be the Ambassador to the United States. He had been educated in

America and knew the expressions and the culture. Americans understood him. But Meir did not like Prime Minister Benjamin Netanyahu or Prime Minister Barak (2001–2006) He said both were self-serving. Having worked under Sharon and Olmert, who went to jail, Meir felt qualified to say that both those men always had the national interest of Israel as their foremost concern, even if it damaged their political interests. He could not say the same about Netanyahu or Barak.

The Iran nuclear agreement finalized in July of 2015 was extremely upsetting to Meir. Signed by China, the European Union, France, Germany, Iran, Russia, the United Kingdom, and the United States, it was supposed to block Iran's pathways to a nuclear bomb.

"This current agreement has many flaws but the most basic flaw," he said, his eyes growing large and angry, "is that inspectors are not allowed to enter the military installations! And where is Iran going to build bombs in the civilian areas? So, this whole agreement is stupid. If you cannot inspect military installations, it is meaningless. Had the Secretary of State and Obama not been so anxious to get an agreement on the table, we might have gotten something better." He looked at Eli with a sad smile. "And now I will go to take a rest."

Chapter 50

On March 7, 2015 over forty thousand Israelis gathered at an anti-Netanyahu rally. It was held on Rabin Square in Tel Aviv under a banner that read: *Israel Wants Change*. The intention of the rally was to unseat Benyamin Netanyahu in the upcoming election later that month. The former Mossad chief, Meir Dagan, delivered the keynote address at the rally.

Meir was passionate, accusing the Prime Minster of fighting only one campaign, the one for his own political survival. Meir said, "I am not a politician and not a public figure. I came here this evening without personal aspirations, not looking for a position and without a grudge or bitterness." He went on to say that he did not fear Israel's enemies, but he did fear Israel's leadership, believing it could lead to the end of the Zionist dream. "To those who say we don't have any alternative, as somebody who worked directly with three prime ministers: there is a better alternative." Newspapers the following day said that Meir Dagan seemed close to tears many times. In actuality, Meir was mortally ill from the cancer that had spread throughout his body. The tears were a result of the chemotherapy treatments he was enduring. Regardless of his physical anguish, his speech galvanized the opposition and was debated on every Israeli TV station and in every newspaper. To this day, it is still mentioned and discussed by various commentators from time to time.

Meir Dagan

Meir Dagan died in Israel one year and ten days later on March 17th, 2016, at the age of 71. His obituary appeared in newspapers around the world.

The funeral took place in the small town of Rosh Pina, his home for many years. Located in the Upper Galilee near Tzfat, Rosh Pina was founded in the late 1800s. Nestled amongst the eastern slopes of Mount Kna'an, it was replete with majestic vistas that included the Sea of Galilee, the Hula Valley, the Golan Heights and Mt. Hermon. Given a full military funeral, Meir's coffin was draped in an Israeli flag. His pallbearers were six senior IDF officers. An Honor guard fired a three-volley salute over the grave.

Over eight hundred people attended the state funeral. For security purposes, the streets had to be closed off to keep back the hundreds more who had come to pay their respects to a man who was seen as the epitome of courage and daring, a man known as *the king of shadows,* who had devoted his life to the security of Israel. Yet, it would not be until years after his death that the vastness of his accomplishments would be finally revealed in the books: *Harpoon: Inside the Covert War Against Terrorism's Money Master* by Nitsana Darshan-Leitner and Samuel Katz, and *Rise and Kill First: The Secret History of Israel's Targeted Assassinations* by Ronen Bergman.

Among the attendees were Prime Minister Netanyahu, President Rivlin, former President Shimon Peres, Defense Minister Moshe Ya'Alon, IDF commander Gabi Ashkenazi and members from every branch of the Israeli government. Lily and Eli sat under the canopy in front of the grave with Meir's wife and family. Their two sons, Ilan and Ron sat behind.

Eli looked at Meir's family. He knew that his brother had never had the time to be the kind of father that he wanted to be. He also knew how much Meir loved his three children. He had a special connection with his oldest daughter Noa. Devoted to her dying father she had made the three-hour drive from Tel Aviv to Rosh Pena several times a week.

Blessed with her father's confidence and charisma, Noa represented her family, giving a heartfelt and emotional eulogy about her father. She acknowledged him as a great soldier and a hero of Israel. And then she reminded all in attendance that Meir was also a devoted father. She related a wonderful story about the time she was scheduled to visit the concentration camps in Poland, as was the custom for sixteen-year-old teenagers in Israel. Noa asked her father to be with her during her departure for Poland. Meir said he would really try but could not promise. On the day of departure, Meir told her at breakfast that he would meet her at the airport. When she arrived with her traveling companions, her father was not there. She was disappointed but she also knew that he was an important man with many responsibilities, and so she put on a brave face.

Waiting to board at the departure gate, a roaring noise brought everyone to the windows. A helicopter had landed, its rotors sending dirt and debris flying everywhere. Her heart pounding wildly, Noa watched as her father stepped onto the tarmac. Entering the building through the security doors, he walked up to his daughter and said: 'I told you I would come.' "That was my Abba," she said, a tear slipping from her eye.

Eli struggled with his emotions, trying to comprehend that his brother was truly gone. And yet he was so proud as he listened to the eulogies that followed. President Reuven Rivlin said of Meir, "You were a living legend. All your life you fought evil, but you remained a sensitive human being." Eli was surprised that the President used the word sensitive to describe Meir. It seemed incongruous considering the nature of Meir's line of work. Netanyahu spoke about the years he spent working with Meir and said, "I was always impressed by his love of the country. He was a Zionist patriot."

But perhaps nothing was more moving than the words said by Shimon Peres. "He never gave up. Not to a drawn sword, not to a painful truth and not in his battle for peace. He was a leader from birth. It wasn't by chance that warriors followed him in battle in both open and secret places. The people trusted him … under his command, which comprised a combination of wisdom, daring, creativity and a winning dash *of chutzpah*, the Mossad became the best organization in the world."

After the funeral, Eli and Lily and their boys sat *shiva*, a week-long mourning period, where friends of the deceased came to pay their respects. The shiva was held in Meir's home overlooking Lake Kinneret. Eli watched as members of the present government, previous government, generals and almost every parliament member filed through those doors.

In the silences, Eli found himself slipping into the past. During their boyhood, Eli remembered the times he took his younger brother swimming. Meir would wrap his legs around Eli's waist, grab his shoulders and hold on for dear life as they splashed and dunked. Eli relived the family picnics along with a memory of Meir doing an acrobatic balancing act in a family photograph.

There were so many shared stories when Meir was young, but it was those-in-between years—between boyhood and manhood—that

Eli lost touch. It was so hard to accept that Meir's friends knew him far better than Eli. A particular close friend was Major General (Aluf) Yossi Ben Hanan, whose iconic picture holding an AK-47 rifle in the waters of the Suez Canal had been on the cover of Life magazine. Meir once told Eli that the magazine cover had assured Yossi's great success with women. Yossi often introduced himself to Eli on the phone by saying, "Here is the brother of your brother." There was no denying that truth. Eli had to shove it aside so he could survive the pain and the regret that he had not been more present in his brother's life.

It seemed to Eli that once he and Meir were young adults, it was their destiny to part. Each followed a separate path. In some respects, each brother was trying to save the world. Meir gave his life to the State of Israel; Eli gave his life to science. As Eli reminisced about their lives, he wondered what they could have done to remain close. What would they have changed? And it came to him like an epiphany. Nothing. Each brother had followed his own destiny.

•••

A year after his death, the first Meir Dagan Conference on Security and Strategy was held on March 21, 2017, at the Netanya Academic College. The purpose of the conference was to highlight Meir's legacy: *defending Israel as a Jewish state and as a beacon of light in the turbulent Middle East facing it current and future threats and promoting an understanding of Israel's regional dynamics and geo-politics. Israel's internal social issues, and of course—Israel's strive for peace and cooperation with its neighbors.* That first conference held several panels: *The Battle over Consciousness and Future Wars, Social Resilience as a factor of National Security, and The Middle East—Today and Tomorrow.*

Hosted by the foremost experts from the military and the government the list included the current and former IDF, Chiefs of Staff,

Mossad Directors, Major Generals, a Brigadier General and the current Defense Minister. President Rivlin spoke via video conferencing. Israel's prize laureate Professor Asa Kasher was the keynote speaker along with many other influential intellectuals. Eli also spoke, talking about Meir's early years.

At the conference Eli met the wife of Eli Cohen, Israel's greatest spy. A movie was made of Cohen's life starring Sacha Baron Cohen that premiered on Netflix in 2019. Learning that Eli Huberman was Meir Dagan's brother, Eli Cohen's widow Nadia shared a story with Eli that he had never known. She said that when Meir became the head of the Mossad he called her and said that if she ever needed anything, she was to call him. When her husband was murdered, she shared that Meir became like a second father to her children. Every big or small thing that they needed; he was there for them. Meir had never mentioned a word of this to anyone; it was a side of Eli's brother that no one really knew. It was a great gift of comfort: seeing the loving and gentle side of Meir, the boy that Eli had helped to raise.

Meir's younger daughter Nitzan waited a year before getting married out of respect for her father. Eli was the closest person the bride had on her father's side of the family and they had become very important to each other. And so, it was Eli who walked her down the aisle and together with Lily stood under the *chuppah,* the marriage canopy, beside Meir's wife Bina. Standing beneath the chuppah with them was a Bedouin, a nomadic Arab. He was a man who had become another brother to Meir. It was not a surprise to anyone. Meir spoke Arabic and had many friends outside the Israeli community. To become a friend of Meir's required certain characteristics—loyalty, integrity, worthiness and honest convictions— be he Jew, Arab, or Bedouin.

Chapter 51

— ••• —

2019

On a previous visit to a conference in Guadalajara, the second largest city in Mexico, Eli had befriended an influential local businessman named Oscar Montano Sam. He encouraged Eli to get involved with the Mexican scientific community and introduced Eli to some important scientists. As was Eli's way, he stayed in touch after returning to the States. Subsequently it was not a surprise when he was invited to assist with research underway in Mexico. Seeing it as an opportunity to take a vacation with Lily, Eli agreed to come in early November of 2019.

During a discussion with his hosts, Eli was astounded to learn that Mexico had an entirely different protocol for research. In America, experiments on a drug's development or establishing potential clinical procedures had to first be presented and approved by specific committees. Just to perform trials in mice required approval by an animal use committee whose responsibilities included ensuring that the animal trials would be performed in an ethical and painless way. Those guidelines caused the studies to be very expensive, and to even consider moving past animal experimentation to a phase 1 human study meant raising many millions of dollars. In Mexico the rules were very different. Once a lab passed intensive inspections to assure every protective measure was in place, the scientists could then work on just about anything. Eli was ecstatic about the possibility of doing animal and human studies in Mexico.

The opportunity came to fruition when he was taken to Tepatitlan near Guadalajara, a small town of one hundred and sixty thousand people. Nearby was a very unusual federal research center affiliated with Mexico's National Forestry, Crops and Livestock Research Institute, a genetic institute established to benefit from the economic life of Mexico. In this Federal Center they maintained and studied plant seeds and cultures as well as animal sperm and eggs and single-cell embryos. It was a quasi-Noah's Ark.

Eli presented his research on his broad-spectrum antiviral drug that focused on Ebola, Corona, HIV, and the Hepatitis C viruses. The institute's director, Dr. Ramon Arteaga-Garibay was intrigued and enthusiastic about collaborating with Eli. To encourage this possibility, Eli's friend Oscar arranged a meeting for Eli with the mayor of Tepatitlan. Eli carefully explained to her and her staff the implications the creation of a multi-spectrum antiviral drug would have—propelling Mexico on to the world stage as the country that could potentially save millions of lives—pointing out that SARS alone killed ten to thirty percent of the people who got infected. After listening, the mayor actually offered to fund Eli's research if the Director General, Dr. Jose Fernando De La Torre Sanchez, approved. As outrageous as it seemed, Eli would only need the approval of two people for his project to proceed. The only problem was that the Director General was abroad.

Eli had recently turned eighty and once in a while, felt his age. Yet suddenly his life was again filled with possibilities and the burden of his years seemed to melt away. But Eli was no fool, he knew that exciting was a long way from reality. But as of January 6, 2020, his dreams seemed to again be within reach.

To his great joy, on January 23, 2020, Eli was invited to return to Mexico to meet the people who could make the decisions that would move his research forward. The initial scientific meeting in Mexico City was successful and Eli was pleased. But he knew that the most crucial meeting would occur the following day when he met with the senior government official Dr. Fernando De La Torre, Director of Mexico's National Forestry, Crops and Livestock Research Institute. During that encounter, Eli was told that Mexico was losing tens of thousands of pigs to a devastating infection caused by two coronavirus strains: one a respiratory infection and the other a diarrhea disease. Since pork was an important export for Mexico, they were interested in Eli's work with the hopes of increasing their pork exports.

It was not the direction Eli had intended for his research, but the pig, which is physiologically close to humans, was certainly a perfect animal model for drug testing. If he could prevent the virus from killing hogs, then he could move on to human testing. He enthusiastically agreed to have the key the experiments done on pigs for the coronavirus at an institute near Mexico City. He returned to Chicago to wait for the formal Letter of Intent from the Mexican government for their ensuing alliance.

• • •

At the beginning of January 2020, an outbreak of pneumonia in Wuhan City, China, was reported to the World Health Organization. It barely made the news. By the end of the month the World Health Organization (WHO) alerted the world that a unique communicable coronavirus to humans had infected over three hundred people in Wuhan City and six of those infected had died. At that time, the WHO also reported that there were confirmed cases in Thailand, Japan, the United States, and the Republic of Korea. Still, the world took little notice and life continued uninterrupted as the virus began escalating. The disease was given the name Covid-19 (Coronavirus disease of 2019).

Eli was aware of the spreading epidemic from the very first reports out of China. Coronavirus was a concern he had harbored since 2002 when an epidemic of SARS-1 Coronavirus appeared in China and within a very short time spread worldwide. In 2012, there was an outbreak of MERS (Middle East Respiratory Syndrome) and from 2014–2016 there was an Ebola epidemic in West Africa, and now there was Covid-19. All of this information added another layer of urgency to his work, as so few non-scientific people understood that all of the above coronavirus diseases were genetically related.

...

On January 30, 2020, Eli received a Letter of Intent from Director General Dr. Jose Fernando De La Torre Sanchez. The letter stipulated an agreement to collaborate in research activities related to the use of Eli's broad-spectrum antiviral drug for the treatment of coronavirus diseases in swine. Eli was thrilled and greatly relieved. That same day he sent a summary to his investment partners relating all that was happening. He explained that his drugs were to be tested on one-day-old piglets that had been infected with the coronavirus. The various experiments would each take about two weeks. Most importantly, they had offered to do the testing free of charge as long as Eli provided them with the drugs and allowed them to be co-authors on any future publications.

Eli related in his summary that he needed to synthesize a large amount of drugs for an initial trial that could last up to two months. To accomplish that, he required a financial infusion of three hundred thousand dollars and additional funds for travel expenses. He specified they would have to supplement their existing patents, as they had a patent in China but not in Mexico. He closed his summary by pointing out that if the results were as he hoped, their drugs would be of interest to many of the large pharmaceutical companies–especially if the new coronavirus epidemic in China was not curtailed. The response back from his investors was immediate and positive.

He needed to get his drugs into Mexico immediately. Sadly, as with all bureaucracies and despite all the promises made, a snag in the permit process upended any swift movement. In fact, Eli was told it could take up to six weeks before the permits would be authorized. To make matters worse, bringing in medical material equipment would take even longer—two to three months. As far as Eli was concerned the collaboration with Mexico's National Forestry, Crops and Livestock Research Institute was finished. He could not, and would not, wait.

Chapter 52

———— ••• ————

Refusing to give up, Eli wrote detailed letters about his research to several foundations and universities. Believing good manners were still important, he was dismayed and angry when his correspondence was ignored. Thankfully, he did hear back from Paul McCray, MD., a highly respected Professor of Pediatrics-Pulmonary Medicine and Professor of Microbiology and Immunology at the University of Iowa. Eli had written to Paul because in addition to his research on cystic fibrosis, he was also known for his work on infectious diseases that included coronavirus. In fact, at the outbreak of the pandemic, Paul's lab was working on the MERS coronavirus.

Initially, Paul expressed an interest in collaborating with Eli and they had numerous back-and-forth E-mails. But to Eli's great frustration, Paul suddenly stopped responding. Eli was angry and disappointed. Contemplating why the sudden disinterest, Eli assumed that Paul must have been contacted by one of the large drug companies to work on COVID-19. Eli understood why Paul would accept such an opportunity. He would have done the same. What he could not accept was the way Paul handled it, never taking the time to explain to Eli what was happening.

•••

Another scientist who worked on coronaviruses was Dr. Craig Day from the Institute of Antiviral Research at Utah State University. In his email to Eli, he explained that his lab had a SARS terminal mouse model and that they were in the midst of developing such a model for SARS-CoV-2 as mice die from that disease that mimics COVID-19.

In biomedical research, a mouse model is created when scientists modify or add/remove a specific gene(s). Then through that process of selective breeding offspring are produced that can simulate human disorders. Such mice are then used for scientific research and for the development and testing of new therapies. It was exactly what Eli was hoping to hear and he asked to have his drugs tested in Craig's mouse model once it was produced.

...

By March 1, 2020, thirty-five countries from around the world were reporting cases of the coronavirus. It was with this knowledge that Eli's son Ron reached out to his friend Allan Golston, president of the Bill and Melinda Gates Foundation's United States Program. Ron told Golston that his father was working on a drug for the coronavirus pandemic. Golston then introduced Eli, through email, to Brad Wilken, Deputy Director of Product Development Operations, and the man leading the Gates foundation's effort in regard to the pandemic. Wilken requested that Eli expound on his research. Eli responded with a detailed description of everything he had been doing as it pertained to the development of his broad-spectrum antivirus drugs. His answer was then forwarded to Ken Duncan and Monalisa Chatterji, the technical leads on the drug side of the project.

Eli did not hear a word from anyone for an entire week. It was agony. He fantasized about what it would be like to have the backing of the Gates Foundation. Then there were the dark times when he would tell himself he was being ridiculous and that he did not have a chance as he was competing with the greatest scientific minds in the world. What Eli forgot was that he was also one of those great scientific minds.

To his great joy, he finally heard from Chatterji on March 8, requesting more information about the molecules and mechanisms being studied. She pointed out "that the near-team approach of the Gates Foundation was to enable the repurposing of already approved drugs and to facilitate advanced clinical candidates for the treatment of Covid-19." He sent his curriculum vitae and copies of his four U.S. patents that dealt with antiviral drugs pointing out that one of the patents dealt specifically with the coronavirus. He knew intellectually that Chatterji was telling him he was not far enough along in the development of his drug, but in his heart he remained hopeful. In the early evening of March 17, she emailed Eli and copied her colleagues saying, "Our immediate focus is on approved drugs and late-stage clinical candidates…the proposed work is not the right option for our response at this time."

As disappointed as Eli was, it would prove to be a mere bump in the road. He still had Dr. Craig Day and his contract with the University of Iowa. Eli sent them a check for fifty percent of the initial cost for testing of his drugs in Petri cultures. Having disposed of all the chemicals and supplies when he closed the NovaDrug lab, it was necessary for Eli to find resources that had experience in producing his drugs. He contacted three different European chemistry companies, sending them the chemical structures for seven distinct drugs that he wanted to be formulated. When completed, five of these freshly synthesized drugs were to be sent to the University of Iowa and two were to be sent directly to Eli. Unfortunately, the drugs had to initially be sent to the European chemistry company's representatives in the United States before they could be shipped to Iowa and to Eli.

By the end of March 2020, thirty-two states in America had issued stay at home orders. By mid-April, Johns Hopkins University reported that 2,984,000 people around the world had been diagnosed with the coronavirus. One hundred twenty-eight thousand had died. The shocking news devastated Eli. He knew that without a curative remedy, a global disaster was imminent.

Five of his drugs had finally arrived in Utah. Eli's first hurdle was to get Utah State University to perform tests on the same human cells Eli had used for his first study on coronaviruses rather than the monkey cells they were currently using. Only then would he have a reference to compare with his previous studies. Eli was anxious for the testing to begin immediately. Delay followed delay. Timely updates were unattainable.

All he could do was wait for the results of those first tests on human cells. Once those results came in, Eli would select two of the most promising compounds. Those two drugs would hopefully be tested in animals using Dr. McCray's SARS-lethal mouse system. That mouse model was indispensable. If it demonstrated that one or more of his drugs blocked the coronavirus in a living being, it meant the drugs worked. They could declare victory. Eli would then take over the next phase of the study, hoping to partner with one of the big drug companies or the National Institute of Health. Because of the pandemic, much of the time-consuming requirements of the FDA could be fast-tracked and his next phase could actually move ahead swiftly.

Above all else, Eli was a realist, used to disappointments and to having to begin again. But this was different. Something deep inside had ignited the sparks of possibility, and like a child opening a present, he was hoping the success of this research was the gift he had wished for. He contacted the NIH and filled out the required paperwork so that they would have some of the information, regardless of the fact that he did not have the final results from the Utah studies. Yet again he had to face the facts. The NIH was more interested in supporting the big pharmaceutical companies because they had the tools to move a drug quickly through the process. The best he could hope for was to be next in line, regardless of the results of his testing.

•••

The negotiations with Mexico to test his drugs on coronavirus in pigs were falling apart. The pandemic had reached every corner of the globe. Most countries were in lockdown. Eli was housebound, stressed and exhausted. Utah, Europe, Mexico, NIH—everywhere he turned required him to jump through hoops. He was desperate for encouragement. That encouragement came in the form of an email from his seventeen-year-old grandson Gabi, the oldest of Ilan's three children. He wanted to know more about his grandfather's research. What was he working on? How did he feel? Was he okay? He cared. For Eli, it was the infusion of love that would carry him to the next phase.

On April 17, 2020, Eli received an email from Ramon Munoz de Loza, Director of Economic Promotion of the Municipal Government of Tepatitlan, Mexico. Once it was translated into English, Eli read that Munoz de Loza wanted a formal agreement with Eli to perform tests on his broad-spectrum antivirus drugs at the National Center for Genetic Resources, along with other institutions of higher learning located in his town. Munoz de Loza's intention was to develop an agreement between the city of Tepatitlan and NovaDrug. He assured Eli that he had the full backing of the mayor. He closed by asking Eli for the terms and conditions necessary to develop the document.

Eli rationalized that the investment in the chemical material needed to work with mice was miniscule compared to the fortune it would cost to acquire the quantities of drugs needed to work with hogs. And since his company NovaDrug would be financing the materials, the partners having agreed to make any additional needed investment, perhaps losing the partnership with the National Forestry, Crops and Livestock Research Institute was a blessing.

Now with the University of Utah and the collaboration in Mexico on board, Eli was feeling as though a lifetime of work was coming together in a time when the entire world was teetering on the edge of chaos. Feeling a surge of confidence, he replied on April 23, listing his requirements. He began by asserting that the tests would be performed only in Petri dishes and in animals. Under no circumstances were tests to be performed on humans. The test sequence would be implemented in two phases. The first phase would be the development of seven different compounds as possible antivirus drugs. In that phase, only Petri dishes would be used to identify the most effective antivirus compounds. In phase two, the most effective compounds identified in phase one would be used on animals. Eli added that he would work with the existing investigators and personnel at the National Center for Genetic Resources but that he wanted additional manpower added to their staff: an experienced virologist, experienced veterinarian and a veterinarian pathologist.

In addition, he asked for clarity on the line of communication, namely asking who his Mexican counterpart for the English/Spanish translation would be. Noting the experimental protocols were imperative. Eli also wanted them to acknowledge that they would be responsible for providing the animals (primarily pigs) for testing. They agreed to everything. The culmination of a lifetime of dedication to his work was converging.

...

By January of 2021 vaccinations for Covid-19 had begun—the largest inoculation event in the history of the world. This did not happen by chance, circumstance or by luck. It happened because dedicated scientists, like Eliezer Huberman, spent fifty years in the fields of cancer and virology and never gave up. It happened because of the men and women who spent their careers working to unravel and identify bacteria and viruses that attack and sometimes destroy life.

Total dedication always takes its toll on families. As a reward for her devotion, Lily has her beloved husband now working in an office from home. Eli has his reward as well. He had missed so many moments with his sons, but he would not miss those moments with his grandchildren.

For Eli there are still challenges and victories to be had but now it is a gentler and quieter quest. Never have the words of Winston Churchill been more meaningful: *success is not final; failure is not fatal: it is the courage to continue that counts.*

A Lifetime of Love

Tributes

—— ••• ——

I want to take this opportunity to thank each of the renowned scientists from around the world that gave so graciously of their time. Those interviews provided me with valuable insight into Eli the scientist and the man. I will be forever grateful. An entire book could be written about each one of these exceptional men and women and so in advance, I ask to be forgiven that I could not write more as I struggled to do an overview of their remarkable careers.

Argonne National Laboratory:

Dr. Alan Schriesheim Ph.D is the retired CEO and Director Emeritus, Argonne National Laboratory. He graduated from Polytechnic Institute of New York University and received his PhD in chemistry from Penn State. He is President of the Chicago Council of Science and Technology and the recipient of *The Order of Lincoln,* the highest honor awarded by the State of Illinois. One of its notable recipients was President Ronald Reagan. Before coming to Argonne, Alan was the general manager of Exxon Engineering and director of Exxon Corporate research. He won the American Chemical Society's George Olah Award for research in petroleum chemistry. He endowed the Schriesheim Distinguished Graduate Fellowship, named for his late wife, Beatrice at Penn State University Eberly College of Science and holds 22 U.S. Patents.

Frank Collart, PhD molecular biologist and the Research Coordinator of the Scientific Focus Area Program: Molecular Mechanism Mediating Environment Sensing and Response for the Department of Energy. He received his PhD from Medical Sciences, Medical College of Ohio. At Argonne National Laboratory, Dr. Collart served as manager of the Robotic Molecular Biology Facility and was Expression Group Leader for the Midwest Center for Structural Genomics. He also directed a research program for the Department of Energy that focuses on the development of genome scale methods for cloning and expression of proteins. From his work with Eli they have three patents and a number of license deals with Roche, Bristol Myers Squibb.

Dr. Yoshimi Homma, PhD, Fukushima, Japan has served as Chief, Professor and is the current Director of the Institute of Biomedical Sciences at the Fukushima Medical University School of Medicine in Fukushima, Japan. He has published over 130 peer-reviewed publications.

Debra A. Tonnetti, PhD, Chicago, Illinois is a tenured Professor of Pharmacology in the Department of Pharmaceutical Sciences in the College of Pharmacy at the University of Illinois at Chicago. She was an Enrico Fermi Postdoctoral Fellow and is the inventor, co-founder and Chief Scientific Officer of TTC Oncology. Her company completed a Phase 1 clinical trial with TTC-352, a new therapeutic drug for breast cancer and is developing PKCa as a predictive biomarker.

Oak Ridge National Laboratory:

Dr. Jacqueline Dayan-Kenigsberg, PharmD, Paris, France was the Director of the Biotechnology, Protein Biochemistry and Macromolecules Control Laboratory, a department of the French National Drug Agency. Jacqueline is considered an expert in biotechnology drugs, vaccines, quality control biological risk and genetic toxicity of drugs, smallpox diagnostic, asbestos metrology, viral safety of biotechnology drugs, allergens standardization, rapid ricin diagnostic, drug counterfeiting and more. She has worked with the US Food and Drug Administration Food Safety Department and the Department of Defense Counterterrorism on rapid diagnosis of ricin in cosmetics. She has 24 publications to her credit. Her training in America was the result of a World Health Organization scholarship.

Amale Laouar, PhD is Assistant Professor at Rutgers University Robert Wood Johnson Medical School. She majored in Biochemistry at the Pasteur Institute in Algiers, Algeria, and pursued a master's degree in immunogenetics and a doctorate degree in Immunology at the Pierre and Marie Curie Institute in Paris, France. Amale served as a senior and leading author on a number of original research studies on gut immunology and cancer. She has a United States patent inventor-ship history and has been funded by the United States Army Medical Research Acquisition Activity Department of Defense and other national granting agencies. She also served biomedical journal editorial boards as well as scientific committees related to grant review from the Nation Institute of Health (NIH) and the Oak Ridge Associated Universities. "

"Eli is really a joy to work with. Being in academia for over two decades, I have known many scientists. Many of them have his genuine intelligence and intellectual curiosity, but very few have his good nature and joie de vivre. I have been fortunate to be one of his mentees."

Professor Dina Raveh PhD, Israel. Dina is a professor (emerita) of Genetics, Ben Gurion University of the Negev. She obtained her BSc and MSc at the Hebrew University of Jerusalem and her PhD at the Weizmann Institute of Science during which she had her first collaboration with Eli Huberman. After a postdoctoral fellowship at the

Genetics Laboratory at Oxford University, Dina joined Eli's group at Oak Ridge Laboratory, TN. Dina spent her career teaching and running a research laboratory at the Ben Gurion University of the Negev during which time she enjoyed periods of research as a visiting scientist at Yale University, US National Cancer Institute, University of Toronto, St Louis University, the University of Hawaii and a final Sabbatical at the University of New South Wales and Auckland University.

University of Wisconsin McArdle Laboratory for Cancer Research:

Dr. Toshio Kuroki MD, PhD is the Academy Director of the World Premier International (WPI) Research Center Initiative and Senior Advisor at the Research Center for Science Systems of the Japan Society for the Promotion of Science. He graduated from Tohoku University, School of Medicine. His career has included, The International Agency for Research on Cancer, World Health Organization, Lyon, France and The Institute of Medical Science at the University of Tokyo where he is Professor Emeritus and the Institute Molecular Oncology, Showa University. Toshio has held positions as President of Japan Cancer Association, President of Gifu University and the Japan Society for the Promotion of Science. He is currently Program Director of World Premier International Research Center Institute. He has published eight books.

Robert Langenbach PhD received his PhD in biochemistry from the University of Nebraska. Robert did postdoctoral work with Dr. Charles Heidelberger at the McArdle Laboratory for Cancer Research, University of Wisconsin. He was an Assistant/Associate Professor at the Eppley Cancer Institute, University of Nebraska Medical Center. Robert then accepted a position at the National Institute of Environmental Health where he is a senior scientist and an Adjunct Professor and Principal

Investigator, Metabolism and Molecular Mechanisms Group (NIEHS) at North Carolina State University. He has 160 peer-reviewed publications to his name, has edited two books and written many chapters. He and Eli have co-authored several publications. He has been a visiting scientist at Oak Ridge National Laboratory.

The following were associated with Eli at the
Weismann Institute, Israel:

Carmia Borek, PhD, Boston, MA. is a Research Professor of Public Health and Community Medicine Nutrition and Infectious Disease Unit at Tufts University School of Medicine. She was the first to show that x-rays transform single normal cells in cell cultures into cancer cells. She was Professor of Pathology at Columbia University. Carmia and Takeo Kakunaga were on the cover of the Journal of Cancer Research (1988). She has served as a consultant and Advisory Board Member with the National Institute of Health, the National Cancer Institute, National Institute on Aging, National Academy of Sciences, Department of Energy, National Institute of Environmental Health Sciences and the Federal Drug Administration. Carmia also worked with the US Army and has been an Expert Witness to the U.S. Senate on environmental issues and health. She has 200 publications to her credit and is the author of over 100 educational articles that appeared in magazines on nutrition and health.

American Association for Cancer Conference:

Joseph Landolph PhD graduated from Drexel University and received his PhD in Chemistry from University of California. He did his post-doctoral fellowship at the University of Southern California. Joseph has served as Assistant Professor of Pathology, Assistant Professor of

Microbiology and Assistant Professor Microbiology, Pathology, and Molecular Pharmacology and Pharmaceutical Sciences at the University of Southern California. He is a consultant in environment issues concerning chemical toxicology and chemical carcinogenesis and has served as an expert witness in forty-five depositions, fifteen trials, and a hundred consulting matters. His publications include forty-four peer-reviewed publications and thirty peer-reviewed articles. Joseph has given over two- hundred lectures and scientific presentations throughout the world. For more than thirty years he and Eli have run the Charles Heidelberger Symposia.

Eliezer Huberman

———— ••• ————

There was simply no way for me to include all of Eli's accomplishments in this book. Yet, I believe as the author that each honor and commitment is noteworthy.

Past and Present Memberships in Professional Societies:

American Association of Advanced Science, American Association Cancer Research, New York Academy of Science, International Society of Differentiation

Honors:

Visiting Professor: Kobe University School of Medicine, Kobe

Doctor Honoris Causa (Honorary Doctorate Engelhardt Institute of Molecular Biology, Moscow Russian Academy of Sciences, Moscow, Commendation presented at the 8th Annual Meeting Japanese Society of Pediatric Oncology in Tokyo, Member, Golden Anniversary Committee McArdle Laboratory, University of Wisconsin, Nakasone Fellow for Cancer Research University of Tokyo Research Fellow, Recognition Award, Tokyo Society of Medical Sciences, Postdoctoral Fellow International Agency for Research on Cancer award.

Committee Membership

Non-Executive Director of Zucero therapeutics limited, Board member, American Committee for the Weizmann Institute of Science Midwest Region, Board member, the Charles and Patricia Heidelberger Foundation for Cancer Research, Scientific Advisory Board, Chair, OPEXA Corporation, International Advisory Board Engelhardt Institute of Molecular Biology, Moscow, Charles Heidelberger Award Committee (Chair), Biotechnology Working Group, State of Illinois, Advisory Committee for Environmental Health Sciences, Massachusetts Institute of Technology, Maria Goeppert-Mayer Distinguished Scholars, Argonne National Laboratory, Medical Advisory Board Leukemia Research Foundation, Biotechnology Inter (National) laboratory Council, Argonne (ANL) Fellow Committee (Chair), Health Sciences Review Committee National Institute of Environmental Health Sciences, Committee on Environmental Chemical Mutagens National Academy of Sciences, Committee on Specific Gene Mutation (Chair) Environmental Protection Agency, Cause and Prevention Scientific Review Committee National Cancer Institute.

Editorial Boards

Associate Editor: Molecular Carcinogenesis, Associate Editor: Pharmacology and Therapeutics, Associate Editor: Molecular and Cellular Differentiation, Associate Editor: Cancer Research, Editorial Board: Teratogenesis, Carcinogenesis, Mutagenesis Journal

Patents

Six U.S. patents owned by the University of Chicago (UC) and the Argonne National Laboratory dealing with IMPDH, a target enzyme for antiviral and immunosuppressive drugs; 1 personal US patent; dealing with lipogenesis; 3 US patents and various corresponding international ones owned by LLC dealing with antiviral drugs.

Patent applications: 1 by UC; involving blood stem cells

Published 210 Scientific papers

Noteworthy

It would take over 80 years for the Russian Ministry of Defense to declassify a document from April 3, 1944 detailing the atrocities perpetrated by the Nazis during their occupation of Kherson. In the document, Lieutenant General Mikhail Rudkov wrote about the suffering of the Ukrainians, Russians, Jews, Gypsies, and other groups, such as the mentally disabled. The Gestapo secret police alone are estimated to have killed up to 17,000 people, stepping up their killing campaign as the Soviet army came close to liberating the city. These documents were declassified, according to the Russian Ministry of Defense, because it is believed they have special relevance today in light of attempts by numerous political forces in both Russia and abroad to rewrite the history of World War II and to impose a new version on the world-to reshape history for political purposes. For further reading: *http://mil .ru/files/files/history_kherson/history.html*